CASES
IN
AUDITING
with supplemental
readings

CASES
IN
AUDITING
with supplemental readings

Roy E. Baker
School of Business and Public Administration
University of Missouri at Kansas City

Prentice-Hall, Inc., Englewood Cliffs, New Jersey

Library of Congress Catalog Card Number: 69–11678

Printed in the United States of America

Current printing (last digit):
10 9 8 7 6 5 4 3 2 1

Prentice-Hall International, Inc., *London*
Prentice-Hall of Australia, Pty. Ltd., *Sydney*
Prentice-Hall of Canada, Ltd., *Toronto*
Prentice-Hall of India Private Ltd., *New Delhi*
Prentice-Hall of Japan, Inc., *Tokyo*

PREFACE

One of the standards of field work prescribed by the American Institute of Certified Public Accountants states:

> There is to be a proper study and evaluation of the existing internal control as a basis for reliance thereon and for the determination of the resultant extent of the tests to which auditing procedures are to be restricted.*

The understanding and evaluation of internal control appears to be the central theme of any generalized functional approach to the study of auditing. The evaluation of internal control presupposes a reasonable knowledge of the accounting system and how the system *should* work in relation to how the system *actually* works. From this evaluation, combined with preliminary testing and knowledge of the work habits of the employees responsible for system implementation, a judgment may be reached as to how much reliance can be placed upon current results. Only at this point can a reasonable audit program be constructed to fit the engagement.

Many text books on auditing devote a great deal of space to describing various types of audit procedures, some of which are mutually exclusive. But many of the problems accompanying these texts do not provide sufficient information for the student to develop skill in selecting, in a particular situation, those procedures which will accomplish the audit objectives of the engagement. The cases in this book have been prepared to provide the setting in which the accounting system and internal control can be seen to interact and provide a framework within which audit procedures may be selected for the engagement under consideration.

In addition to providing perspective on internal control, many of the cases readily demonstrate the interrelationships between various parts of the accounting system. For example, it is quite difficult to examine audit procedures for purchases without also considering the effects of the system upon accounts payable, inventories, and cost of goods sold.

---

* "Auditing Standards and Procedures," *Statements on Auditing Procedure*, No. 33, American Institute of Certified Public Accountants, New York, 1963, p. 16.

v

The cases and readings included in this book should be useful in conjunction with any of the available auditing texts. They may be used in a non-procedures oriented course in lieu of existing problems and questions or they may be used in the more traditional course as a supplement to problems and questions. In my own classes, the cases frequently served as a springboard for exploring the system-audit procedure relationship in terms of testing and audit program design.

Part One of the book contains cases relating to legal liability, independence, and professional ethics. Included is the landmark case of *Ultramares Corp.* v. *Touche* as well as more recent developments such as the *Hedley Byrne* decision in the English courts.

Part Two is concerned with internal control, systems analysis, and audit procedures in particular. Some of the cases may be used in more than one setting where the systems interrelationships warrant. Usually, on a second exposure, the conclusions reached in the first discussion are improved and reinforced.

Part Three deals with statement presentation and the auditor's report. Included are cases dealing with principles of consolidation, pooling-of-interests, and post-balance sheet date events.

Part Four develops material related to electronic data processing in somewhat greater detail than found in currently available audit text books. The material is built around on understanding of the techniques of decision tables and flowcharting as an integral part of the documentation of EDP systems. An ability to understand either, or both, of these techniques should be helpful to the auditor as he encounters EDP systems, even though he is not trained in the techniques of programming. In addition, one case illustrates the use of test decks in auditing EDP systems.

Part Five presents a brief review of the Securities and Exchange Commission and the various statutes it is charged with supervising. Two articles dealing with cash fraud are included along with two review cases. One review case is a rather complex situation involving EDP equipment. The other, although comprehensive, does not require any knowledge of electronic data processing.

ACKNOWLEDGMENTS

I would like to express my appreciation to the following for permission to use material previously published by them:

Institute of Chartered Accountants in England & Wales
American Institute of Certified Public Accountants

Editors, *The Journal of Accountancy*
Editors, *Management Services*

In addition, my appreciation to Sheller-Globe Corporation and to Getty Oil Company for permission to reproduce substantial portions of their annual reports to stockholders, and to the many companies who provided auditors' opinions and footnotes for Part Five.

I would also like to express my gratitude to Professor Howard F. Stettler, School of Business, University of Kansas and Professor Samuel R. Hepworth (now deceased), Graduate School of Business Administration, the University of Michigan for their valuable contributions, and to the numerous partners and staffmen of many CPA firms, who must remain nameless, for their many hours of discussion and counsel. Their contribution to the development of these cases is deeply appreciated. Of course, any errors of commission and omission are mine alone.

Roy E. Baker

CONTENTS

PART ONE

Legal Liability
Independence
Professional Ethics

MARYLAND CASUALTY CO. V. COOK   3

ULTRAMARES CORP. V. TOUCHE   7

HEDLEY BYRNE & CO. LTD. V. HELLER & PARTNERS LTD.   15

C.I.T. FINANCIAL CORP. V. GLOVER   20

GRAIN STORAGE INVESTIGATION   35

CONNER DRUG COMPANY   52

MAYTOWN INVESTMENT CLUB   53

PART TWO

Internal Control
Systems Analysis
Audit Procedures

OBJECTIVE INTERNAL CONTROL EVALUATION   57
  by R. Gene Brown

WHITNEY OFFICE EQUIPMENT   67

WILLETT MANUFACTURING COMPANY   68

ALLISON WHOLESALE COMPANY   70

GREEN'S DISTRIBUTORS   73

FOTO-PRESS INCORPORATED 78

WAGNER WIRE DISTRIBUTORS 84

MEMORIAL HOSPITAL 88

NOBLE COMPANY 91

FORBES ELECTRONICS COMPANY—A 93

HAYNES FOOD PROCESSORS, INCORPORATED 94

THE HAGIN CONSTRUCTION COMPANY 97

FORBES ELECTRONICS COMPANY—B 102

STUART PRODUCTS 104

PART THREE

Statement Presentation
Auditors' Reports

MATERIALITY 109
by Donald Rappaport

J. H. TURNER & SONS 121

HOMEWAY AERO-SPACE COMPANY 123

SHELLER-GLOBE CORPORATION 125

BEST-OF-CROP FOOD COMPANY 128

MCBEDE MANUFACTURING COMPANY 129

GETTY OIL COMPANY 133

PART FOUR

Electronic Data Processing
Internal Control Aspects
Selected Audit Techniques

THE INTRODUCTION OF COMPUTERS TO BUSINESS SYSTEMS 143
by Richard J. Guiltinan

THE AUDITOR'S RELATIONSHIP
WITH THE ELECTRONIC DATA PROCESSING MANAGER 151
by J. Kenneth Hickman

THE EFFECT OF EDP ON INTERNAL CONTROL   157
   by Robert E. Schlosser
   and Donald C. Bruegman

GUIDE TO REVIEW OF INTERNAL

CONTROL IN EDP SYSTEMS   171

DECISION TABLES AND FLOWCHARTS   177

MONUMENTAL MANUFACTURING COMPANY   186

JAMESTOWN NATIONAL BANK   187

MURPHY METALS CORPORATION   188

BLAZ-PRUF ASBESTOS COMPANY   189

PART FIVE

**Supplemental Material
The SEC and Disclosure
Fraud
Review Cases**

THE SEC AND DISCLOSURE   199

FBI INVESTIGATION OF FRAUD   220
   by John Edgar Hoover

MARSHALL GLASS WORKS   228

WYANDOTTE PRODUCTS CORPORATION   240

CASES
IN
AUDITING
with supplemental
readings

PART ONE

**Legal Liability
Independence
Professional Ethics**

MARYLAND CASUALTY CO. v. COOK

District Court of the United States, 35 F. Supp. 160
(E.D. Michigan, 1940)

TUTTLE, DISTRICT JUDGE. Dexter G. Conklin was appointed city treasurer by the City of Flint, Michigan. This appointment was confirmed by the City Commission. The period of employment was continuous, beginning April 5, 1928, and ending October 24, 1935. The employment was discontinued by resignation. The resignation was given by reason of and immediately following discovery of misappropriations and embezzlements by said Dexter G. Conklin.

* * *

The City of Flint carried fidelity bond insurance for its protection, said fidelity bonds providing that if Dexter G. Conklin should embezzle, misappropriate or misapply funds belonging to the City of Flint then the surety on such fidelity contracts was to be chargeable for such loss.

* * *

First, as to Dexter G. Conklin, defendant herein. He was dishonest and embezzled moneys belonging to the City of Flint during each and all of the years in question. He had different ways of embezzling and misappropriating the money. Principally, such moneys collected by him and misappropriated by him were delinquent personal property taxes owing to the City of Flint. For one example, he collected delinquent taxes voluntarily paid by the taxpayer and then issued what has been termed a temporary receipt and no record was made of the tax payment in his office whatever. For another example, he issued the official receipt of the City of Flint, but duplicate copies of such receipt supposed to be recorded in his office were destroyed and no record of the taxpayer having paid such item was made. For another example, he, as permitted by the statutes of the State of Michigan, seized personal property of the taxpayers and by authorization of law sold these assets of the taxpayers who were delinquent for the purpose of satisfying the tax indebtedness. Having done this, he issued the so-called temporary receipt and no record of payment of the taxes appeared in his office.

For another example, he altered the delinquent tax rolls by increasing the amount shown to be owing in an amount sufficient so that

3

his books balanced by reason of his collection of the tax money which he had embezzled.

* * *

The embezzlements and misappropriations resulted in a loss to the Maryland Casualty Company of $12,917.30. That is the amount of their payment to the City of Flint. In addition thereto, expenses have been incurred by the Maryland Casualty Company Investigation of $51.85, making a total loss to this company of $12,969.15.

The embezzlements and misappropriations resulted in a loss to the United States Fidelity & Guaranty Company of $3,148.21. That is the amount of their payment to the City of Flint. In addition thereto, expenses have been incurred by the United States Fidelity & Guaranty Company in investigation of $11.35, making a total loss to this company of $3,159.56.

These losses to the Maryland Casualty Company and to the United States Fidelity & Guaranty Company resulted entirely by reason of the fraud and embezzlements of Dexter G. Conklin, in an official capacity and while acting as fiduciary for the City of Flint.

* * *

The Maryland Casualty Company, and the United States Fidelity & Guaranty Company, sureties on fidelity bonds on behalf of Dexter G. Conklin, City Treasurer, on the making good of his defalcations, are subrogated *pro tanto* to the City of Flint's right of action as against Jonathon Cook, d/b/a Jonathon Cook & Company, Public Accountants, for his negligence in the auditing of the books of the City of Flint, in consequence of which negligence the earlier defalcations of Dexter G. Conklin as City Treasurer were not discovered, and the City Treasurer, Dexter G. Conklin, was left in a position to commit subsequent defalcations.

* * *

I have quoted at length hereinbefore from the specifications for the audit and the contract for the audit. The contract made the specifications a part of the audit and required that the audit engagement be performed in accordance with the specifications.

* * *

While I have reached the conclusion and interpreted this contract for the audit to require a complete audit within the broad aspects of the meaning of that word, it does not make any difference in deciding as to negligence or non-negligence whether I interpret it as a complete audit within the broad aspects of this contract or whether I say it is a combination cash and balance sheet audit. I say that because if I follow the testimony in this case of all of the certified public accountants who have testified they all agree that reasonable care should be used in test checking or in some other way to see that the figures in the controls are in balance with the detailed ledgers. There was not a reasonably careful audit performed by the defendant auditor on either basis, whether it be on the basis of the complete audit or on the basis of the combination cash and balance sheet audit. I reach that conclusion for several reasons as follows:

1. The auditor made no attempt to circularize the delinquent accounts outstanding. If there had been any attempt made the probabilities are that the discrepancies would have been discovered. Certainly there should have been some attempt made at circularization. It would not necessarily have been a 100 per cent circularization, but there should at least have been a test circularization. The delinquent accounts should have been canvassed and selected persons contacted either by personal call, by telephone, or by a form letter.

2. Alterations of the tax rolls. There were many items of alterations of the tax rolls. The alterations were very crude. He did not even use the same kind of ink. There are many ways in which these alterations could have been discovered by this defendant auditor. The particular rolls could have been totaled and then compared with the rolls in the assessor's office, which were not altered, and the discrepancies would have immediately come to light. This auditor paid no attention to the original assessor's rolls. These rolls are a part of the books and records of the City of Flint, and hence were required to be audited and examined.

3. When this defendant auditor or his representatives started to make his monthly audits and his annual audits it was incumbent upon him to audit various delinquent tax rolls including the current tax roll. He should have carefully examined the 1926, 1927, 1928, 1929, and 1930 delinquent tax rolls as well as the 1931 tax rolls. He should have determined whether or not the delinquent balance outstanding on each and every one of those tax rolls balanced with the controls. It is my belief and finding that this was not done. The auditor was unable to produce work sheets. The auditor said he thought that the delinquent tax rolls for several years were totalled in their entirety, and that then the totals taken from the controls for the corresponding years were added and the two then compared. Even if done, this, in my judgment, is not reasonably prudent or careful auditing work.

4. This defendant auditor found the delinquent balances outstanding from these tax rolls on the basis of the total obtained over the period of years to be out of balance on the basis of the total obtained from the controls over the period of years. He says that the only thing that he did

was to mention it verbally to the Director of Finance, and then he proceeded in the annual report to certify the exact balance to be a stated figure on the delinquent taxes, when actually it was not true, and he had no knowledge whatsoever of what the delinquent balance outstanding was. The auditor did not balance these books or require the City to do so. He should have required the City of Flint to bring these books into balance. It was not done.

5. When this auditor ran tapes, he used figures superimposed upon the tax roll in lead pencil. By that I mean this City Treasurer's office for their convenience had placed out at the extreme edge of the page in lead pencil what they claimed represented the delinquent balances outstanding, and when this auditor ran his tapes he used those pencil figures without checking those figures with the figures in ink to determine whether or not the pencil figures were accurate. Many of them were not accurate and a careful check would have so disclosed.

6. This auditor failed to audit the control as maintained in the City Treasurer's office, either with the control in the Director of Finance's office or with the tax rolls themselves. Had he audited such book in comparison with either the controls or the rolls, he would have found the records decidedly out of balance. It is the failure to do these things that forces me to the conclusion that this auditor failed to faithfully perform his audit engagement. With a reasonable degree of care the many defalcations would have been discovered. It is the failure upon the part of the auditor to do these things which makes it clear that he did not make the audit he had contracted to make, and he did not do what a reasonably prudent auditor would and should have done under the circumstances. He was negligent.

For the failure to perform this audit engagement in accordance with the terms of this contract as a reasonably prudent and careful auditor would and because of such negligence, the defendant auditor, Jonathon Cook, must respond in damages.

* * *

Is the negligence of the defendant auditor the proximate cause of the damage for which this suit against Jonathon Cook is brought?

The evidence as to all of the shortages and peculations which appear upon the books and records of the City of Flint during the yearly audit engagement of the defendant auditor must be considered. Those marks of irregularity were there in the record.

An auditor performing an audit on the basis of this contract and these specifications and doing his work as a reasonably prudent, careful auditor would have done his work, would have, and should have, discovered some of these many, many irregularities; and, having discovered some of them, all of the others would have been found.

One of the purposes of the audit was to determine whether or not any of the employees of the City of Flint, including the City Treasurer, were embezzling or misappropriating or defrauding the City of Flint of its money. These irregular items were apparent from the books. If they had been brought to the attention of the City of Flint by the auditor, the Treasurer's services would have been terminated and the City would then not have been put to the further loss suffered by it by reason of the subsequent misappropriations and peculations by this City Treasurer occurring after the negligent performance of the contract by the auditor. Restatement, Contracts, Sec. 330.

It was fairly within the contemplation of the parties to this contract that this work should be properly done. It was negligently done and thus the defaulting City Treasurer was permitted to continue on in his work. The auditor is obligated to respond in damages for the amount of the shortgages accruing after the negligent· performance of the audit engagement.

ULTRAMARES CORP. v. TOUCHE

(255 N.Y. 170, 174 N.E. 441, 1931)

CARDOZO, CHIEF JUDGE delivered the opinion of the court:

The action is in tort for damages suffered through the misrepresentations of accountants, the first cause of action being for misrepresentations that were merely negligent, and the second for misrepresentations charged to have been fraudulent.

In January, 1924, the defendants, a firm of public accountants, were employed by Fred Stern & Co., Inc., to prepare and certify a balance sheet exhibiting the condition of its business as of December 31, 1923. They had been employed at the end of each of the three years preceding to render a like service. Fred Stern & Co., Inc., which was in substance Stern himself, was engaged in the importation and sale of rubber. To finance its operations, it required extensive credit and borrowed large sums of money from banks and other lenders. All this was known to the defendants. The defendants knew also that in the usual course of business the balance sheet when certified would be exhibited by the Stern Company to banks, creditors, stockholders, purchasers, or sellers, according to the needs of the occasion, as the basis of financial dealings. Accordingly, when the balance sheet was made up, the defendants supplied the Stern Company thirty-two copies certified with serial numbers as counterpart originals. Nothing was said as to the persons to whom these counterparts would be shown or the extent or number of the transactions in which they would be used. In particular there was no mention of the plaintiff, a corporation doing business chiefly as a factor, which till then had never made advances to the Stern Company, though it had sold merchandise in small amounts. The range of the transactions in which a certificate of audit might be expected to play a part was as indefinite and wide as the possibilities of the business that was mirrored in the summary.

By February 26, 1924, the audit was finished and the balance sheet made up. It stated assets in the sum of $2,550,671.88 and liabilities other than capital and surplus in the sum of $1,479,956.62, thus showing a net worth of $1,070,715.26. Attached to the balance sheet was a certificate as follows:

> Touche, Niven & Co.
> Public Accountants
> Eighty Maiden Lane
> New York
> February 26, 1924

Certificate of Auditors

We have examined the accounts of Fred Stern & Co., Inc., for the year ending December 31, 1923, and hereby certify that the annexed balance sheet is in accordance therewith and with the information and explanations given us. We further certify that, subject to provision for federal taxes on income, the said statement, in our opinion, presents a true and correct view of the financial condition of Fred Stern & Co., Inc., as at December 31, 1923.

> Touche, Niven & Co.
> Public Accountants.

Capital and surplus were intact if the balance sheet was accurate. In reality both had been wiped out, and the corporation was insolvent. The books had been falsified by those in charge of the business so as to set forth accounts receivable and other assets which turned out to be fictitious. The plaintiff maintains that the certificate of audit was erroneous in both its branches. The first branch, the asserted correspondence between the accounts and the balance sheet, is one purporting to be made as of the knowledge of the auditors. The second branch, which certifies to a belief that the condition reflected in the balance sheet presents a true and correct picture of the resources of the business, is stated as a matter of opinion. In the view of the plaintiff, both branches of the certificate are either fraudulent or negligent. As to one class of assets, the item of accounts receivable, if not also as to others, there was no real correspondence, we are told, between balance sheet and books, or so the triers of the facts might find. If correspondence, however, be assumed, a closer examination of supporting invoices and records, or a fuller inquiry directed to the persons appearing on the books as creditors or debtors, would have exhibited the truth.

The plaintiff, a corporation engaged in business as a factor, was approached by Stern in March, 1924, with a request for loans of money to finance the sales of rubber. Up to that time the dealings between the two houses were on a cash basis and trifling in amount. As a condition of any loans the plaintiff insisted that it receive a balance sheet certified by public accountants, and in response to that demand it was given one of the certificates signed by the defendants and then in Stern's possession. On the faith of that certificate the plaintiff made a loan which was followed by many others. The course of the business was for Stern to deliver to the plaintiff documents described as trust receipts which in effect were executory assignments of the moneys payable by purchasers for goods thereafter to be sold. When the purchase price was due, the plaintiff received the payment, reimbursing itself therefrom for its advances and commissions. Some of these transactions were effected without loss. Nearly a year later, in December, 1924, the house of cards collapsed. In that month, plaintiff made three loans to the Stern Company, one of $100,000, a second of $25,000, and a third of $40,000. For some of these loans no security was received. For some of the earlier loans the security was inadequate. On January 2, 1925, the Stern Company was declared a bankrupt.

This action brought against the accountants in November, 1926, to recover the loss suffered by the plaintiff in reliance upon the audit, was in its inception one for negligence. On the trial there was added a second cause of action asserting fraud also. The trial judge dismissed the second cause of action without submitting it to the jury. As to the first cause of action, he reserved his decision on the defendants' motion to dismiss, and took the jury's verdict. They were told that the defendants might be held liable if with knowledge that the results of the audit would be communicated to creditors they did the work negligently, and that negligence was the omission to use reasonable and ordinary care. The verdict was in favor of the plaintiff for $187,576.32. On the coming in of the verdict, the judge granted the reserved motion. The Appellate Division affirmed the dismissal of the cause of action for fraud, but reversed the dismissal of the cause of action for negligence, and reinstated the verdict. The case is here on cross-appeals.

The two causes of action will be considered in succession, first the one for negligence and second that for fraud.

1. We think the evidence supports a finding that the audit was negligently made, though in so saying we put aside for the moment the question whether negligence, even if it existed, was a wrong to the plaintiff. To explain fully or adequately how the defendants were at

fault would carry this opinion beyond reasonable bounds. A sketch, however, there must be, at least in respect of some of the features of the audit, for the nature of the fault, when understood, is helpful in defining the ambit of the duty.

We begin with the item of accounts receivable. At the start of the defendant's audit, there had been no posting of the general ledger since April, 1923. Siess, a junior accountant, was assigned by the defendants to the performance of that work. On Sunday, February 3, 1924, he had finished the task of posting, and was ready the next day to begin with his associates the preparation of the balance sheet and the audit of its items. The total of the accounts receivable for December, 1923, as thus posted by Siess from the entries in the journal, was $644,758.17. At some time on February 3, Romberg, an employee of the Stern Company, who had general charge of its accounts, placed below the total another item to represent additional accounts receivable growing out of the transactions of the month. This new item, $706,843.07, Romberg entered in his own handwriting. The sales that it represented were, each and all, fictitious. Opposite the entry were placed other figures (12–29), indicating or supposed to indicate a reference to the journal. Siess when he resumed his work saw the entries thus added, and included the new item in making up his footings, with the result of an apparent increase of over $700,000 in the assets of the business. He says that in doing this he supposed the entries to be correct, and that his task at the moment being merely to post the books, he thought the work of the audit or verification might come later and put it off accordingly. The time sheets, which are in evidence, show very clearly that this was the order of time in which the parts of the work were done. Verification, however, there never was either by Siess or by his superiors, or so the triers of the facts might say. If any had been attempted, or any that was adequate, an examiner would have found that the entry in the ledger was not supported by any entry in the journal. If from the journal he had gone to the book from which the journal was made up, described as "the debit memo book," support would still have failed. Going farther, he would have found invoices, seventeen in number, which amounted in the aggregate to the interpolated item, but scrutiny of these invoices would have disclosed suspicious features in that they had no shipping number nor a customer's order number and varied in terms of credit and in other respects from those usual in the business. A mere glance reveals the difference.

The December entry of accounts receivable was not the only item that a careful and skillful auditor would have desired to investigate. There was ground for suspicion as to an item of $113,199.60, included in the accounts payable as due from the Baltic Corporation. As to this the defendants received an explanation, not very convincing, from Stern and Romberg. A cautious auditor might have been dissatisfied and have uncovered what was wrong. There was ground for suspicion also because of the inflation of the inventory. The inventory as it was given to the auditors, was totaled at $347,219.08. The defendants discovered errors in the sum of $303,863.20, and adjusted the balance sheet accordingly. Both the extent of the discrepancy and its causes might have been found to cast discredit upon the business and the books. There was ground for suspicion again in the record of assigned accounts. Inquiry of the creditors gave notice to the defendants that the same accounts had been pledged to two, three, and four banks at the same time. The pledges did not diminish the value of the assets, but made in such circumstances they might well evoke a doubt as to the solvency of a business where such conduct was permitted. There was an explanation by Romberg which the defendants accepted as sufficient. Caution and diligence might have pressed investigation farther.

*   *   *

We are brought to the question of duty, its origin and measure.

The defendants owed to their employer a duty imposed by law to make their certificate without fraud, and a duty growing out of contract to make it with the care and caution proper to their calling. Fraud includes the pretense of knowledge when knowledge there is none. To creditors and investors to whom the employer exhibited the certificate, the defendants owed a like duty to make it without fraud, since there was notice in the circumstances of its making that the employer did not intend to keep it to himself.

*   *   *

A different question develops when we ask whether they owed a duty to these to make it without negligence. *If liability for negligence exists, a thoughtless slip or blunder, the failure to detect a theft or forgery beneath the cover of deceptive entries, may expose accountants to a liability in an indeterminate amount for an indeterminate time to an indeterminate class.*[1] The hazards of a business conducted on these terms are so extreme as to enkindle doubt whether a flaw may not exist in the implication of a duty that exposes to these consequences. We put aside for the moment any statement in the certificate which involves the representation of a fact as true to the knowledge of the auditors. If such a statement was made, whether believed to be true or not, the defendants are liable for deceit in the event that it was false. The plaintiff does not need the invention of novel doctrine to help it out in such conditions.

[1] Emphasis added.

The case was submitted to the jury, and the verdict was returned upon the theory that, even in the absence of a misstatement of a fact, there is a liability also for erroneous opinion. The expression of an opinion is to be subject to a warranty implied by law. What, then, is the warranty, as yet unformulated, to be? Is it merely that the opinion is honestly conceived and that the preliminary inquiry has been honestly pursued, that a halt has not been made without a genuine belief that the search has been reasonably adequate to bring disclosure of the truth? Or does it go farther and involve the assumption of a liability for any blunder or inattention that could fairly be spoken of as negligence if the controversy were one between accountant and employer for breach of a contract to render services for pay?

*   *   *

Even an opinion, especially an opinion by an expert, may be found to be fraudulent if the grounds supporting it are so flimsy as to lead to the conclusion that there was no genuine belief back of it. Further than that this court has never gone.

*   *   *

Our holding does not emancipate accountants from the consequences of fraud. It does not relieve them if their audit has been so negligent as to justify a finding that they had no genuine belief in its adequacy, for this again is a fraud. *It does no more than say that, if less than this is proved, if there has been neither reckless misstatement nor insincere profession of an opinion, but only honest blunder, the ensuing liability for negligence is one that is bounded by contract, and is to be enforced between the parties by whom the contract has been made. We doubt whether the average business man receiving a certificate without paying for it, and receiving it merely as one among a multitude of possible investors, would look for anything more.*[2]

2. The second cause of action is yet to be considered.

The defendants certified as a fact, true to their own knowledge, that the balance sheet was in accordance with the books of account. If their statement was false, they are not to be exonerated because they believed it to be true.

*   *   *

We think the triers of the facts might hold it to be false. Correspondence between the balance sheet and the books imports

[2] Emphasis added.

something more, or so the triers of the facts might say, than correspondence between the balance sheet and the general ledger, unsupported or even contradicted by every other record. The correspondence to be of any moment may not unreasonably be held to signify a correspondence between the statement and the books of original entry, the books taken as a whole. If that is what the certificate means, a jury could find that the correspondence did not exist, and that the defendants signed the certificates without knowing it to exist and even without reasonable grounds for belief in its existence. The item of $706,000, representing fictitious accounts receivable, was entered in the ledger after the defendants' employee Siess had posted the December sales. He knew of the interpolation, and knew that there was need to verify the entry by reference to books other than the ledger before the books could be found to be in agreement with the balance sheet. The evidence would sustain a finding that this was never done. By concession, the interpolated item had no support in the journal, or in any journal voucher, or in the debit memo book, which was a summary of the invoices, or in anything except the invoices themselves. The defendants do not say that they ever looked at the invoices, seventeen in number, representing these accounts. They profess to be unable to recall whether they did so or not. They admit, however, that, if they had looked they would have found omissions and irregularities so many and unusual as to have called for further investigation. When we couple the refusal to say that they did look with the admission that, if they had looked, they would or could have seen, the situation is revealed as one in which a jury might reasonably find that in truth they did not look, but certified the correspondence without testing its existence.

In this connection we are to bear in mind the principle already stated in the course of this opinion that negligence or blindness, even when not equivalent to fraud, is none the less evidence to sustain an inference of fraud. At least this is so if the negligence is gross.

* * *

The defendants' attempt to excuse the omission of an inspection of the invoices proved to be fictitious by invoking a practice known as that of testing and sampling. A random choice of accounts is made from the total number on the books, and these, if found to be regular when inspected and investigated, are taken as a fair indication of the quality of the mass. The defendants say that about 200 invoices were examined in accordance with this practice, but they do not assert that any of the seventeen invoices supporting fictitious sales were among the number so selected. Verification by test and sample was very likely a sufficient audit as to accounts regularly entered upon the books in the usual course of business. It is plainly insufficient, however, as to accounts not entered upon the books where inspection of the invoices was necessary, not as a check upon accounts fair upon their face, but in order to ascertain whether there were any accounts at all. If the only invoices inspected were invoices unrelated to the interpolated entry, the result was to certify a correspondence between the books and the balance sheet without any effort by the auditors, as to $706,000 of accounts, to ascertain whether the certified agreement was in accordance with the truth. How far books of account fair upon their face are to be probed by accountant, in an effort to ascertain whether the transactions back of them are in accordance with the entries, involves to some extent the exercise of judgment and discretion. Not so, however, the inquiry whether the entries certified as there, are there in very truth, there in form and in the places where men of business training would expect to find them to be. The defendants were put on their guard by the circumstances touching the December accounts receivable to scrutinize with special care. A jury might find that, with suspicions thus awakened, they closed their eyes to the obvious, and blindly gave assent.

We conclude, to sum up the situation, that in certifying to the correspondence between balance sheet and accounts the defendants made a statement as true to their own knowledge, when they had, as a jury might find, no knowledge on the subject. If that is so, they may also be found to have acted without information leading to a sincere or genuine belief when they certified to an opinion that the balance sheet faithfully reflected the condition of the business.

Whatever wrong was committed by the defendants was not their personal act or omission, but that of their subordinates. This does not relieve them, however, of liability to answer damages for the consequences of the wrong, if wrong there shall be found to be. It is not a question of constructive notice, as where facts are brought home to the knowledge of subordinates whose interests are adverse to those of the employer.

* * *

These subordinates, so far as the record shows, had no interests adverse to the defendants', nor any thought in what they did to be unfaithful to their trust. The question is merely this, whether the defendants, having delegated the performance of this work to agents of their own selection, are responsible for the manner in which the business of the agency was done. As to that the answer is not doubtful.

* * *

HEDLEY BYRNE & CO. LTD. v. HELLER & PARTNERS LTD.
(1963) 2 All E. R. 575, 1963 W. L. R. 101

Facts of the Case

Heller & Partners Ltd. were bankers for a company who had engaged Hedley Byrne & Co. Ltd. as its advertising agents. Hedley Byrne had undertaken personal liability for certain of the advertising they had placed. Consequently, they asked Heller & Partners Ltd., through their own bankers, about the credit worthiness of the client.

Heller replied that the client was a ". . . respectably constituted company, considered good for its ordinary business engagements. . . ." The reply, however, specifically stated that the reference was ". . . without responsibility on the part of the bank or its officials."

Hedley Byrne proceeded to place advertisements on the faith of this reference and suffered a loss when the client was unable to meet its commitments. Heller & Partners were held not liable by the Court of Appeal in accordance with the rule of law stated in *Candler* v. *Crane Christmas & Co.*, i.e., no contractual relationship existed between the parties.[1] An appeal to the House of Lords upheld the decision of the Court of Appeal. Although the result achieved by the House of Lords is consistent with that in *Candler,* the reasoning is not. The decision in favor of Heller turned on the fact that a disclaimer was given, not that there was no contractual relationship between the parties.

Lord Reid, in his opinion, reasoned thusly:

> I can see no logical stopping place short of all those relationships where it is plain that the party seeking information or advice was trusting the other to exercise such a degree of care as the circumstances required, where it was reasonable for him to do that, and where the other gave the information or advice when he knew or ought to have known that the inquirer was relying on him. I say "ought to have known" because in questions of negligence we now apply the objective standard of what the reasonable man would have done.

[1] *Candler* v. *Crane Christmas & Co.* (1951) 2 K. B. 164; (1951) 1 All E. R. 426 C. A. dealt with the contractual relationship between client and auditor. The rule of law was expressed in the following excerpt from that opinion:
". . . negligent misstatement is not actionable in the absence of any special contractual or fiduciary relationship. . . . The practice of a profession, art, or calling which, from its nature, demands some special skill, ability, or experience, carried with it a duty to exercise to a reasonable extent, the amount of skill, ability and experience which it demands. . . . [However] where the prospect of physical injury is absent, the duty to exercise skill is only contractual."

A reasonable man, knowing that he was being trusted or that his skill and judgement were being relied on, would, I think, have three courses open to him. He could keep silent or decline to give the information or advice sought; or he could give an answer with a *clear qualification that he accepted no responsibility* [2] for it or that it was given without that reflection or inquiry which a careful answer would require; or he could simply answer without any such qualification. If he chooses to adopt the last course, he must, I think, be held to have accepted some responsibility for his answer being given carefully, or to have accepted a relationship with the inquirer which requires him to exercise such care as the circumstances require.

If that is right, then it must follow that *Candler* v. *Crane Christmas & Co.* was wrongly decided.

The same reasoning is supplied in another opinion, this time by Lord Morris of Borth-Y-Gest, as follows:

My lords, I consider that it follows and that it should now be regarded as settled that if someone possessed of a special skill undertakes, quite irrespective of contract, to apply that skill for the assistance of another person who relies on such skill, a duty of care will arise. The fact that the service is to be given by means of, or by the instrumentality of, words can make no difference. Furthermore, if, in a sphere in which a person is so placed that others could reasonably rely on his judgment or his skill or on his ability to make careful inquiry, a person takes it on himself to give information or advice to, or allows his information or advice to be passed on to, another person who, as he knows or should know, will place reliance on it, then a duty of care will arise.

The decision was interpreted to be broadly applicable to third-party situations where no contractual relationship existed. In particular, it was thought, accountants were covered by the decision although neither party to the action was an accountant. Subsequently, the Council of the Institute of Chartered Accountants in England and Wales submitted the case to legal counsel for advice on the question of accountants' liability for negligence to third parties. The following article is the official statement issued by the Institute to its members and discusses the implications of the decision with respect to auditors.

"Accountants' Liability to Third Parties— The *Hedley Byrne* Decision" [3]

The Council of The Institute of Chartered Accountants in England and Wales has taken legal advice on the question of accountants' liability

---

2 Emphasis added.

3 *Accountancy*, the journal of the Institute of Chartered Accountants in England and Wales, Vol. 76, no. 865 (September, 1965), pp. 829–30. Reproduced by permission.

for negligence in the light of the decision of the House of Lords in Hedley Byrne & Co. Ltd. *v.* Heller & Partners Ltd. *(1963), and the statement was approved for publication by the Council of the Institute on August 4. The statement refers solely to accountants' liabilities to third parties and does not purport to deal with liabilities arising from contractual or fiduciary relationships. Its contents have counsel's approval.*

Introduction

1. The decision of the House of Lords in the case of *Hedley Byrne & Co. Ltd.* v. *Heller & Partners Ltd.* (1963) indicates that actions for professional negligence may rise if financial loss is suffered by third parties through their reliance on the professional skill and judgment of persons with whom they were not in contractual or fiduciary relationship.

2. Until the *Hedley Byrne* case it had been generally believed that an accountant could not be held liable for financial loss suffered through his professional negligence by a third party with whom he was not in a contractual or fiduciary relationship. In this connection reliance had been particularly placed on the decision of the Court of Appeal in *Candler* v. *Crane Christmas & Co.* (1951). The *Hedley Byrne* case has, however, introduced new considerations.

3. The effect of the *Hedley Byrne* decision is that someone possessed of a special skill may, quite irrespective of contract, be considered to have undertaken to apply that skill for the assistance of another person and thereby to have accepted a duty of care to that person. A negligent though honest misrepresentation which causes financial loss to another may thus in certain circumstances give rise to an action for damages at the suit of a person with whom no contract exists.

4. The implications are of particular concern to practicing accountants, an important part of whose work consists in preparing, examining or expressing an opinion on, financial statements of various kinds which may be relied on by persons other than those for whom they were originally prepared and for other purposes than those originally intended; but the implications should not be overlooked by any accountant who knows that his professional skill exercised in an independent capacity, whether gratuitously or not, will be relied on by others.

Counsel's Advice

5. Counsel has advised that the *Hedley Byrne* decision is much more restricted in its effect than may first appear, and has drawn attention to the development of the law in this sphere overseas, referring particularly to the cases of *Ultramares Corporation* v. *Touche* (255 N.Y. 170) in the United States and *Herschel* v. *Mrupi* (1954, S.A. 464) in

South Africa. In this connection the *Ultramares* case is of particular interest. There the Court decided that auditors were not liable for negligence to a plaintiff who lent money on the strength of accounts on which the auditors had reported but which they did not know were required for the purpose of obtaining financial assistance or would be shown to the plaintiff. In so deciding the Court recognized that it would be quite wrong to expose the auditors to a potential liability "in an indeterminate amount for an indefinite time to an indeterminate class."

6. In Counsel's view, third parties entitled to recover damages under the *Hedley Byrne* principle will be limited to those who by reason of accountants' negligence in preparing reports, accounts or financial statements on which the third parties place reliance suffer financial loss in circumstances where the accountants knew or ought to have known that the reports, accounts or financial statements in question were being prepared for the specific purpose or transaction which gave rise to the loss and that they would be shown to and relied on by third parties in that particular connection. There is no general principle that accountants may be liable for damages if a report or statement which proves to have been prepared negligently by them is shown casually or in the course of business to third parties who suffer loss through reliance on the report or statement.

Practical Applications

7. The application of these principles may be illustrated by reference to some of the types of work commonly carried out by practicing accountants:

8. (a) *The position of clients' creditors.* Clients commonly produce their financial accounts to third parties in support for requests for credit or loans. An action for damages by third parties if they suffer financial loss through reliance on the accountants' reports or statements would be likely to succeed only if it could be shown that the reports or statements were made negligently and that the accountant knew or ought to have known at the time he was preparing them that they were required for this purpose, for example, of being shown to bankers or others in order to obtain credit or the continuance of existing credit facilities.

(b) *Auditors and shareholders.* In Counsel's view the object of annual accounts is to assist shareholders in exercising their control of the company by enabling them to judge how its affairs have been conducted. Hence a decision by the shareholders collectively taken on the basis of negligently prepared accounts and resulting in improper payments by or financial loss to the company could result in liability. No claim by an individual shareholder, however, would succeed in respect of loss suffered through his own investment decisions made on the strength of misleading company accounts supported by an auditors' report containing negligent misrepresentations, since the purpose for which annual accounts are normally prepared is not to enable individual shareholders to make investment decisions. But if the audited accounts comprised in effect part of a document of offer, and the auditors knew or ought to have known that the accounts were intended to be so used, they could be liable to third parties for financial loss suffered through reliance on a negligent auditors' report in connection with the offer.

(c) *Taxation.* Although they themselves may not be charged with the task of agreeing the assessment, practicing accountants often know that the accounts they are preparing or reporting on will also be submitted to the Inland Revenue and form the basis of the client's assessment to tax. There would, in Counsel's view, be no grounds for action by the Revenue to recover any tax claimed to have been lost by reason of reliance on negligent misstatements by the accountant, since in fact any ultimate loss suffered by the Revenue through failure to recover tax lost must be attributed to the death, decamping or insolvency of the taxpayer, not to the negligence of his accountant.

Where the accountant is instructed to agree his client's tax liability with the Inland Revenue he is in law the taxpayer's agent and the law relating to principal and agent applies to the exclusion of the *Hedley Byrne* principle.

Conclusion

9. The *Hedley Byrne* decision has modified the liability of accountants for professional negligence in an important, but limited, respect. It has not introduced a new concept of negligence: for an action in damages under the *Hedley Byrne* principle to succeed, negligence must first be shown. But accountants may now be held in law to owe a duty of care to persons other than those with whom they are in a contractual or fiduciary relationship and may be liable for neglect of that duty if, but only if, they know or ought to know that a financial report, account or statement prepared by them has been prepared for a specific purpose or transaction, will be shown to a particular person or class of persons, and may be relied on by that person or class of persons in that particular connection.

10. Accountants have always recognized that they have a responsibility to third parties in these circumstances, even if it was hitherto considered to be unenforceable in law, and it is recognized best practice that, in the interest of all concerned, the extent to which the accountant accepts responsibility should be made clear beyond possibility of misunderstanding. . . . The *Hedley Byrne* decision underlines the importance of observing best practice; and Counsel has further advised that where an accountant specifically restricts the scope of his report or ex-

presses appropriate reservations in a note attached to and referred to in the financial statements he has prepared or the report which he has made thereon, this can constitute a disclaimer which will be effective against any action for negligence brought against him by third parties.

C.I.T. FINANCIAL CORP. v. GLOVER
224 F. 2d 44 (2nd Cir. 1955)

Decision of the United States Court of Appeals, before Clark, Chief Judge, Medina, Circuit Judge and Dimock, District Judge.

CLARK, CHIEF JUDGE. The plaintiff, Commercial Investment Trust Financial Corporation (C.I.T.), sued the firm of Barrow, Wade, Guthrie & Company (B.W.G.), certified public accountants, to recover for losses incurred by plaintiff through the bankruptcy of its debtor, Manufacturers Trading Corporation (M.T.C.), in October, 1948. In the course of its lending business plaintiff had lent M.T.C. some $1,440,000 on October 17, 1945, and had failed to call in its loan thereafter, in alleged reliance on defendants' statements concerning the financial condition of M.T.C. The complaint stated five different causes of action, alleging negligence and gross negligence in pre-loan and post-loan audits, and also charging, in a fifth count, concealment of prior errors in each subsequent audit. Plaintiff's appeal does not contest the propriety of Judge Ryan's action in dismissing the first and fifth counts, but instead concentrates its attack on the jury verdict for the defendants on the remaining counts.

In response to special interrogatories, the jury found that plaintiff had established defendants' duty to it under the second and fourth counts relating to gross negligence, but not on the third count, which had charged ordinary negligence in the post-loan audits. On all three counts the jury further concluded that plaintiff had failed to prove defendants' representations false or misleading in any material respect. It is this latter finding which resulted in the defendants' verdict that the plaintiff particularly attacks on this appeal as erroneous in law and in fact.[1]

[1] The relevant interrogatories and replies were as follows:
On the second cause of action the jury answered the first two questions. Question No. 1 was, "Were the statements and certification issued for the period ending June 30, 1945 made by the defendants with reason to believe that it would come to the notice of and would be relied upon by those with whom Manufacturers Trading Corporation and its subsidiaries would transact business or seek the granting of credit and the making of loans to Manufacturers Trading Corporation and to its subsidiaries?" which the jury

The contentions of the parties as to the facts can be briefly summarized as follows. Plaintiff claimed that defendants' audits were fatally inadequate for failure to disclose overvaluation of M.T.C.'s loans to its debtors. Plaintiff argued that defendants should have pointed out the necessity for larger reserves due to the stagnancy of certain collateral, and due to its concentration in certain types of merchandise and in certain individual debtors, including Joseph Sachs, the brother of M.T.C.'s president, Alfred H. Sachs. This was the gist of the complaint, although reference was also made to alleged misclassifications of particular items as accounts receivable, rather than as inventory loans.

The defense relied on this special nature of M.T.C.'s business and on plaintiffs' knowledge of this. Defendants maintained that M.T.C. in its financial transactions had always relied primarily on the borrower's collateral, rather than on his general financial condition. Accurate appraisal of the value of such collateral in the event of the debtor's not infrequent insolvency and bankruptcy was always extremely difficult, and M.T.C.'s past income had resulted from Alfred H. Sachs' peculiar genius in such valuation. Defendants claimed that they had never asserted their own special competence to make such appraisals, but that they had inserted in their audit reports appropriate disclaimers qualifying their general assertions about M.T.C.'s financial stability. Further, they claimed that M.T.C.'s business was such that accountants had to rely to a great extent on management statements about the nature and the value of the collateral, and that, since the audit reports disclosed this reliance, defendants were not liable for whatever factual errors might have occurred.

---

answered in the affirmative. To Question No. 2, "Were the representations contained in the statement and certification for the period ending June 30, 1945 false or untrue in a material respect?" it answered "No."

With respect to the fourth cause of action, two questions were again considered. Question No. 1 was, "Were the statements and certifications of the audit reports of defendants for the period subsequent to June 30, 1945, made by defendants with reason to believe that they would come to the notice of and would be relied upon by those with whom Manufacturers Trading Corporation or its subsidiary would transact business in the granting of credit and the making of loans to Manufacturers Trading Corporation? Answer yes or no with respect to each period." The jury answered "Yes" to each period, and answered "No" to each period in response to Question No. 2, which read, "With regard to any period for which your answer to Question No. 1 is in the affirmative, state whether representations contained in the statement and certification for this period were false or untrue in a material respect, and if so, for which period."

The first two questions relating to the third cause of action were also unanimously decided. Question No. 1 was, "Did the defendants conduct the audits subsequent to June 30, 1945 and make reports and representations and certifications therein with particular knowledge that they were to be submitted to and were made for the primary benefit of and were to be relied upon by the plaintiff?" This the jury answered "No, on the basis of the emphasis on 'primary.'" Nonetheless it went further and answered the second question, "Were the audits and reports subsequent to June 30, 1945 false and untrue in a material respect as a result of defendants' negligence?" in the negative.

In addition, the defense asserted the factual correctness of the audits as made and claimed that plaintiff's inquiries of Sachs in response thereto showed adequate disclosure of M.T.C.'s weaknesses.

On all these points there was a sharp conflict of testimony. However we might ourselves have resolved this conflict, we cannot say that the jury's verdict was so clearly mistaken as to warrant reversal unless some error of law was committed.

In this connection the plaintiff strongly urges that the jury's verdict must have been based on the defendants' disclaimer, and that this issue should have been decided by the judge as a matter of law in plaintiff's favor. Each audit report had a disclaimer in these or similar words: "While it was not within our province to pass upon or assume responsibility for the legal or equitable title to the commercial receivables purchased by the companies or the valuation of any security thereto accepted and held by them, it was apparent from their books and records and by opinion of counsel, that their contractual and assignment forms are adequate for their legal protection in connection with the collection and liquidation of commercial receivables purchased." Plaintiff asserts that, as a matter of law, this disclaimer was limited to denying responsibility for the valuation of collateral and that defendants' responsibility for the valuation of receivables was unaffected by the disclaimer. But the jury could reasonably find that this dichotomy between face value and collateral was meaningless in the kind of transactions in which M.T.C. had been engaged, and that this fact had been adequately brought home to plaintiff, with the result that the disclaimer applied to the valuation of both collateral and receivables. With a proper charge, as given, the meaning of the disclaimer was therefore correctly left to the jury.

The plaintiff claims further that the instructions to the jury were erroneous in charging that in order to establish a duty to the plaintiff for ordinary negligence in preparation of the post-loan audits, the jury had to find that these reports had been made for the "primary benefit" of the plaintiff. Whatever the propriety of this charge, and we incline to think it was correct, see *Ultramares Corp.* v. *Touche et al.,* 225 N.Y. 170, 174 N.E. 441, 74 A.L.R. 1139; *O'Connor* v. *Ludlam,* 2d Cir., 92 F. 2d 50, *certiorari denied* 302 U.S. 758, it could not have affected the outcome of the case. It is true that the jury indicated that its finding of absence of duty under count three, with which we are here concerned, was predicated on the emphasis on primary benefit. The jury went on, however, to find that defendants' representations had not been negligently false or misleading, and this second finding alone bars recovery on this count.

Finally, plaintiff complains of the prejudicial tactics of the counsel for defense during the trial. Plaintiff's objection to the defendants' insistence on a jury trial, as was concededly their right, is surely not meant to be taken seriously. Defense counsel did indulge in numerous minor undesirable maneuvers, including repeated leading questions and unwarranted interruption of opposing cross-examination with argumentative statements. All this was properly censured and excluded by the trial judge. . . . Furthermore, and of even greater importance, Judge Ryan's charge to the jury was outstandingly careful and complete and dispassionately presented to the jury all the important contentions of both sides. On this record, viewed as a whole, we do not think that reversal is justified.

Plaintiff argues vigorously the importance of this case in holding accountants to strict liability for their audits, and, in effect, for increasing that liability. But we do not believe we should attempt to go beyond the standards of the market place, as reflected in current judicial decisions. So when, after a fair and carefully conducted trial under existing law, a jury has found for the defendants, the function of the courts should be considered fulfilled.

Judgment affirmed. (All concur.)

APPENDIX

C.I.T. FINANCIAL CORP. v. GLOVER
224 F. 2d 44 (2nd Cir. 1955)

[Note: Justice Clark, in his opinion giving the decision of the Court of Appeals in this case, made reference to the quality of Judge Ryan's charge to the jury. Portions of the charge to the jury are reproduced here.]

This suit is brought by C.I.T. Financial Corporation, a Delaware corporation, engaged in the financing business, against a number of individuals who were the partners in a firm of accountants known as Barrow, Wade, Guthrie & Co. The suit is in the federal courts by reason of the diversity of citizenship between the plaintiff and the defendants. . . .

In substance, it is plaintiff's contention that it was damaged by defendants in that relying on defendants' false, inaccurate and misleading statements and representations contained in their reports of audits as to the financial condition of Manufacturers Trading Corporation and of its subsidiary, Manufacturers Discount Company, it was led into making and continuing loans to Manufacturers in the belief that the latter was in the financial condition and position as represented and stated in the defendants' reports, when in fact it was not; that these reports and the representations they contained were certified by defendants in their capacity as certified public accountants; that at the time defendants prepared and certified their reports on audits they knew that for the purpose of obtaining credit and of obtaining a continuance of credit already granted, Manufacturers would submit these reports of audits to those with whom they transacted business, such as plaintiff, that these reports would be relied upon by such persons, and that defendants intended that reliance be placed on these reports, since the purpose of the auditing and of the preparation of the reports by defendants was to assist their client Manufacturers in obtaining credit.

With reference to the reports issued on the audits made by the defendants after the period ending June 30, 1945, the plaintiff also contends in the third cause of action, and with what force is for you to say, that these reports and audits were made by the defendants with actual knowledge that they were to be furnished to and submitted to the plaintiff by Manufacturers and were for plaintiff's benefit, who was so specifically identified to the defendants, in compliance with the terms of the indenture loan agreement made between plaintiff's subsidiary and Manufacturers on October 17, 1945, at the time the loan was made.

The complaint in this suit alleges five separate claims or what are called in law counts or causes of action. I have withdrawn from your consideration the first and fifth of these, so that you are required to give your verdict only as to the remaining three claims, that is, the second, third and fourth causes of action. I have taken the first and fifth claims from your consideration entirely for reasons of law with which you are not to be concerned, and the fact that this has been done is not to be considered by you in any manner in reaching your verdict or in your consideration of the evidence in this case.

Specifically, then, in its claim, which is stated in the complaint as the second cause of action, plaintiff alleges that defendants certified two statements and reports of audits as true and accurate concerning Manufacturers' financial condition and the business transacted by it for the year ending December 31, 1944, and for the six-month period ending June 30, 1945; that by their certification they represented that they had examined the accounts, books and records of Manufacturers as they were engaged to do by Manufacturers; that such reports and certifications did not reflect the true financial condition of Manufacturers in the following respects: that the commercial receivables shown on its books were worthless and uncollectible, or in fact did not exist; that some of the loans and receivables shown on the books to be secured by collateral were not so secured because there was no collateral or that the collateral was insufficient to cover the loans or was valueless; that the reserve set upon the books for doubtful accounts was inadequate; that the collection and replacement of the commercial receivables was much less rapid than shown; and that Manufacturers had made substantial loans to clients who were in no position to pay them back.

It is further claimed in this second cause of action that plaintiff, believing the accuracy of these audit reports and relying on them, did on October 17, 1945, enter into a loan indenture agreement and did cause its subsidiary Commercial Investment Trust Incorporated to lend to Manufacturers the sum of $1,440,000 in exchange for three notes of Manufacturers as security for the loan. Plaintiff claims, too, that these audits of December 31, 1944, and of June 30, 1945, made and certified by defendants, were fraudulently and recklessly made; that defendants knew that the books and records of Manufacturers which they represented that they had examined were false, and did not represent its true financial position as of the date of the audit periods, and that these representations would not have been made by defendants in reports of their audits had they not acted fraudulently, namely, with gross negligence, arising from a wilful disregard of the facts known to them or which they would have known if they had made the audits and examinations in the manner they represented they had. The plaintiff claims that in reliance upon these false reports it made the loan of $1,440,000 to Manufacturers which was a total loss, and seeks recovery of the defendants for this amount and interest.

In its next claim, called the third cause of action, plaintiff alleges that defendants were negligent in the semi-annual reports prepared and certified by the defendants and issued by them after the loan was made which reports they represented to be true and accurate audit reports for the six-month periods ending on June 30th of the years 1946, 1947 and 1948 and ending on December 31st for the years 1945, 1946 and 1947, and that these reports did not reflect and present the true worth and business of Manufacturers; that when defendants prepared and issued these audit reports they knew of the loan indenture agreement of October 17, 1945, between plaintiff's subsidiary and Manufacturers, and of the purchase of the notes by plaintiff and knew of the terms and provisions of the agreement; that they knew that one of the purposes for the preparation of the reports of the semi-annual audits and the annual audits after June 30, 1945, was that they were to be submitted by Manufacturers specifically to plaintiff pursuant to the loan indenture agreement; that these semi-annual and annual audits and reports after June 30, 1945, were for the purpose of keeping plaintiff informed of Manufacturers' financial condition; that defendants knew of this and prepared their reports of these audits for this purpose; that by reason of this plaintiff claims defendants were under a continuing duty to plaintiff to use reasonable care and skill in the preparation of their reports and certifications which they did not exercise and employ, and that had they used reasonable care and skill the true condition of Manufacturers would have been revealed and been made known to defendants; that by reason of defendants' negligence plaintiff did not know that Manufacturers had breached the provision of the agreement which gave plaintiff the right to accelerate and demand immediate payment of the notes or that a fraud had been perpetrated on it by Manufacturers in obtaining the loan in October, 1945; that had this been known by plaintiff, it would have demanded immediate payment of the notes it held of Manufacturers and would have been able to enforce collection of Manufacturers' obligations, if not in whole, in part; and that because of defendants' negligence in not preparing accurate and true audits and reports the notes in plaintiff's hands became worthless and uncollectible to plaintiff's damage.

In the next claim, called the fourth cause of action, plaintiff alleges the same misrepresentations in the semi-annual audits and reports for the years 1946, 1947 and 1948 and the annual audits and reports for the years 1945, 1946 and 1947, and charges the defendants with fraud in that the defendants knew that the reports and certifications they made were false or that they made such reports without knowledge or without an opinion in good faith as to the truth or falsity of said reports; or in wilful disregard of facts known to them or which they should have known had they conducted their examinations and prepared their audits in the manner in which they represented they had; and that had the true facts been known by plaintiff it would have demanded immediate payment of the notes it held of Manufacturers and would have been able to enforce collection of Manufacturers' obligation, if not in whole, in part; and that because of defendants' fraud in not preparing accurate and true audits and reports the notes in plaintiff's hands became worthless and uncollectible to plaintiff's damage.

Defendants deny that they made negligent or grossly negligent or fraudulent reports and representations of the affairs of Manufacturers and contend that their reports and audits were issued and conducted with care and in accordance with generally accepted auditing standards; that plaintiff did not rely on defendants' reports; that plaintiff made its own investigation of the affairs of Manufacturers and of its subsidiaries and of its financial worth before making the loan and continued its own independent investigation after the making of the loan and conducted its own supervision of the loan and the administration of the loan; that plaintiff was fully aware and advised of the affairs of Manufacturers and of the nature of its business and relied when making the loan and continuing it not only on its own judgment but on the judgment of Alfred H. Sachs and others (Alfred H. Sachs, you will recall, was the president of Manufacturers) as to the value of collateral held by Manufacturers; that Alfred H. Sachs was regarded by plaintiff as one who was an expert in such matters and particularly in the evaluation of collateral given as security for loans of this type; that plaintiff knew that the ability to evaluate collateral was vital to the success of Manufacturers' business; that defendants were not employed to evaluate collateral, that they did not do so, and that they disclaimed any responsibility for such evaluation as was made; that they did not represent or certify to the valuation of collateral held by Manufacturers or the collectibility of the loans made by Manufacturers or the adequacy of the reserve set upon the books of Manufacturers against receivables.

* * *

One of the first questions to be decided is just what the defendants did represent. Defendants have pointed out to you what has been called their disclaimer or qualification which is contained in the June 30, 1945 report, and similar or identical statements in the other reports, reading:

> While it was not within our province to pass upon or assume responsibility for the legal or equitable title to the commercial receivables purchased by the companies or the valuation of any security thereto accepted and held by them, it was apparent from their books and records and by opinion of counsel that their contractual and assignment forms are adequate for their legal protection in connection with the collection and liquidation of commercial receivables purchased.

Defendants contend that by this disclaimer or qualification anyone who read their reports would take notice that the defendants assumed no responsibility for the valuation of the collateral held by Manufacturers Trading Corporation. This much plaintiff apparently concedes, but plaintiff contends that this disclaimer did not permit the defendants to close their eyes to facts and to give up the alertness which an accountant should apply during his audit.

Plaintiff contends that if the defendants had reasonable ground to suspect that the collateral was not worth the amounts which the management thought it was worth, the disclaimer did not cover the situation. There was testimony of expert accounting witnesses bearing on this issue. The question of the accounting principles involved is a question of fact which you, as jurors, are to decide and the true meaning and application of the disclaimer or qualification, in light of that testimony and the other facts of the case, is for you to decide. . . .

Defendants also state that because of the peculiar and special nature of the business of Manufacturers Trading Corporation and its subsidiary, that of making loans against collateral of all different types and sorts, the disclaimer as to responsibility for the valuation of collateral extends to the valuation of the receivables themselves, and that therefore, defendants are not responsible for the valuation of the receivables of Manufacturers Trading Corporation shown on its balance sheet. Plaintiff contends that on the fair reading of the language of the disclaimer in light of standard accounting practices it does not extend to the valuation of the receivables. Plaintiff further urges that the defendants expressed an opinion on the valuation of the receivables when they expressed their opinion that the balance sheet presented the financial condition of Manufacturers Trading Corporation and its subsidiary with a reserve for doubtful accounts set forth against the receivables. Defendants answer that the remarks about the reserve for doubtful accounts in the body of its report were not their own representations, but were those of the management, and that this was made clear by the comments in the reports.

Plaintiff contends, however, that it is a principle of auditing that if an accountant withholds an expression of opinion on so large a portion of the total assets of the enterprise as to amount to a withholding of the expression of an opinion on the financial statements as a whole, then the accountant has no right, as a matter of auditing principle, to express any opinion on the financial statements, and he must refrain from signing a report. Since the receivables amounted to over 80 per cent of the total assets of Manufacturers Trading Corporation, plaintiff contends that this asserted auditing principle is applicable here. Therefore, plaintiff contends, both as a matter of the reading of the report by itself, and on the basis of the report in the light of the foregoing asserted auditing principle, that the defendants did express an opinion on the valuation of the receivables. On these points, both parties offered expert accounting testimony, and the defendants vigorously contend that the qualified opinion was entirely proper in view of the very nature of Manufacturers' business, of the special skill and experience of Alfred H. Sachs, its president, in the realization upon collateral which the company had in the past been obliged to possess and liquidate when large loans secured by collateral were in default.

There has also been much testimony concerning the adequacy of the reserves set up for the receivables. Plaintiff has contended that if the reserves had been built up to what it contends was a proper amount by charge to expense for the audit periods, these deductions would have resulted in the showing of losses instead of profits. The defendants, of course, deny these contentions, and here again state that they relied, and they contend properly so according to standard accounting procedure and practice, upon the representations of management as to the adequacy of the reserves, of the collectibility of the accounts and of the amounts which could be realized on the collateral and so plainly stated in their reports. Here, the issue is again for the jury to decide.

* * *

I shall now endeavor to give you the law which governs the duty and the obligations of the defendants to the plaintiff in this case, and particularly of the limitations of that duty and of those obligations as it applies to each of plaintiff's three claims or causes of action which you are to consider.

An accountant is employed to report, after examination, review and consideration of factual representations of management, his own professional opinion that the statements of management fairly present the financial position and results of operations. An accountant does not make factual representations as to the contents of financial statements; these are the statements of the management and unless the accountant expressly states to the contrary he does not assume responsibility for them, but he does assume responsibility for his own opinion and represents that in order to form such an opinion he has complied with generally accepted auditing standards.

His duty in examining the books is not merely for the purpose of ascertaining what they do show, but also for the purpose of satisfying himself that they showed the true financial position of the company. If you should find that the defendants had knowledge of such facts as would reasonably have caused them to suspect that the books and records of Manufacturers and of its subsidiary materially failed to reflect the true financial condition of the company, the failure to indicate in the report of audits which they issued can only be justified by an actual check-up. A refusal to see the obvious, a failure to investigate the doubtful, if sufficiently gross, may furnish evidence leading to an inference of fraud so as to impose liability for losses suffered by those who rely on the balance sheet. In other words, heedlessness and reckless disregard of consequences may take the place of deliberate intention to defraud.

You will recall that I pointed out to you that in the second and fourth causes of action, plaintiff charges the defendants with fraud and with gross negligence amounting to fraud; and that in the third cause of action alone plaintiff charges the defendants with simple negligence, that is with neither gross negligence nor with fraud.

It is most important that you keep the allegations of these various causes of action separate and distinct, that is, the second and fourth from the third, for as to each the principles of law which are to guide you in determining the liability of the defendants to plaintiff for any damage it may have suffered are entirely different.

* * *

With particular reference to the second and fourth causes of action wherein plaintiff alleges that defendants were guilty of fraud and of gross negligence amounting in fact to fraud, I am now going to instruct you on some general principles of law governing the liability of accountants such as defendants to a person in the position of plaintiff.

Bear in mind that the defendants were not under contract to plaintiff or in its employ; they were engaged to audit and examine by Manufacturers Trading Corporation, not by plaintiff. With respect to plaintiff and anyone who was not their employer therefor, although as certified public accountants the defendants represented themselves to be skilled and capable in the audit and examination of books and records, the defendants did not assume thereby to guarantee or to insure the accuracy of their reports, or the financial condition of Manufacturers or of any company whose books they examined. Consequently, plaintiff in the absence of any contractual agreement or business relation with defendants, and none is alleged in the second and fourth causes of action, cannot recover on these two causes of action for defendants' negligence, that is, for carelessness or honest blunders or an error in judgment in the examination and audit of Manufacturers Trading Corporation's books and records. So that, even if Manufacturers Trading Corporation's books were falsified, and defendants because of their failure to do a workmanlike job were deceived and did not know of the falsification, they may not be held liable to plaintiff on the second and fourth causes of action solely because they were negligent. In order for plaintiff to recover from defendants on a showing of ordinary negligence, it is necessary that it establish that defendants when they submitted their audits and certifications knew that although they were performing this work at the request of Manufacturers Trading Corporation, the audits and certifications were for the primary benefit of plaintiff and that plaintiff was specifically identified to defendants as a person for whose primary benefit these audits and certifications were being made. . . .

In the second and fourth causes of action plaintiff does not contend that any such relationship such as a contractual relationship or business arrangement existed between it and defendants, nor does it contend that defendants knew specifically of the existence of plaintiff as a person for whose primary benefit the audits and certifications were being made. It is therefore necessary for plaintiff to establish to your satisfaction by a preponderance of the credible evidence with respect to the second and fourth causes of action that defendants in preparing these audits and certifications and in examining the books and records were guilty of fraud as I shall later explain that term; and this it does allege.

* * *

Fraud presupposes an intent to deceive another. The fraud which plaintiff contends the defendants practiced on it was the wilful representation of certain facts as true when they knew them to be false, or the representation of facts to be true to their knowledge when they had no such knowledge and were totally indifferent or uninformed to whether the facts were true or false. An intent to deceive must be present before one can be said to be guilty of fraud. The requisite intent may be inferred from knowledge on the part of the defendants that what they were stating to be true was in fact false, or it may be inferred from the lack of an honest belief on their part that what they stated was true. The answer therefore lies in the state of mind of defendants; did they honestly believe that the audits and certifications they made were true and accurate? If they did have such belief whether it was reasonable or not for them to entertain it is immaterial, for if they honestly believed what they said then they had no intent to deceive.

If the defendants represented a fact as true to their knowledge, then whether they believed it to be true or not, defendants are liable for deceit in the event that it was false.

Fraud includes the pretense of knowledge when knowledge there is none.

Knowledge of falsity is an indispensable element, except where a representation has beeen put forward as one of one's own knowledge, or in circumstances where the expression of opinion was a dishonorable pretense.

Even an opinion, especially an opinion by an expert, may be found to be fraudulent, if the grounds supporting it are so flimsy as to lead to the conclusion that there was no genuine belief back of it.

With respect to an omission or concealment on the part of defendants, the test is: Was the omission and concealment deliberate? If it was deliberate, then an intent to conceal may be inferred. Here you must remember that one is held to intend the necessary consequences of his acts and doings. The defendants represented in their reports that they made audits of the books and accounts of Manufacturers Trading Corporation and of its subsidiary. If the audits which they in fact made were so superficial as to be only a pretense of audits and not real audits, then the element of knowledge or falsity of their representation is present— for they were representing a fact as true and that they had knowledge of its truth when in fact they had none. This does not mean that they are liable for mistakes and omissions in their audits if the audits were genuine and honest audits. Whether the audits were real and in good faith or a pretense of audits is a question of fact for you to determine. The honesty or the lack of honesty of the belief of the defendants, the issue in determining the intent of the defendants, can only be determined by you from all the evidence in the case, from the testimony, the exhibits, and the impression the witnesses made on you when they testified.

The fact that the audit actually sets forth the condition of the Manufacturers Trading Corporation and its subsidiary as shown upon the books of that company, does not prevent it from being a false audit, provided that it is shown to your satisfaction by a preponderance of credible evidence that defendants had knowledge that the books did not correctly show the actual condition of the company. Knowledge on the part of employees of the defendants who were working on the books is in law knowledge on the part of the defendants.

Naturally you can only determine the state of mind of the defendants from their actions, from what they did, from the information they had as that has been revealed to you by the evidence in the case. And, in determining this you may take into consideration their motive, if any, whether they stood to gain or lose by practicing a deception on plaintiff, as such inducement might bear on the true state of their mind or knowledge; but aside from this, defendants' motive is wholly immaterial, and it is not necessary that defendants derived any benefit from the fraud they are alleged to have committed.

When you consider the question whether the defendants made representations known to them to be untrue, or in reckless disregard of their truth or falsity, you must answer this by a determination of what the defendants' knowledge and intention was at the time of the making of each audit and report and not by a determination of what it was at a subsequent date.

It is this reckless indifference to the truth or falsity of a statement certified and stated to be true to a person's knowledge, when in fact there is no such knowledge of its truth or falsity, and from which an intent to deceive may reasonably be inferred, that the law calls gross negligence amounting to fraud. It is this intent to deceive, inferred from all the surrounding circumstances which distinguishes gross negligence from ordinary negligence, in which one acts unintentionally and carelessly.

For ordinary negligence under these two causes of action, the second and fourth, the defendants cannot be held liable to plaintiff; for gross negligence amounting to fraud as I have just defined it to you defendants may be liable on these two causes of action to plaintiff or anyone to whose attention and notice defendants might reasonably have expected their audit reports to come.

* * *

To entitle plaintiff to recover on either the second or fourth causes of action, the plaintiff must convince you by a preponderance of the credible evidence of these five matters:

1. That the particular audit reports which are the basis of its claims . . . were made by the defendants with knowledge that they would be acted upon by the plaintiff and those similarly situated who transacted business with Manufacturers Trading Corporation and its subsidiary.
2. That the statements and representations were false or untrue.
3. That the defendants made the representations known to them to be untrue or in reckless disregard of their truth or falsity.
4. That the plaintiff acted in reliance upon the representations made by the defendants; and
5. That the plaintiff thereby suffered financial damage.

I have told you that you must find that there was reliance on the part of the plaintiff on the misrepresentation by defendants of a fact and this must be a misrepresentation of a material fact. That is necessary, for unless it is as to a material fact you may not find that it was the cause of loss to plaintiff. Plaintiff's reliance need not be exclusive. By this I mean that it is not necessary that plaintiff relied solely on the defendant's representations and nothing else before coming to a decision, but it is necessary and important that you find that defendants' fraudulent act, if you find that one was committed, played a substantial part in bringing about plaintiff's decision.

In determining whether plaintiff relied substantially upon the audit reports, you will consider the nature of the business plaintiff was conducting; the experience, intelligence and business ability of plaintiff's officers who conducted or approved the dealings had with Manufacturers; their actions and such independent investigation that you find they may have made or did not make; the amount of the sums involved; the evidence of the conversations, correspondence and communications these officers had with Alfred H. Sachs, with the defendants and with others; the audit reports themselves and all other evidence which you feel will aid you.

If you find that irrespective of the audit reports and the representations they contained, the plaintiff would nevertheless have loaned the moneys which it did, and that the audit reports and defendants' statements were not an inducing cause of the making of such loans, then in such event I instruct you that the action of the defendants, even though fraudulent, was not the proximate cause of the loss to the plaintiff. If, on the other hand, one of the inducing causes of the making of the loans was the alleged and fraudulent representations of the audit reports and plaintiff relied upon them in making the loans, then, even if this reliance was not the sole ground upon which plaintiff based its actions, nevertheless defendants would be liable if the audit reports relied upon were false and fraudulent. But if plaintiff's action, in making the loan, or in continuing it, was not induced by the audit reports but by any other and different reason shown by the evidence, then in that event the inducing cause of the dealings between plaintiff and Manufacturers Trading Corporation and its subsidiary was not the representation of the audit reports and hence there would not be any liability on the part of the defendants.

* * *

Negligence

This brings us now to a consideration of the third cause of action. In this claim, you will recall that plaintiff charges the defendants with ordinary negligence in that, pursuant to the loan indenture agreement between plaintiff and Manufacturers Trading Corporation and subsequent to the making of the loan in October, 1945 the defendants with knowledge of the terms of this agreement submitted semi-annual and annual audit reports from December 31, 1945 through June 30, 1948 and that the plaintiff was specifically identified to defendants as a person for whose primary benefit these audits and certifications were being made.

Although in this cause of action plaintiff does not contend that defendants were in its employ or that it had a contract with them, it does allege that defendants knew of the agreement between it and Manufacturers Trading Corporation and that when they prepared their audit reports they knew specifically that plaintiff would make use of them and that they had been prepared for plaintiff's benefit. In this respect, this third cause of action differs from the second and fourth causes of action; in those plaintiff does not allege that defendants knew of plaintiff as a specific person who would make use of their audits and to whom they would be submitted and for whose primary benefit they were intended; here in the third cause of action it does so contend. If this is so, then defendants owed to plaintiff the duty of care and diligence which they owed to Manufacturers Trading Corporation and in whose actual employ they were. It is by virtue of the knowledge of defendants of this situation which knowledge plaintiff contends the defendants had—knowledge, to wit, that plaintiff was specifically identified to defendants as a person who would make use of and rely on their audits—that the duty of care which they owed to Manufacturers was extended to include plaintiff.

Defendants are not to be held liable for mere negligence if their reports were made primarily for the benefit of Manufacturers Trading Corporation as a convenient instrumentality for use in the development of its business, and only incidentally or collaterally for the use of plaintiff. The test is then, did defendants know that the audits and certifications were being made for the primary benefit of plaintiff, and was plaintiff so specifically identified to the defendants? If this has not been established to your satisfaction by a preponderance of the credible evidence, your verdict shall be for the defendants on this third cause of action. If this has been established to your satisfaction by a preponderance of the credible evidence, then the defendants in preparing their audits would be liable to plaintiff for carelessness, blunders and errors in judgment, which were the result of failure to exercise that degree of care which a reasonably prudent accountant employed on a like and similar task would exercise. Apply, of course, when determining the degree of care required of the defendants, the standards of recognized accounting practice and procedure as you find them from the evidence which has been presented.

* * *

GRAIN STORAGE INVESTIGATION

Monday, May 28, 1962
House of Representatives
INTER-GOVERNMENTAL RELATIONS SUBCOMMITTEE
OF THE COMMITTEE ON GOVERNMENT OPERATIONS,
Washington, D.C.

The subcommittee met in executive session, pursuant to call, at 5:25 P.M., in room 1501-B, New House Office Building, Hon. L. H. Fountain (chairman of the subcommittee) presiding.

Present: Representatives L. H. Fountain, Neal Smith, Ross Bass, Florence P. Dwyer, and Odin Langen.

Also present: James R. Naughton, counsel; Daniel A. Kavanaugh, associate counsel; Edward Hanna, certified public accountant, General Accounting Office; Robert Manuel, minority counsel; and James A. Lanigan, general counsel, Government Operations Committee.

* * *

TESTIMONY OF WINN P. JACKSON, CERTIFIED PUBLIC ACCOUNTANT, LUBBOCK, TEXAS

MR. NAUGHTON. Mr. Jackson, did you receive by mail, prior to leaving Lubbock, a copy of the rules of the subcommittee?

MR. JACKSON. Right.

MR. NAUGHTON. Which indicate the rights of witnesses.

MR. JACKSON. Yes.

* * *

MR. NAUGHTON. Mr. Jackson, would you like the committee to postpone this hearing in order for you to have an opportunity to secure counsel?

MR. JACKSON. No; I believe not. I don't have anything to hide. Like I say, I wasn't doing anything that I thought was wrong. I need to get back to Lubbock at the earliest possible minute.

MR. FOUNTAIN. Well, under those circumstances, then, why don't you go ahead, Mr. Jackson, and tell us just exactly what transpired, the circumstances under which Mr. Estes contacted you, and what arrangements he made with you and what you did in consequence thereof.

MR. JACKSON. All right. First of all, may I give you my name and where I was raised and a little background?

MR. FOUNTAIN. Yes; and your full background.

MR. JACKSON. I was born in Hedley, Texas, and afterward my family moved to a farm six miles southwest of Levelland, Texas, which is thirty miles west of Lubbock, where I was raised. Upon finishing high school in 1945 I went to the Navy; and upon discharge, honorable discharge in 1946, I entered Baylor University in Waco. Then upon graduation with the class of 1950 I went to work in the Houston area. I understand at that time, before 1945—I don't know what this Mr. Estes was doing, but I had no reason to have known him and I certainly didn't. I was employed in the Houston area for approximately eight years.

MR. FOUNTAIN. By whom?

MR. JACKSON. First by Dow Chemical Co. at Freeport, which is south of Houston.

MR. FOUNTAIN. How long were you there?

MR. JACKSON. Two and a half years, until January of 1953, when I moved up to Houston and went to work for—I was in the auditing department of Dow Chemical Co., internal audit. I moved up to Houston in January of 1953 as assistant chief accountant for Trans Texas Airways. I left there in October of 1954 and went to work for Union Oil & Gas Corp. of Louisiana in their accounting department.

After that I decided I wanted to take the CPA exam and try to become a CPA. I began studying then in my spare time to take the exam. I took it the first time in May 1954 and passed half of it, and then passed the remaining in May of 1956.

In October or November of 1956, then I became employed by a firm of CPA's in Houston with the name of Shifftey, O'Garrett & Carter, for whom I worked until November of 1958. Now, it was while I was with Schifftey, O'Garrett & Carter that I discovered that I liked public accounting very much and I wanted to establish my own office some day, and I had to make up my mind whether to open it down there in that area where I was at that time, or move back to my home area; and I decided on the latter. So we moved to Lubbock with the intention—and I went to work for Castle & Co., CPA's in Lubbock. But I knew that if and when the opportunity ever presented itself that I would try to open my own office somewhere. This came about in February of 1960 that I agreed to stay with Mr. Castle until April, after tax season—April 15, at which date I did open my office for the practice of public accounting.

I started off with one client, I guess you would say. However, it was a firm where I was spending four hours—in other words, half a day; and my fee was $90 a week. That gave me the other half-day to get out and meet people. Pretty soon I began to pick up small bookkeeping accounts and tax work.

Now, I was located in Lubbock in a building where there was an insurance agent also as well as real estate. In June 1960 a man by the name of E. H. Patterson from Roswell, New Mexico, purchased all of the capital stock of South Plains Grain, Inc., at Levelland. This was a corporation. He purchased it from two individuals over there that started it and that owned it.

MR. BASS. Who were they?

MR. JACKSON. One of them was McInroe and the other one's name was Kirby Rogers. He had no previous grain-storage experience. He hadn't been in the grain storage before, but heard it was pretty good, so that's the reason that he bought that. He was more of a promoter type of individual rather than a real businessman, as we normally think of one.

MR. FOUNTAIN. Who was that?

MR. JACKSON. E. H. Patterson of Roswell, New Mexico. He, of course, had to have a Texas agent. Each corporation in Texas must have a registered agent, of course. He asked me if I would like to be secretary of that corporation because he did need one, and I agreed that I would.

However, just prior to that, let me back up just a little bit. It so happened that this insurance agent in the building where I had my office in Lubbock was carrying the insurance policies of South Plains Grain, Inc. So he was over there—it must have been about July—talking to the insurance agent relative to the insurance. The subject got around to accounting or bookkeeping, and he sent him back there to see me. We talked, and I agreed that I would take care of his—set up his books and do his bookkeeping for him over there because he didn't know a debit from a credit himself. And the warehouseman who he had employed did not either. He was a grain man, but he didn't know anything about bookkeeping other than how to write checks and make bank deposits, which he did. I didn't do that part of it. I merely posted the journals and the general ledger.

Now, at this time, as far as I know—and he never indicated otherwise to me—Mr. Patterson did not know Mr. Estes, had never met him. But he, being a promoter type of individual that he was, met him somewhere between July and August.

MR. FOUNTAIN. What year is that?

MR. JACKSON. Sir?

MR. FOUNTAIN. What year?

MR. JACKSON. Of 1960.

MR. FOUNTAIN. 1960?

MR. JACKSON. Yes. They started talking about the grain business, and evidently started to making big plans for the storage facility at Levelland. They thought it would be a good idea to add several million bushels more capacity storage there and make it a nine house, which is a terminal-type storage that can issue official weights and grades. They have railroad scales. So for this purpose they decided that they would go 50-50 in the ownership. This was about August, I would say, of 1960. They wanted to own it 50-50.

MR. SMITH. How did you know this? Did they tell you or were you there during their conversations?

MR. JACKSON. Well, I will get to that in just a second.

MR. SMITH. All right.

MR. JACKSON. For this purpose, they arranged with an attorney in Plainview—Mr. Lucian Morehead—to draw the agreement between them. Mr. Patterson requested that I be present with any records in the case of South Plains Grain, in case the attorney needed to refer to them in drawing up this agreement between them. It was more or less a partnership agreement, although South Plains Grain was more or less a corporation.

Because of the fact, I guess they thought they needed some records there because their agreement specified—I remember one item that Mr. Estes had to match Mr. Patterson's expenditures for the capital stock and contributions to working capital of the corporation before he was to receive his one-half of the stock. So they made this agreement September 30, 1960. Thereafter, or soon thereafter, Mr. Estes began to put money in the corporation over there and they began to look around for somebody, some finance company, I suppose, that would finance their additional plant facilities.

MR. FOUNTAIN. Was it a corporation or a partnership?

MR. JACKSON. It was a corporation.

MR. FOUNTAIN. They incorporated?

MR. JACKSON. South Plains Grain, Inc.—incorporated.

So they began to look around for somebody that would finance their planned additional facilities over there. Mr. Patterson found a broker in Fort Worth by the name of Sneed, who in turn had contact with a broker in New York by the name of George Birmingham, who wanted to talk to them about their proposed additional expansion. Of course at that time the grain storage was most good. Now, let's back up one point.

This meeting here on June 30 with the Plainview Terminal was the first time that I had met Mr. Estes.

MR. BASS. June 30, 1960?

MR. JACKSON. September 30; I'm sorry.

MR. BASS. 1960?

MR. JACKSON. That's right. That's the first time I had met him and I had only begun to hear some reports about him after I started to work for South Plains Grain. Of course they were in the grain business, too. I was employed and doing work for Mr. Patterson, who was a nice man, even though he wasn't a real good businessman.

But after the September 30 agreement, then they wanted to expand the facility and they found this broker who in turn had another broker, and they wanted to talk to him. So they made an appointment in Fort Worth to meet this broker from New York.

MR. BASS. Mr. Jackson, let me ask you one question. You said this man was not a good businessman. Now, are you indicating that prior to the time that Mr. Patterson went in business with Mr. Estes he was not doing very well in the grain storage business?

MR. JACKSON. He had never been in the grain storage business before.

MR. BASS. But he owned one when he went in. Was he making any money before—I mean after the time he bought this corporation until he met Mr. Estes? Was he getting any business?

MR. JACKSON. Well, they had some grain in storage over there, but what I was saying was that Mr. Patterson didn't know the grain storage business.

MR. BASS. So actually he didn't have much grain in storage then until he met Estes. Is that what you are saying?

MR. JACKSON. Well, the storage capacity that South Plains Grain had when Mr. Patterson bought it was approximately 450,000 bushels. I would say that they probably had about 360,000 to 380,000 in storage.

MR. BASS. That is pretty good.

MR. FOUNTAIN. Was that before they formed the corporation?

MR. JACKSON. Yes, sir.

MR. FOUNTAIN. That was Mr. Patterson himself who had that?

MR. JACKSON. It was a corporation before he bought it.

MR. FOUNTAIN. The corporation.

MR. JACKSON. That's right. The corporation had been formed two or three years before.

MR. SMITH. Did Estes get 50 per cent of the stock transferred to him then?

MR. JACKSON. No.

MR. SMITH. How did he acquire 50 per cent of the stock interest?

MR. FOUNTAIN. What you are saying is that Mr. Patterson purchased the stock in the corporation?

MR. JACKSON. One hundred per cent.

MR. FOUNTAIN. What you are saying is that Mr. Patterson purchased the stock in the corporation and thereafter took Mr. Estes in and Mr. Estes contributed on a 50-50 basis?

MR. JACKSON. Right. Then he began to contribute money into the corporation to—

MR. FOUNTAIN. Pursuant to a written understanding they had?

MR. JACKSON. Right. To match Mr. Patterson's expenditures.

MR. SMITH. But there was no transfer of stock from Patterson in Texas?

MR. JACKSON. Not at that time.

MR. SMITH. Then at that time you had a partnership between Patterson and Estes. Right?

MR. JACKSON. Well, the agreement drawn up by the attorney was really between Mr. Patterson and Mr. Estes.

MR. SMITH. I see.

MR. JACKSON. It was not—I am almost positive with South Plains Grain being partners with the agreements.

MR. FOUNTAIN. Contracts between them as individuals.

MR. JACKSON. Right.

MR. FOUNTAIN. Or between Mr. Patterson as the owner of the stock of the company and Mr. Estes.

MR. JACKSON. Between them as individuals, I believe.

MR. FOUNTAIN. Do you know whether or not Mr. Patterson agreed to transfer a certain percentage of the stock upon the condition that Mr. Estes pay into the corporation a certain sum?

MR. JACKSON. A like amount, right; and he did. He agreed to transfer one-half the stock to Mr. Estes upon such time that Mr. Estes matched his contributions.

MR. BASS. Did they do this with cash or with stock certificates and some other interest?

MR. JACKSON. Did he do what?

MR. BASS. Did Mr. Estes put his part in the corporation in cash or in stock certificates in another corporation?

MR. JACKSON. He did it in the form of cash.

MR. BASS. In the form of cash?

MR. JACKSON. Yes.

MR. FOUNTAIN. When you say cash, you mean check?

MR. JACKSON. Check. Well, I assume that it was. I didn't make deposits and I never saw the checks myself. But they were made.

MR. FOUNTAIN. All right, go ahead.

MR. JACKSON. All right. I am going to cover that point in just a minute. But this meeting was set up in Fort Worth with the brokers. Here again Mr. Patterson suggested that I come along because he felt like the New York broker was wanting to know about South Plains Grain and the accounting records. So he also talked Mr. Estes into taking him and myself down there in his plane. So Mr. Estes had his pilot and they picked Mr. Patterson and myself up at Lubbock and we went to Fort Worth.

MR. FOUNTAIN. Whose plane did you go in?

MR. JACKSON. Mr. Estes' plane. Of course on the plane I got a little further acquainted. This was the second meeting with him. He was telling me about all the businesses that he had, how well he was doing, and how much money he was making; and that he was doing this church work also, and he gave a good bit away to charity.

MR. BASS. Gave you a real snow job, didn't he?

MR. JACKSON. Well, I believe you refer to it as that.

That was the main thing going down there. Coming back from Fort Worth he began to ask me specifically about depreciation rates and methods on grain-storage facilities. I told him at the time that I couldn't give him a very good answer, you know without doing some research on it, but I would be glad to do it when I got back to Lubbock, and he said, "Well, fine."

So after we arrived back to Lubbock, the next day or so I did research on depreciation of grain-storage facilities for taxes. This was for tax purposes, income-tax purposes. I even consulted with a tax attorney, a friend of mine in Lubbock, relative thereto. In a couple of days or three I wrote him a one-page finding of my research. He wrote back fairly soon, thanked me for it, and said he appreciated it very much.

MR. FOUNTAIN. This was research you did and sent to Mr. Estes?

MR. JACKSON. Right, on depreciation of grain-storage facilities for tax purposes.

He wrote me back in a few days and thanked me for it and said he appreciated it and please send him a bill for it. I sent him a $15 bill for it which he promptly paid.

MR. LANGEN. Can I interrupt you?

MR. JACKSON. Yes, sir.

MR. LANGEN. Who was your attorney friend here who supplied you with the information on depreciation?

MR. JACKSON. Ed Smith.

MR. LANGEN. Ed Smith?

MR. JACKSON. Yes. He is a CPA and an attorney. He specialized in income tax depreciation.

MR. NAUGHTON. Excuse me; did Mr. Smith know this was for Mr. Estes?

MR. JACKSON. No, I didn't tell him. I knew the firm he worked for had a tax case going on depreciation of grain-storage facilities.

MR. NAUGHTON. As far as you know, Mr. Smith doesn't know Mr. Estes?

MR. JACKSON. Oh, no.

MR. NAUGHTON. Or never has had any connection with him?

MR. JACKSON. Oh, no, he has none. Now, this was the only other contact I had with Mr. Estes until through the end of the year, except for one or two times when I made up these lists of contributions that Mr. Patterson had put in and that Mr. Estes had put in.

He, of course, immediately after they went in agreement, began to put moneys in South Plains Grain, and they were in the process of expanding, adding on some additional grain storage. They had to put in new rail facilities, and in one column I would list Mr. Patterson's and in the other Mr. Estes'—what they had in.

So other than preparing one or two of those lists between then and after the first of the year, until about the latter part of January—that's all the contact I had with him. But in the meantime I had found out that he was on the board at Lubbock Christian College—what I thought was a Christian businessman, and everything that I could hear on him was just wonderful, you know. I just thought that a fellow like that must really have something on the ball.

So in the latter part of January or at the first part of February when he called me—

MR. FOUNTAIN. What year?

MR. JACKSON. Of 1961. When he phones and asked if—well, at first he said, "You know, I have a good many businesses and pretty large operations." He said, "I don't feel like that I need a complete overall certified audit. However, I do need help in one of my businesses at various times." He said, "I was wondering if you would be interested in doing whatever work I might need at these scattered places on the basis of $500 a month retainer."

I said "Yes," because naturally I felt, I would never have a client like that, you know, probably again, and that my ship had really come in. So I managed to squeak out a "yes." Then this request for a financial statement followed in a few days.

MR. FOUNTAIN. Was that in writing?

MR. JACKSON. In writing.

MR. FOUNTAIN. What did he say to you?

MR. JACKSON. He wanted me to put it on my own stationery.

MR. FOUNTAIN. What did he tell you?

MR. JACKSON. Well, that's about it. He said, "I am going to send you, or I am sending you a financial statement and would you please put it on your stationery."

MR. FOUNTAIN. In other words, he prepared this particular statement himself?

MR. JACKSON. Right; and then it was mailed to me. I told Mr. Estes that I would have to check it out; I would have to do some checking. This was on the telephone.

MR. FOUNTAIN. What did you tell him on the telephone?

MR. JACKSON. Over the telephone and he said, "Well, why?" He said, "It is all right, there is nothing wrong with it." He said, "You know it's right to the penny." Everybody thought that he was such a Christian gentleman and, with his wide reputation, I made the mistake of believing him.

MR. FOUNTAIN. Then what did you do?

MR. JACKSON. So I prepared it on my own stationery.

MR. FOUNTAIN. So you prepared this statement on your stationery, with the firm name of Jackson & Rogers, certified public accountants?

MR. JACKSON. Right.

MR. FOUNTAIN. Lubbock, Texas. Will you read that statement to us and state whether or not the attached sheets were also prepared by him and whether or not that is an exact copy of the information which he furnished to you to be supplied him over your signature?

MR. JACKSON (reading):

MR. BILLIE SOL ESTES,
Pecos, Texas.
Dear Sir: We have examined the balance sheet presented in condensed form of Billie Sol Estes as of December 31, 1960. Our examination was made in accordance with generally accepted standards and accordingly included such tests of the accounting records and such other auditing procedures as we considered necessary in these circumstances, except that our examination did not

include the generally accepted auditing procedure of observing and testing the methods used in determining inventory quantities, prices and amounts.

By reason of the limitation of the scope of our examination as to inventories, no opinion may be expressed as to the fairness of the presentation in the accompanying balance sheet of the financial position of Billie Sol Estes as of December 31, 1960.

Respectfully,

JACKSON & ROGERS,
BY WINN P. JACKSON,
Certified Public Accountant.

Dated February 14, 1961.

MR. FOUNTAIN. Will you describe to the committee what the attached sheets are, and if those sheets contain the same information which he furnished you?

MR. JACKSON. The attached sheet—the first page—is a list of his various assets. Under the first caption we have "Current Assets." Under the second caption, "Land and Depreciable Assets." Under the third caption, "Other Investments and Assets." And then the total assets.

The second page consists of his liabilities—

MR. NAUGHTON. Excuse me. Do you want the amounts there, Mr. Chairman?

MR. FOUNTAIN. Yes, you might have those.

MR. NAUGHTON. Do you want to give us the total amount?

MR. JACKSON. The total amount of assets shown to be $20,087,416.38. On page 2 of the balance sheet is the liabilities and net worth section. Under "Liabilities" you have first "Current Liabilities" and then the second caption, "Long-Term Debt." The total liabilities shown are $6,352,461.63, leaving a net worth of $13,734,954.75.

MR. NAUGHTON. Excuse me; at that point how much were the inventories that are shown on that statement?

MR. JACKSON. The inventories of merchandise for resale is shown to be $942,701.13.

MR. FOUNTAIN. Is that an exact duplicate of the statement which you supplied him on your stationery?

MR. JACKSON. Yes, sir; it appears to be.

MR. FOUNTAIN. Did Mr. Estes tell you the purpose for which he wanted to use that statement?

MR. JACKSON. I can't remember at the time whether he did or not. I said "Now I will have to check that out. I will have to audit the figures on this"—on the balance sheet which he mailed me, which was just like this one, of course. When he said "You know everything is right and there's nothing wrong with it." I believe at that time is when he indicated to me, "The only place it is going is somewhere up in the Agriculture Department."

MR. FOUNTAIN. Did you make any examinations of books or records of any kind or nature or description before preparing that statement?

MR. JACKSON. No, sir. I did not.

MR. FOUNTAIN. You simply submitted the statement which he had prepared in the form in which he had prepared it and mailed it to him?

MR. JACKSON. Right. At the time I certainly didn't have any reason to doubt his net worth.

MR. FOUNTAIN. Let me ask you this question. As a certified public accountant, just what does that statement mean?

MR. JACKSON. As a certified public accountant, that means that—nothing, in effect, because of the fact it says (reading):

> No opinion may be expressed as to the fairness of presentation in the accompanying balance sheet of the financial position of Billie Sol Estes.

Now that is what accountants or CPA's refer to as a disclaimer, because of the fact they have not been able to examine statements or records sufficiently to warrant giving an opinion, or even a qualified opinion.

MR. SMITH. But the disclaimer only went to inventories, didn't it?

MR. JACKSON. No. The description of the work done on the described inventory. But the disclaimer says no opinion may be expressed, and that applies to all assets and liabilities. I didn't feel like I could give any other kind of report or opinion other than a disclaimer.

MR. FOUNTAIN. Of course you said (reading):

> We have examined the balance sheet presented in condensed form of Billie Sol Estes as of December 31, 1960.

Did you examine the balance sheet?

MR. JACKSON. Right.

MR. FOUNTAIN. And the balance sheet was identical with this?

MR. JACKSON. Right; except let me point out one item. For instance, I think land and depreciable assets he had listed like fixed assets, and I just called it land and depreciable assets. That is the caption I liked better, but I didn't change anything else as far as the figures.

MR. FOUNTAIN. But he presented you no balance sheet which contained any more information than that contained on these sheets?

MR. JACKSON. That's right.

MR. FOUNTAIN. Now, you state (reading):

> Our examination was made in accordance with generally accepted
> auditing standards.

You say you made no examination?

MR. JACKSON. Except—there's a semicolon there.

MR. FOUNTAIN (reading):

> . . . and accordingly included such tests of the accounting records
> and such other auditing procedures as we considered necessary in
> the circumstances.

What would a certified public accountant have in mind when he
says "included such tests of the accounting records and such other auditing procedures as we considered necessary in the circumstances."

MR. JACKSON. First of all, every audit that you make is different, see;
and an auditor has to decide when he gets into the audit as to how much
or what extent he carries his procedures, because if you get into making
an audit of a company and they have good internal control, checks and
balances and such, you wouldn't carry your audit procedures to such an
extent as opposed to another audit that you did for a company and they
didn't have good internal control or good checks and balances.

Then also, there are many times when you get into doing an audit
perhaps you run into something that maybe you feel you need to extend
certain auditing procedures. So that's the reason you say, "in the circumstances." You felt it to be necessary in the circumstances.

MR. FOUNTAIN. And then you say (reading):

> . . . except that our examination did not include the generally
> accepted auditing procedures in determining inventory quantities,
> prices, and amounts.

Now what did you mean by that?

MR. JACKSON. Well, of course, the request came to us after the first
of the year; and the balance sheet, being presented as of December 31,
1960, we could not go back and observe or test the inventories as of that
date because that date had already passed and it would just be an im-
possibility. So we had no means at all or no reason to give any kind of
an idea otherwise.

MR. FOUNTAIN. Now you say in your next paragraph (reading):

> . . . no opinion may be expressed as to the fairness of the presen-
> tation in the accompanying balance sheet of the financial position
> of Billie Sol Estes as of December 31, 1960.

Now, I am puting the first part of it at the end for emphasis—"by
reason of the limitation of the scope of our examination as to inventories." Just what would normally be meant by that?

MR. JACKSON. Exactly that no opinion was being rendered at all on
the financial position of Mr. Billie Sol Estes as of December 31, 1960.

MR. FOUNTAIN. Why was that stated, "by reason of the scope of our examination as to inventories"? What does that mean?

MR. JACKSON. Our profession requires that before we can render an opinion on a financial statement that we must do two positive things, and that is: (1) that we must observe and test the inventories—and what I mean by that is that when the company is taking their inventory at the end of their accounting year we must be there to observe and satisfy ourselves that it is all counted and listed. And when we test them, the prices, we go back to their purchase invoice and data to get the cost to compare with their cost prices that they use to make the extensions of the amounts.

MR. SMITH. Doesn't that indicate that you are satisfied that he has the assets that he says, except that you don't know whether or not he has his inventory?

MR. JACKSON. No. Any time an accountant—at least, the layman might misunderstand, just like a lot of us don't understand a lot of things about law, you know. But any CPA, when you say no opinion may be expressed, regardless of what your reasons or what you did or didn't do, when you get down and say, "No opinion may be expressed," it means exactly that and nothing else.

MR. SMITH. This accountancy jargon, then, that means something doesn't necessarily look like what it means?

MR. JACKSON. No; I wouldn't say that. It should be obvious to anyone that when you say no opinion may be expressed, that that is exactly the meaning.

MR. FOUNTAIN. You are saying by reason of one item, but actually are expressing no opinion as to the fairness of presentation in the accompanying balance sheet of the financial position of Billie Sol Estes as of December 31, 1960.

MR. JACKSON. Right.

MR. FOUNTAIN. Mr. Hanna is a certified public accountant who is associated with the subcommittee in its investigation. I will yield to you, Mr. Hanna.

MR. HANNA. Thank you. Mr. Jackson, with reference to the scope paragraph, you indicated that in certain businesses you are required to examine the internal control and determine the extent of your test. You may be required to go to a certain extent for one company and to a lesser extent for a second company.

What is the purpose for determining the extent to which you are going to make your test? What do you do for your own satisfaction in making the test? What is the general purpose of the scope paragraph?

MR. JACKSON. I don't know if I quite understand what you mean, Mr. Hanna.

MR. HANNA. Why do you do certain tests only in one company where internal control is good, whereas in the second company internal control may be terrible and you would extend your tests? Why do you have the different extents? What are you doing by extending your test in the second company where internal control is bad?

MR. JACKSON. Oh, only for the reason that, if you had some reason to doubt—

MR. HANNA. But what are you trying to do with your testing? What is the purpose of your testing?

MR. JACKSON. To form an independent opinion.

MR. HANNA. That is to satisfy yourself, is it not, as to the accuracy of the statement made?

MR. JACKSON. Right.

MR. HANNA. Therefore, in your "scope" paragraph you said that you made the tests to the extent that you deemed necessary and, as a result of these tests, you are qualifying the scope because inventory could not be tested. Therefore, in your "opinion" paragraph you are stating that, because of the limitation of your scope and inventory, you may not express an opinion.

Now, what about materiality? We have inventory that is less than $1 million. We have total assets that are $20 million. Do you consider inventory to be a material item in that respect?

MR. JACKSON. Well, I did not—I do not know whether I would or not. Of course, as I look at it, when you get into checking inventories a lot of times you pick up other errors, many errors in other accounts. And inventory usually is a big item for an accountant to consider and look at, regardless of how small or how large a company is.

And certainly—I probably, from inexperience—maybe I could have written a report that would have been a little plainer, you know to the average person to read. But at the same time, I was endeavoring, to the best of my ability, to get the fact over that I could not express an opinion on his financial statement.

MR. HANNA. There were other assets that were much more material than inventory. Now, if your tests were as necessary under the circumstances, then you, by reason of deduction, must have necessarily assured yourself that the other assets were reasonably fair as a result of your tests.

MR. JACKSON. Well, not necessarily. In my own mind thinking, because, not having been able to examine inventories to me was a big item at that time. And I felt like, for that reason, that I could not express an opinion on it.

MR. HANNA. But we had land stated in there, I believe, somewhat in the area of $2 million. Now, the effect that your scope has is to say that the tests that you made, under the circumstances, you had no question whatsoever about. Had you had a question, you were required, under the rules of your profession, to make a full disclosure. And you only qualified for inventory—a rather insignificant item.

MR. JACKSON. Well, I might—it might—ended up being worded that way, but it was not meant that way, in my own mind at the time.

MR. FOUNTAIN. But anyway, this is the exact language which he gave to you?

MR. JACKSON. No, he did not give me the language.

MR. FOUNTAIN. Oh, he did not give you the language?

MR. JACKSON. I worded that myself. And admittedly, maybe I did not—in looking back, and now I have the advantage of hindsight, you might say—maybe I used bad judgment in wording the report.

MR. FOUNTAIN. Let me ask this. Maybe we had better get the record straight. I gathered that he sent this to you written out in this form.

MR. JACKSON. No.

MR. FOUNTAIN. Oh, he did not?

MR. JACKSON. He only sent this here—from here over.

MR. FOUNTAIN. The two attached sheets?

MR. JACKSON. Yes.

MR. FOUNTAIN. You yourself worded this statement?

MR. JACKSON. That is right.

MR. HANNA. Mr. Chairman, may I ask a question?

MR. FOUNTAIN. Yes.

MR. HANNA. What prompted you to select inventory? Were you aware of what the bulk of Mr. Estes' income was? Did inventory play a principal part in producing income for Mr. Estes?

MR. JACKSON. Well, I did not really know at the time what most of his income was from.

MR. HANNA. So inventory, then, you could not say whether or not it was material?

MR. JACKSON. Well, I felt that anytime according to the rules and regulations of the profession that I have read that we could never give any other kind of report on anybody, other than a disclaimer like that, unless we had observed and tested the inventories, see. So I was merely complying with that regulation as I understood it.

MR. HANNA. Are you referring back to the McKesson-Robbins case?

MR. JACKSON. No; not specifically.

MR. HANNA. What prompted you to use the specific language that you did for the inventories?

MR. JACKSON. Well, that is a good question. I do not know now. I hadn't had very much experience in, of course, writing reports like that, or, you know, making opinions, and I was just merely trying to express— write up a disclaimer in the best way that I knew how, really. And I can only say again that evidently I was taken by a man that was a little smarter than I was.

MR. LANGEN. Mr. Chairman.

MR. HANNA. You were not suggested to use that language?

MR. JACKSON. No. I made it up myself. Yes, sir?

MR. LANGEN. Just let me ask this of you as an accountant. Suppose you were at the other end of the line and received a report like this, worded the way that one is. What would that mean to you when you got that? Would this be something that you would rely on as an accounting of a man's interests and his net worth?

MR. JACKSON. No, sir. As an accountant, I would file it in the waste-basket as far as depending on it for anything. Because anytime that you cannot get a CPA to express an opinion, you cannot depend on the audit work or what was done to establish the figures that are—is the way I understand it.

MR. SMITH. Don't CPA's generally limit the scope of their opinion.

MR. JACKSON. Oh, I do not know what the general—I would not say whether that would be general or not.

MR. FOUNTAIN. You could just say, based on the examination of the information supplied by the man for whom you were making the audit?

MR. JACKSON. That is right. There are many unqualified opinions given, in which they say, you know, everything is right, as far as they can determine.

MR. NAUGHTON. If it was not worth anything, it meant nothing, why do you suppose Billie Sol wanted it?

MR. JACKSON. I just don't know.

*   *   *

MR. SMITH. This statement you put on this balance sheet: Wouldn't you think that a person that was not a CPA would look at that and think that that represented the financial situation?

MR. JACKSON. Well, sir, a person that was not a CPA—like I mentioned a while ago, I am not going to try to say that I used good judgment. Perhaps now—and especially having backsight or hindsight to be able to take advantage of, maybe I did use bad judgment in wording my report.

But certainly at the time I thought I was wording it where anybody would have understood that when I said "no opinion may be expressed" that that would—

MR. SMITH. Then why did you put all the qualification on it? Why didn't you say "This balance sheet shouldn't be taken any stock in," instead of taking all this roundabout wording if you didn't expect it to mislead somebody?

MR. JACKSON. Well, you know, all of our mistakes we wish we could go back and do them over, especially when I wish I had—

* * *

MR. NAUGHTON. Couldn't you just have said, "This is an unaudited balance sheet from figures prepared by Mr. Estes"?

MR. JACKSON. I could. I could have said a lot of things. I have rewritten it in my sleep or laying awake nights. Since February or March, I guess I have rewritten it a dozen times already. I could have said it a lot of ways, as far as that goes.

* * *

MR. NAUGHTON. Would you describe your contacts with the Department of Agriculture employees after Mr. Estes was arrested?

MR. JACKSON. They just sent a couple of their what they called investigators to talk to me and find out my interpretation of what I meant by my report that I—

MR. NAUGHTON. Did you tell them the same story that you have told us today?

MR. JACKSON. I don't recall if I gave them—I probably didn't give them the detail that I've given you.

MR. NAUGHTON. Did you tell them that you destroyed the working papers?

MR. JACKSON. Yes.

MR. NAUGHTON. You did tell them—

MR. FOUNTAIN. What working papers did you have?

MR. JACKSON. Well, I didn't have many to start with. A copy of the balance sheet.

MR. FOUNTAIN. You did not have anything to destroy except the duplicate of what he had sent you?

MR. JACKSON. Right. And of course when this thing blew up, well —I don't know; I didn't feel like I had any further use for any of the material at all. And certainly I just wanted to rid my mind of it.

* * *

CONNER DRUG COMPANY

George Greenway and Owen Sylvester are partners in a small public accounting firm. Much of its work involves tax returns and "write-up" or "bookkeeping" services for a number of small businessmen. A few audits are performed, usually on non-write-up clients, to satisfy bank loan requirements. Today, Mr. Greenway asked Mr. Sylvester into his office to tell about a meeting he had had with a prospective client.

"Alfred Conner, who operates the Conner Drug Company, was just here and has asked us to review his accounting system. He would like a recommendation for any needed improvements and would want us to install any changes that are approved. In addition, he asked if we could audit his financial statements to be submitted to his bank in support of a loan he is negotiating.

"It seems that Mr. Conner has secured leases at two new shopping centers and hopes to open two new retail outlets. He plans to incorporate the business to aid him in securing capital for the expanded operations. Since we do no write-up work for Mr. Conner, my initial reaction was quite favorable to accepting the engagement.

"When we discussed our fee schedule, however, a complication entered the picture. Mr. Conner has suggested that our fee be paid in cumulative, non-voting, non-participating preferred stock, which would be redeemable within five years from the date of incorporation. He indicated that we would be retained as auditors at least until the preferred stock had been redeemed.

"After Mr. Conner left, I called his attorney and he indicated that it is fairly common practice for attorneys to accept stock in a new corporation in payment of their fees. He assured me the practice is not contrary to the legal profession's Canons of Ethics. I also discussed the engagement with Mr. Conner's banker and he indicated that the bank will want audited statements at least annually for the duration of any loans.

"I told Mr. Conner I would have to discuss the matter with my partner and that I would call him tomorrow and give him an answer. What do you think? Should we accept the engagement?"

PONDER and PREPARE

1. What response should Mr. Sylvester make to his partner?
2. If he decides the firm should decline the engagement, what reasons would form the basis for this decision?

MAYTOWN INVESTMENT CLUB

Jeff Bowman is a staff accountant for one of the national firms of certified public accountants and is active in one of the local civic organizations. One evening, after the regular meeting, Jeff joined a group of members who were discussing the formation of an investment club. In general, the men were interested in investing in securities, but concluded that, individually, none could afford the risks inherent in limited diversification. An investment club, on the other hand, would limit the risks to the individual member and permit greater latitude in portfolio selection. The group agreed to meet again the following week and formalize plans for organization.

At the organization meeting, twenty-two men agreed to establish the club and also agreed upon the following general rules and regulations:

1. The club would be incorporated and be called Maytown Investment Club.
2. The enrollment fee for all members would be $25. Enrollment fees would be set aside for administrative expenses such as incorporation fees, supplies, periodic audits if needed, brokerage fees, bank service charges, and so forth.
3. Each member would make monthly contributions of $25. With the funds from enrollment fees available for brokerage charges, the club hoped to maintain monthly contributions invested at full value.
4. Participation units would be issued to each member, in multiples of $25, with fractional interests carried to three decimal places.
5. New members would be admitted on the same terms as the charter members. Current members could withdraw upon thirty days notice and would be paid the net asset value of their participation units upon withdrawal.
6. Weekly meetings would be held to review the club's portfolio and to make decisions about buying and selling securities.
7. Each member would have one vote, irrespective of his participation units; a majority vote of all members attending a meeting would be required to determine club activities.
8. Each member would share in capital gains, capital losses and dividends in proportion to his participation units of investment.

Jeff Bowman was an active member of the group organizing the investment club and drafting the rules and regulations. The other members felt he would be a valuable member by being able to provide technical advice to the club. However, before committing himself to membership, Jeff decided he should check with one of the partners of his firm.

PONDER and PREPARE

1. Should Jeff join the club if the members agree not to purchase any securities issued by any of the clients of Jeff's firm?
2. Would your answer differ if Jeff was a partner in the firm?
3. If, instead of an investment club, Jeff was considering an investment in a mutual fund which, in fact, owned securities issued by several clients, should Jeff invest if
   (a) he is a junior staffman?
   (b) he is a partner?

PART TWO

Internal Control
Systems Analysis
Audit Procedures

OBJECTIVE INTERNAL CONTROL EVALUATION

By R. Gene Brown *

It would be difficult to overstate the importance of the review and appraisal of internal control by the public accountant and its use as the very foundation and justification for a program of testing and sampling.[1]

Questionnaires, flow charts, and procedural work sheets are the tools most commonly used in this review. Regardless of the *method* employed to evaluate internal controls, the primary *objective* is the same: to assist in determining economically and effectively the extent of testing necessary.

To this end, the auditor *measures* the degree of effectiveness of internal control which exists. He does not ascertain the existence or absence of internal control. The results of the measurement are relative and are subjectively stated, e.g., excellent, very good, poor. The auditor's opinion with regard to the adequacy or inadequacy of internal controls forms the foundation for any initial plan for testing.

Unfortunately, at least three problems arise in practice as a result of this subjective evaluation of internal controls. First, several auditors might judge the effectiveness of a given system of internal control quite differently. Because of different personal standards, what is satisfactory to one auditor might be unsatisfactory to another. This condition develops primarily from the use of different methods of appraisal, but can also arise because auditors place different emphasis on the relative importance of various factors of internal control.

The second major problem stems from the nature of the evaluation mechanism itself. Because appraisal is time-consuming, it is a great temptation to rush through the survey and not accord it the importance it deserves. Equally tempting is the possibility of postponing the preparation of the survey until the "real" auditing is completed. These problems are complicated by the fact that most techniques for evaluation are uninteresting and are a burden on the auditor's client as well as on the auditor.

A third problem is the difficulty in judging the overall effectiveness

* Reprinted from *The Journal of Accountancy*, Vol. 114, no. 5 (November 1962), pp. 50–6, by permission of the publishers.

1 Saul Levy, "Internal Control and Legal Responsibility," *The Journal of Accountancy*, February 1957, p. 29.

of internal controls within individual areas of audit attention—a problem intensified by the breadth of the work required in appraising the controls, and by the complex interrelationships among various accounts.[2]

Questionnaire Offers Five Advantages

A practical tool is needed to help the auditor solve these practical problems. It is suggested that one way of ameliorating this situation is to use a quantified internal control questionnaire.

The questionnaire is chosen over the flow chart, procedural work sheets, and other evaluation mechanisms for the following reasons:

1. It permits the use of a standardized approach and working papers prepared in advance.
2. It is faster and more efficient to use.
3. System weaknesses are more obviously isolated for audit attention.
4. It can be used by less highly trained audit personnel.
5. Most important of all, it provides a standard against which to measure existing internal controls—a feature noticeably lacking in other techniques.

Measurement implies some sort of yardstick against which an attribute can be compared. The internal control questionnaire is an attempt to construct such a yardstick, but unfortunately it can be likened to a yardstick with no printed scale. Without intermediate markings, the measurement process is crude at best.

The measurement process has been described as follows:

> The first stage in the development of a full-fledged operational definition of a scientific quality is an intuitive feeling for the quality. The second stage is the discovery of a method of comparison so that it can be said that A has more of the quality in question than B. The third stage is the establishment of a set of standards, which thereby provide categories to which values of the quality can be assigned by means of the comparison test. The fourth step requires a scheme for the interrelation of the standards.[3]

At present, internal control appraisal is at the end of step two of a measuring process. It is now logical and desirable to consider progressing toward step three, the assigning of values. A quantified internal control questionnaire is one method by which this can be done.[4] Basically, the idea of a quantified questionnaire can be stated as follows:

---

[2] The questionnaire illustrated in *Montgomery's Auditing*, 8th ed., contains 917 questions.

[3] E. B. Wilson, Jr., *An Introduction to Scientific Research* (New York: McGraw-Hill Book Company, Inc., 1952), p. 164.

[4] Quantified questionnaires have been used for years in the social sciences, e.g., sociology.

1. A questionnaire for internal control appraisal for any given audit can be so designed as to represent a conceptually perfect (or wholly satisfactory) system. It can and should include all questions relative to internal accounting controls which might affect the fairness of financial data generated by the system.
2. Within the questionnaire, certain questions are more significant than others; that is, the absence of adequate control is more significant in certain areas than in others.
3. Since certain questions are of greater significance than others, the auditor must decide, judiciously, upon the materiality of the various questions. Since the auditor goes through this thought process anyway, why not attempt to formalize it?
4. This decision, this ranking of questions in terms of materiality, demonstrates that it should be possible to assign numerical values to the questions.
5. Such numerical weights would provide a basis for an objective measurement of the degree of adherence of the particular internal control system to the conceptually perfect (or wholly satisfactory) system visualized by the questionnaire.

Basis for Assigning Values

A difficult problem in the quantification of the internal control survey is determining the value to be assigned to each question. As mentioned above, some questions are obviously more significant than others. Concerning internal controls in the cash area, for example, the auditor will usually consider it serious if bank balances are not reconciled periodically. On the other hand, he will find it less disturbing if petty cash vouchers are not approved prior to disbursement and/or replenishment. Reconciliation of bank balances and approval of petty cash disbursements are both recognized as elements of a complete internal control system, but the opportunities for defalcation or material misstatement of reported financial data are much more serious in the former case.

Such reasoning exemplifies the value judgment necessary at present in evaluating internal controls. Since reconciliation of cash is very important, a weakness in his area would lead the auditor to extend his normal tests and even change their timing. He probably would not do so because of nonapproval of petty cash vouchers; perhaps he would do no more than comment to management that approval prior to disbursement is a sound element of internal control.

Since there is such a difference in materiality between these two elements of internal control in the cash area, it should be possible to recognize this difference by some given quantitative rating scale. The range of such a scale is not significant to the argument. It could be 1 to 5, 1 to 10, or even 1 to 100. In any such scale the high numbers would correspond to the more material items. Certain arguments seem to favor a small range of values for the scale. A primary consideration should be the relative degree of uniformity involved in the decision as to a particular value and the high degree of conformity which would result.

In reference to the cash examples above, and assuming a scale with a range of values from 1 to 5, few auditors would disagree with a weighting of 4 or 5 for the cash reconciliation and 1 for petty cash approvals. The basis for the weighting of each question in the internal control survey is the judgment of the auditor.

The initial reaction to this statement might be that, since the auditor is using his judgment to assign the values, any objectivity in approach is lost. Nothing could be further from the truth! Although judgment can never be removed from the audit process, it can be refined. There is no such thing as an exact, applied science. Only in the abstract can science be exact. The minute an abstract model is adapted to a real-life situation, it becomes inexact. The fact that the input values are subjectively derived does not mean that the quantified internal control questionnaire is unscientific. The initial data of all applied sciences are furnished by qualitative description.[5] The quantified internal control survey provides an objective means for the review and appraisal of internal controls.

To quantify the internal control questionnaire, the auditor must decide upon a range of values to be used, evaluate the materiality of each question in the survey, and assign the proper weight to each question. For purposes of the example outlined herein, the rating scale of 1 to 5 was used. The exhibits at the end of the article illustrate how this process can be accomplished.

Inspection of the questionnaire page will reveal that the only change from the way questionnaires are customarily used involves the two vertical columns at the left-hand side of the page. These columns usually read "yes" and "no." In the example, they are titled "Assigned Value" and "Result of Test." The assigned value is the materiality rating determined for each question. Question 8 (c), Exhibit One, is deemed to be relatively insignificant and so carries an assigned value of one. Formerly the auditor would place a check mark in the appropriate "yes" or "no" column. If the answer to the question is affirmative in the quantified questionnaire, the appropriate point value is entered in the "Result of Test" column. If tests reveal that the response to a particular question is negative, a zero is placed in this column. Within the method described in this article, the answer must be either yes or no; hence the numerical value must be either the total assigned or zero. The questions in this particular questionnaire are so written as to preclude partial credit.

[5] Dagobert D. Runes, *Twentieth Century Philosophy* (New York: Philosophical Library, 1947), p. 112.

Determining Control Effectiveness by Area

Following the completion of questions for a given area of audit attention, the values placed in the "Result of Test" column are totaled. This total provides the basis for determining the overall internal control effectiveness for the pertinent area. The total is then measured against the total possible for the given area and stated as an "effectiveness index," whose derivation can be expressed as follows:

$$\text{Effectiveness Index} = 100 \left[\frac{\text{Sum of the actual values resulting from testing}}{\text{Sum of the potential values for that audit area}} \right]$$

The computation of the internal control effectiveness index for a specific example can be illustrated as follows: Assume that the total possible points in the area of cash (reflecting the conceptually perfect or wholly satisfactory system envisioned by the questionnaire) amount to 127. A total of 111 points is earned by virtue of affirmative responses to the questionnaire. Thus,

$$\text{EI} = 100 \left[\frac{111}{127} \right]$$

$$= 100 \ [0.888]$$

$$= \ 89 \ \text{per cent}$$

The auditor now has a quantitative statement of internal control effectiveness for this area, and can use it rationally and precisely to determine the extent of testing required in relation to cash.

Using the tools presently available in auditing, the auditor has no truly objective means of measuring internal control effectiveness; he must rely solely on "yes" and "no" answers. The use of a quantified internal control survey retains the advantages of "yes" and "no" answers, but indicates the affirmative response with a numerical value and the negative with a zero. The revised questionnaire gives the auditor more than he now has without removing any of the present advantages.

Other Benefits of Quantified Survey

Some of the advantages of the quantified internal control survey have already been mentioned, but the list of significant benefits is summarized below:

1. It removes nothing from the auditor's techniques for evaluating internal controls; rather, it extends and strengthens them.

2. It gives the auditor an overall quantitative measure of internal control effectiveness for each area of audit attention.

3. The quantitative measure brings a new objectivity to the statement of results. Assuming that national, intrafirm, or individual audit standards can be set for minimum internal control acceptability, the auditor can more easily measure a particular system against such standards.

4. It will permit the auditor to make a valid trend analysis on recurring engagements. A year-by-year improvement in internal control effectiveness would show up distinctly in the ratings. For example, if the effectiveness index were 78 per cent in 1958, 82 per cent in 1959, 84 per cent in 1960 and 91 per cent in 1961, the auditor could justifiably consider adjusting his amount of testing. At present, since improvements in internal control are not so obvious, the testing levels of prior years are occasionally maintained for some time until improvements become clearly recognizable.

5. The conclusions of the auditor relative to internal controls will be more easily demonstrable to other interested persons. As a result, the quality of work can be more easily controlled, within both the profession and the firm. Since the index summarizes the results for the auditor, he is not forced to attempt a subjective evaluation involving many complex and interrelated questions which in aggregate practically defy precise verbal description.

6. The internal control effectiveness index will assist in the effective implementation of statistical sampling. Because of the inexactness of present internal control measurement techniques, attempts to apply statistical sampling have been little more than abstractions of a conceptually precise tool. Since the degree of confidence (risk) and/or the level of accuracy required for statistical sampling are based on the evaluation of internal controls, these decisions can be more easily made if an objective measurement of internal controls is available.

7. It should remove some of the drudgery from the auditors' preparation and subsequent review of the questionnaire. The prospect of determining numerical ratings of the various facets of internal control would certainly warrant the increased attention and interest of both the auditor and the management of the firm subject to examination.

Possible Arguments or Objections

Aside from the natural human resistance to change, there are several objections which might arise regarding a quantified internal control questionnaire.

Probably the first and immediate objection would be that the auditor's judgment is being superseded or impeded. Any such argument is unsound. To do his job effectively, the auditor must be equipped with both technical proficiency and good judgment. The quantification of the internal control survey adds to his technical tools, but not at the expense of his judgment. It must be remembered that the input values are still derived judiciously. The results of the internal control survey help the auditor choose the appropriate risk and desired accuracy for subsequent testing; he can do so more easily because there is a more precise statement of the degree of effectiveness of internal control.

A second objection might be that the proposed quantification is too mechanical. However, it is no more mechanical than the present questionnaire. Instead of check marks, the auditor places numerical values in the appropriate columns. Any approach to surveying internal controls that provides for an affirmative or negative response is bound to be somewhat mechanical. Even though the tool that provides the auditor with information about the status of internal controls tends to be mechanical, the evaluation and utilization of the results are not. The auditor will still use the questionnaire results in the manner judged most appropriate for the particular audit.

A third major criticism might be that question-weighting is of dubious value, particularly since it is impossible to weight the various questions accurately. All questions are important, so the argument might run, or they would not be included in the questionnaire. To argue in this manner denies the fact that the questions have varying significance in their relation to the amount of testing to be done. It should be obvious to the experienced auditor that many questions are extremely material, while others may be necessary to internal controls but are considerably less important in their potential effect on audit testing. Probably the real source of any dissatisfaction with question-weighting is the obvious uncertainty over what values to assign rather than whether weighting is conceptually worthwhile. It is true, of course, that equally experienced auditors might assign different values to a given question during their initial experience with this method. Certain individual weights assigned to the internal control survey illustrated in Exhibits One and Two might well be questioned in certain respects. However, this should not cause immediate concern. The primary argument for the moment is that the internal control questionnaire can and should be quantified. The latitude and uncertainty in assigning weights will significantly decrease as familiarity with the technique is acquired.

Judgment, Experience are Required

Any new product can be improved. The primary source of information for determining final questionnaire values (if it is really desirable to do so) will result from a considerable distillation of audit experience. Initially, the flexibility in values that could be assigned provides the necessary means for implementing diversity in audit judgment. It is questionable whether such diversity should (or would) continue unresolved for any length of time. However, in the interest of promoting new ideas and techniques, it must be tolerated temporarily. To hand the quantified questionnaire to an experienced auditor without permitting him to participate in the process of assigning values is tantamount to accepting failure prior to trial. It is possible, of course, that someday it may be possible to set rather specific national auditing standards. However, due to the current state of the art, this is not a feasible short-term objective.

The fourth crticism which might be voiced is that the use of a standardized questionnaire, which is relatively common, would not lend itself to quantification. This is because certain weaknesses are more important in some engagements than in others. However, certain arguments seem to favor a standard questionnaire. The major one is that even though the emphasis on the various sections of the questionnaire might vary with each engagement, the particular questions within each area of audit attention are of the same relative importance. For example, emphasis on the cash portion of an audit would be much more significant for a retail outlet than for a branch manufacturing plant. Nevertheless, monthly cash reconciliation is equally important for both. The emphasis on the cash portion of the audit will vary between the two jobs; but within each section of the questionnaire, the relative importance of each question would be roughly the same. In essence, this is one of the peculiar advantages of the quantified questionnaire; even though the same techniques of analysis are used, the results of the particular analysis provide sufficient flexibility for use in almost all audit engagements. Whether it is possible to construct a questionnaire applicable to most engagements remains to be seen, but the successful use of many standardized audit programs suggests that it is.

A final possible criticism is that the use of an overall rating for each area obscures the significance of individual questions. For example, it is argued that four negative responses for questions weighted one po:nt each is not identical in materiality with one negative response for a four-point question. This argument is sound. The auditor must consider each question as well as the total effectiveness index. He does this at present and should continue to peruse the responses to the individual questions. There are two reasons for assigning values to individual questions in the questionnaire. The first, as previously mentioned, is to permit a summary statement in quantitative terms about internal control effectiveness for an individual area of audit concentration. The second objective is to give an indication of the relative importance of *each question*. The intent is not to shift the emphasis in evaluating internal control from specific problem areas to a general overall evaluation. The computation of the internal control effectiveness index does not eliminate the necessity of considering the answer to each question in the survey. The analysis by area of audit attention permits an overview of the complex interrelationships of internal controls, while the perusal of individual questions permits the auditor to plan his testing in detail. In addition, the numerical values assigned to each question will assist the inexperienced auditor in picturing the significance of negative responses.

Questionnaire is Not the Final Answer

It is felt that suggested limitations or disadvantages of the quantified questionnaire are relatively insignificant when compared with its advantages.

It should be pointed out that the main thesis of this article is that serious consideration should be given to developing more objective methods for evaluating internal control. The questionnaire method was selected because at first glance it seems to be a way of doing so within the framework of present techniques. It is not implied that all auditors do or should use a questionnaire in evaluating internal control. In fact, due to the increasing importance of that preliminary phase of the audit dealing with the internal control appraisal, it is quite likely that several different techniques will be used in the future. It is hoped that one or more of them will be so constructed as to yield a *quantitative* statement of internal control reliability.

GENERAL
PART I—INTERNAL ACCOUNTING CONTROL

Assigned Value	Result of Test	
5		1. Is a chart of accounts in use? (A formal chart of accounts is a list of accounts, systematically arranged, indicating account names and numbers.)
3		2. Is the chart of accounts supplemented by definitions of items to be recorded in the various accounts? (The definitions of items to be included in the accounts promote consistency in recording and summarizing accounting transactions.)
5		3. Is an accounting manual in use? (Such a manual should prescribe procedures to be followed in recording and summarizing accounting transactions.)
2		4. Is the assignment of accounting duties and responsibilities expressed in the form of an organization chart? (Such a chart is a formal expression of assignments, showing functional responsibilities; these assignments may also be expressed in the form of job descriptions.)
5		5. Are all postings to general and subsidiary ledgers required to be supported by entries in books of original entry or journal entries?
5		6. Are ledger entries clearly referenced to indicate their source?
		7. Are journal entries:
5		(a) Standardized for content and identification?
5		(b) Supported by readily identifiable data?
3		(c) Reviewed and approved by a responsible employee?
		8. Are the original recording and summarizations of accounting transactions reviewed to assure adherence to:
2		(a) Chart of accounts?
2		(b) Accounting manual instructions?
1		(c) Assignments indicated by the organization chart? (These reviews may be made by department heads, the chief accounting officer, or other assigned personnel. When a formal chart of accounts, accounting manual, or organization chart is not in use, a file of instructions may contain equivalent data.)

---

[6] Norman J. Lenhart and Philip L. Defliese, *Montgomery's Auditing* (New York: Ronald Press, 1957), p. 643 for Exhibit One and p. 668 for Exhibit Two, reproduced by permission of the publisher. The two columns headed "Assigned Value" and "Result of Test" and the numerical values were added by this writer and do not appear in the book.

ACCOUNTS RECEIVABLE
PART I—INTERNAL ACCOUNTING CONTROL

Assigned Value | *Result of Test*

3   21. Are statements of accounts regularly sent to *all* customers? (Periodic statements provide opportunities for debtors to report differences. If it is not the practice to send statements regularly to all customers, objectives might be partially attained by other means. For example:
(a) Statements might be mailed only to customers with delinquent balances.
(b) A delinquent notice to an installment or budget account customer when payments are not received as due is a form of statement to the customer.
(c) Bills from public utilities and other companies furnishing services may serve the dual purpose of invoice and statement.)

22. Are credit memorandums for returned merchandise, price adjustments, special discounts, and damage claims:
5   (a) Under numerical control?
2   (b) Issued promptly on receipt of proper authorization?
4   (c) Recorded promptly when issued?
2   (d) Approved by a responsible person?
(Undue delay in recording these credits may result in a substantial overstatement of accounts receivable.)

23. Are aging schedules:
3   (a) Prepared periodically?
1   (b) Reviewed by a responsible person?
(The review should include consideration of the amount of allowance to be provided for doubtful accounts.)

24. Is approval of a responsible person required for:
5   (a) Payment of customer credit balances?
2   (b) Write-off of uncollectible amounts?

25. Are accounts receivable that have been written off:
5   (a) Under accounting control?
2   (b) Reviewed periodically by an informed person?
(Frequently these accounts are transferred to a bad debt ledger under memorandum control.)

WHITNEY OFFICE EQUIPMENT

Whitney Office Equipment is a small wholesaler of office equipment, stationery, and supplies. Most of its business is on open account due within 30 days. Certain items of equipment may be sold on extended credit of 60 to 120 days provided the buyer gives a promissory note as evidence of the debt. Whitney Office Equipment has an agreement with its bank, The Bank of Commerce, for discounting notes, with recourse. Discounting is not a regular practice, however, occurring only when cash needs require additional funds on short notice.

Mr. Adam Strong, the cashier, has been employed by Whitney in various positions for the past nine years. He was promoted to cashier four years ago. His duties include receiving and disbursing cash, maintenance of the notes receivable file, maintenance of accounts and notes receivable control accounts, and the authorization of non-cash adjustments to individual customers for sales returns, allowances, and bad debts. He also approves all vouchers for payment.

In addition to Mr. Strong, there are two clerks who divide the routine bookkeeping duties including posting the individual customers' accounts. Each clerk is able to perform all of the various bookkeeping jobs, and individual jobs are assigned on a random basis rather than having specific duties for each clerk. Mr. Clay Whitney, one of the partners, maintains the partners' accounts and most of the general ledger. Mr. Whitney signs all checks and either he or Mr. Strong must approve new accounts. Either one may endorse checks for deposit and notes for collection or discounting.

The Bank of Commerce, as part of its loan portfolio evaluation, has requested audited financial statements from Whitney. Whitney has not been audited previously, and Johnson & Kerr, CPA's, have been engaged. As part of the audit, the auditors sent positive confirmation requests to all out-of-town open accounts and notes. Negative confirmation requests were sent to all local accounts with balances of $250 or more. The number of confirmations sent out included 30 per cent of the open accounts and 70 per cent of the dollar balances. No unusual replies were received.

PONDER and PREPARE

1. Given the present number of employees, prepare a work flowchart that will provide reasonable internal control over record keeping activities.

2. Compare the actual situation with your flowchart and list existing weaknesses and what you have done to correct them.

WILLETT MANUFACTURING COMPANY

The Willett Manufacturing Company produces a specialty product that is distributed regionally through gift shops. It is a relatively small operation, having no outside sales force. All orders result from regular mail solicitation and distribution of descriptive brochures. About 70 per cent of all sales received are credit sales, with the balance being cash sales. Of the cash sales, the majority enclose checks in payment, with a few orders including cash rather than check or money order.

All incoming mail is opened by Mr. Willett's secretary, and receipts for credit and cash sales and all sales orders are turned over to the book-keeper for processing. The bookkeeper prepares remittance advices for later posting to the accounts receivable cards and also prepares the sales invoices to be sent to the customer, with a copy of the invoice forwarded to the shipping department as authorization to ship the merchandise. The customer's copy of the invoice is used as a posting medium prior to mailing. There is no regular check on credit of customers, and losses due to uncollectible accounts have been small in relation to total sales.

As a senior accountant for J. P. Strycker & Company, Certified Public Accountants, you arrived for the annual audit on December 10th. Upon your arrival, the bookkeeper witnessed the count of cash on hand and provided you with the following bank reconciliation which he had prepared:

Balance per books, November 30		$45,363.89
Add: Outstanding checks #9621	$457.70	
#9623	496.32	
#9632	348.67	1,202.69
		$46,566.58
Less: Undeposited receipts		9,246.58
Balance per bank		$37,320.00
Deduct: Unrecorded bank credit (NSF check)		100.00
Correct cash balance, November 30		$37,220.00

In a routine check of the records preparatory to working on the cut-off reconciliation, an examination of the cash account showed a balance of $45,363.89 which included the undeposited receipts, at November 30. There were, however, no postings for the month of December. Examination of the check register showed the following checks to have been issued from December 1 through December 9:

#9633	$222.31		#9638	$187.77
9634	63.12		9639	576.45
9635	151.37		9640	64.30
9636	738.76		9641	190.89
9637	462.41		9642	109.80

The cash receipts journal had seven entries totaling $5,923.66 as being received from customers.

When questioned about the NSF check, the bookkeeper admitted he was holding it for redeposit since the customer had assured him that there would be sufficient balance by December 15 to cover the check. The bookkeeper had not thought it necessary to make any entries in the records and as a result, the customer's ledger card showed the balance as paid in full.

Later in the afternoon, a messenger from the office delivered the cut-off bank statement to you. In processing the cut-off statement, you found the following cancelled checks included by the bank:

#9562	$279.00	#9623	$496.32	#9635	$151.37
9583	360.00	9632	348.67	9636	738.76
9584	607.80	9633	222.31	9638	187.77
9621	457.70	9634	63.12	9639	576.45

There was one deposit recorded, on December 4, in the amount of $9,246.58. The bank balance on the statement was $42,077.31. The cash count amounted to $3,523.01 plus the $100 NSF check.

PONDER and PREPARE

1. Prepare a bank reconciliation as of December 9, indicating the actual cash balance of the company.
2. If needed, prepare a corrected bank reconciliation as of November 30, indicating the actual cash balance of the company.
3. Assuming the October 31 reconciliation is known to be correct, describe what has happened.
4. Taking only the specific information given, what specific features of good internal control are missing? How can they be corrected?

ALLISON WHOLESALE COMPANY

The Allison Wholesale Company handles a complete line of hardware. In general, it purchases for its own account but will occasionally take items on consignment that are being test marketed by one of the manufacturers from whom it regularly purchases. The company conducts a nation-wide business from its home office in Kansas City and through 32 branch offices located in major cities throughout the country. It maintains 42 warehouses with at least one warehouse supporting each branch office; the remaining ones are smaller facilities located in heavy sales areas.

In most cases, branch offices supply customers directly from the local warehouse. Allison maintains a fleet of trucks and makes deliveries to customers within a 25-mile radius of the warehouse. Customers outside the delivery zone receive shipments by prepaid truck freight. Since some of the larger customers have their own vehicles, only about 50 per cent of the sales are delivered by Allison. If the local warehouse is temporarily out of stock, the branch office may order from the central warehouse in Kansas City for direct delivery to the customer, usually by truck freight; or, the branch may back-order the goods and have delivery made to the local warehouse and then to the customer. The decision is made on the basis of the size of the individual order and the item involved. Thus, large orders or specialty item orders would normally be shipped direct from the central warehouse while smaller orders of a high volume item would be back-ordered and shipped from the local warehouse when received.

The size of retail hardware outlets varies from extremely large dealers to small family owned and operated neighborhood stores. As a result, detailed credit information is maintained for each customer and a credit limit is established and revised periodically. If the customer is a poor credit risk, he must take delivery on a C.O.D. basis. As a convenience to small customers, each branch is permitted to make over the counter cash sales much like a retail outlet.

Each branch office maintains a small sales force which calls upon major customers in the territory. Salesmen ordinarily prepare orders each evening and mail them to the branch, although in urgent situations the salesmen may phone in an order for immediate attention. In addition, other orders are received by mail and phone directly from the customer who orders from the company catalog. Of course, orders are received directly from the customer in person for over-the-counter cash sales.

Nash, Bennett & Carson, CPA's, have been engaged to audit the activities of the branch office located in Syracuse, New York. Preliminary visits to the client's office revealed the following facts:

Billing: A four-copy sales invoice is prepared for each order received, regardless of source. In general, the original goes to the customer, the second copy is retained for the office use, and the third and fourth copies are sent to the shipping department. The forms are not pre-numbered; however, on credit sales, the credit manager assigns a number as he approves credit.

Shipping: Copies three and four of the sales invoice are used by the shipping department in preparing the order for shipment. When the order has been assembled and packaged, copy four of the sales invoice is included as a packing slip. Copy three is used to prepare shipping instructions for company delivered orders and bills of lading for freight shipments. In either case, the driver signs copy three as evidence that the order has been transferred to his custody. When the customer picks up his own order, he signs the receipt. Once delivery has been made, copy three of the sales invoice is used to update the perpetual inventory records maintained at the warehouse and then the invoice is filed alphabetically. The inventory records are kept in quantities only.

Credit Sales: If the sales order is a credit sale, all four copies of the invoice are forwarded to the credit manager for his approval. If credit is approved, the credit manager assigns a number to the invoice and initials the second and third copies in a special box that indicates the type of sale—credit or C.O.D. His approval on copy three is the authorization for the shipping department to release the goods. The original and second copy of the invoice are sent to the assistant credit manager and copies three and four are sent to the shipping department.

The assistant credit manager verifies unit prices and extensions on the invoice and mails the original to the customer. The second copy is then used by the accounting clerk as a posting medium in preparing the sales journal. The invoice is filed alphabetically by customer. The company uses a "ledgerless" form of accounts receivable wherein the file of sales invoices represents the accounts receivable detail. As remittances are received, the office copy of the sales invoice is removed, stamped paid, and filed by date of payment.

C.O.D. Sales: The credit manager, in reviewing sales invoices, makes the decision regarding C.O.D. sales. No C.O.D. sales are authorized that cannot be delivered by an Allison truck. Once the decision has been made, copies three and four of the sales invoice are initialed in the appropriate place and forwarded to the shipping department. The original and second copy of the invoice are turned over to the cashier who verifies unit prices and extensions. The original is given to the driver as his authority to make the collection and is delivered to the customer. The second copy is retained by the cashier until the driver makes settlement. This copy is then stamped paid, and forwarded at the end of the day to the accounting clerk for posting to the sales journal.

Cash Sales: Cash sales may result from over-the-counter sales or from mail orders which include full payment. The original and second copies of the sales invoice are given to the cashier who stamps them paid upon receipt of the cash. The original invoice is given to the customer for over-the-counter sales and included with the packing slip in the case of mail orders. The second copy, after being stamped paid, is sent to the accounting clerk for posting.

Mail: Mail is opened by the secretary to the credit manager. Remittances on accounts receivable are given to the credit manager for his review and then turned over to the cashier. Mail orders are turned over to the billing clerk who prepares the sales invoices. Cash sales orders, with remittances attached, are first sent to the cashier, and then routed as previously described. Credit sales orders are forwarded to the credit manager for his approval.

At the daily deposit cut-off time, the cashier delivers checks and cash to the assistant sales manager, segregated as to credit sales collections and cash sales collections. The assistant sales manager then prepares remittance lists for credit collections, makes up the bank deposit, and the cashier takes the deposit to the bank. The assistant sales manager uses the remittance lists to update the accounts receivable file by pulling the company's copy of the sales invoice and stamping it paid. He also verifies allowable cash discounts and handles correspondence relative to unauthorized discounts taken by customers.

The credit manager authorizes non-cash adjustments to accounts receivable, but must obtain approval from the home office in Kansas City before authorizing the write-off of an account as uncollectible. At the time of the examination, he had in his custody some remittances that were received during the last month of the fiscal year. All represented NSF checks returned by the bank.

PONDER and PREPARE

1. Evaluate the billing and collection procedures.
2. Redesign the procedures to strengthen internal control and improve efficiency.
3. Describe the kinds of irregularities that might occur under the procedures now in effect for handling cash collections. Do your procedures effectively limit the possibility of irregularities? Describe.

GREEN'S DISTRIBUTORS

The Company was founded as a wholesale distributor of cigars in 1890. Today, the company handles a full line of tobacco products, candy and confections, magazines and paper bound books. The central office is located in the midwest and services customers in the metropolitan area and a four-state "fringe" area extending about 250 miles radially from the office.

Company salesmen call on all metropolitan customers at least once a week and on out of town customers at least once a month. More frequent calls are made where sales volume warrants a visit. In town customers place orders with Company salesmen and receive delivery on a two-day basis. Out of town customers are supplied with a catalog and frequently place phone or written orders between calls by salesmen.

All customers are supplied with a "want" book containing sheets which are perforated on the bound edge. The sheets contain space for the customer to write down merchandise desired at the next delivery date. When the salesman calls, he examines inventory levels and suggests additional merchandise as needed. If acceptable to the customer, the salesman notes these additional items in the "want" book. Prior to leaving, the salesman obtains the customer's signature on the "want" sheet, which he then sends to the office as a basis for shipping and billing.

Out of town customers need only mail the "want" sheets, with signature, to the office to have orders filled between visits by salesmen. Most customers rely on the salesmen to select and stock the paperback book racks, but will normally have a pre-selected list of magazines and periodicals that are delivered on a regular basis without subsequent reordering. Unsold copies of magazines, periodicals, and books are returned by the customer for full credit against his account. The Company, in turn, receives credit from the publisher for these items.

Sales Orders

When "want" lists are received from either the salesman or through the mail, customer service representatives enter stock order numbers on the lists and prepare sales orders. A telephone order, when received, is entered directly on the sales order form with no intermediate form preparation.

A standard five-part sales order is prepared and distributed as follows:

Original: Processed through perpetual inventory records, warehouse, and billing.
Second: Packing list included with shipment.
Third: Sent to purchasing department for merchandise control use.
Fourth: Sent to salesman.
Fifth: Sent to customer.

The original copy plus packing list are forwarded to the clerk who maintains perpetual inventory records on a visible record index file. Quantities ordered are entered on the appropriate stock card and unit costs and unit sales prices are entered on the original copy of the sales order. Total sales prices are extended and added by the inventory clerk.

Where the inventory records indicate an item is out of stock, the inventory clerk prepares a back-order set in three parts. The first two parts, identical to the original sales order and packing list, are filed by item pending receipt of stock. The third copy is sent to the purchasing agent for follow-up. The original sales order is marked to indicate any back-orders and is processed as noted below for instock items. Back-orders are similarly processed when merchandise is received and the order may be filled.

From the inventory section, the sales order is then forwarded to the addressograph section where a clerk locates an addressograph plate for the customer. If the total order does not exceed the credit limit embossed on the plate, the operator prepares an invoice set entering only the data on the addressograph plate. If no plate exists—e.g., a new customer—or if the credit limit has been exceeded, the sales order is forwarded to the credit manager for, prior approval before the preparation of the invoice set.

The sales order, packing list and invoice set are then forwarded to the dispatcher who enters a seven-digit identifying number on all copies received by him. The number is composed of two digits representing the current month, two digits representing the day, and three digits identifying the order. The three digit identifying number is reset to 001 at the start of each day. The dispatcher forwards the sales order and packing list to the warehouse where the order is filled and shipped to the customer. The packing list is included with the order. The warehouse will note on the sales order any shipping details, such as shipped by company truck or shipped by freight.

The company has a "uniform" charge schedule for freight on shipments, which is billed to each customer regardless of whether shipment is by company truck or commercial truck. Bills of lading prepared for commercial shipments are forwarded to the accounts payable clerk to be matched against monthly freight bills rendered to the company.

After the sales order has been returned from the warehouse, the dispatcher matches sales order with the invoice set and the two are sent to the billing section.

Billing

For billing purposes, the company uses a combination typewriter-card punch-accounting machine manufactured by one of the leading data processing equipment companies. When the sales order and invoice set are received in the billing section, the invoice set is placed in the typewriter and is completed by entering the customer's account number, the sales order number and an itemized listing of all items that were shipped along with a memorandum listing of any items that were backordered. The machine, in a separate operation, accumulates total sales and total cost of sales in accumulators. A set of three kinds of punched cards is generated for each invoice set:

1. A receivable summary card indicating customer account number, sales order number, and total sales for the invoice.
2. One or more cards, one for each stock item included on the invoice, which shows stock number, number ordered and shipped, unit cost price and total cost, unit sales price and total sales price.
3. A commission card containing the salesman's number, the customer's number, and total dollar value of the sale.

The invoice set is a four-part set and is distributed as follows:

Original: To customer
Second: Attached to the sales order and filed by customer
Third: To the accounting office
Fourth: To the salesman

The third copy of the invoice, along with the punched cards, are forwarded to the accounting office. The accounting office prepares daily runs of the sales and cost of sales analyses cards, producing a daily sales journal and a cost of sales report. Totals from this run are compared with the daily totals developed at the time of invoice preparation. Daily sales and cost of sales totals are manually posted to monthly summary sheets, and manually posted to the general ledger on a monthly basis.

Accounts Receivable

The receivable summary cards representing the daily invoices are merged into the open invoice ledger file (accounts receivable subsidiary ledger) by a punched card sorting process. The open invoice cards are removed from the file when payment, indicated by remittance advices, or cancellations, indicated by credit memos, are received from the cashier or credit section. When cash remittances or credit memos cannot be immediately identified with an open invoice, unapplied cash or credit cards are key-punched and merged into the open invoice file. A form is prepared for such items to be sent to the customer, asking for an identification of the invoice being paid. The forms are routed to the credit section daily for action.

At the end of each month, open invoice cards are tabulated to produce customer's statements. A second run prepares an aged trial balance, using the sales invoice number as a basis for aging. Copies of the aged trial balance are sent to the credit office for any necessary action. A listing of unidentified cash remittances/credit memos outstanding at the end of the month, is also prepared and sent to the credit office for necessary follow-up.

Attached as Exhibit One is a partial organization chart obtained from the client. It has not been verified by observation or questioning.

PONDER and PREPARE

1. Based upon the above information, list the strong and weak points in the system of internal control.
2. Based on your evaluation of internal control, what auditing procedures would you consider necessary in testing sales and accounts receivable?

GREEN'S DISTRIBUTORS
ORGANIZATION CHART

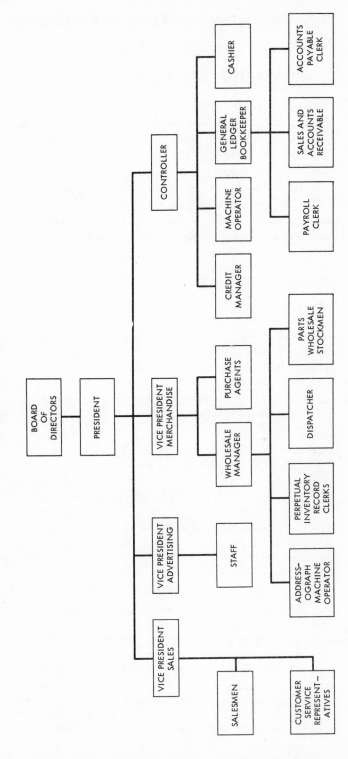

FOTO-PRESS INCORPORATED

Foto-Press Incorporated is a medium sized company specializing in the manufacture of newspaper presses utilizing the photo offset process of printing. It also has a line of small presses for the letterpress type of operation designed specially for the job shop. The company has prospered over the years, gradually expanding its operations each year.

In order to remain competitive, the company has recently completed the testing of a new machine capable of processing four-color pictures for use with the photo offset process. The machine will handle both locally produced photographs as well as pictures transmitted by radio, microwave, or other electronic processes. Work has begun on three production models, two to be used for purposes of demonstration, one of which has been sold.

Major orders for photo offset presses are custom built to individual customer specifications. Letterpress equipment is manufactured in three different models with four sizes in each model line. Letterpress equipment is manufactured only on customer order, with the customer specifications restricted to one of the four stock sizes in each model line. No letterpress machines are produced for inventory. A job-order cost accounting system is used for all major equipment production.

The company also manufactures about 75 per cent of the component parts used in the various presses produced. The balance of the parts, mostly electrical motors and control components, are purchased from outside suppliers. The company maintains a reasonable inventory of component parts both for its own use and for replacement orders received from customers. The only components not manufactured for inventory are special purpose parts that can be used on a very limited number of installations. Purchased parts are not carried in inventory for customer replacement orders; but the company will assist the customer in obtaining these parts. Component parts are manufactured in a separate part of the plant on a continuous basis, with process cost procedures employed for accumulating inventoriable cost information.

Raw materials are purchased by the purchasing department, on order of the production supervisor. Prenumbered purchase orders are used and prepared in four parts. The original is forwarded to the supplier, a copy is sent to the receiving department to be used as a receiving report, a copy is sent to the accounting department, and a copy is retained in a follow-up file until the order has been received. When notified by the receiving department that the order has been received, ile copies of the purchase order are transferred to a "completed file" for uture reference.

When merchandise is received, the receiving department checks actual receipts against the quantities on their copy of the receiving eport. If all material has been received, the purchase order is initialed and sent to the accounting department. If there is any shortage (or overage) in the delivery, the receiving report is amended to show actual receipts prior to sending it to the accounting department. On deliveries that are short, a memo is prepared in the receiving department indicating the shortage and the name of the supplier. A copy of the memo is sent to the purchasing department for their follow-up file and one is retained by the receiving department until the balance of the order is received. The third copy of the memo is sent to the accounting department as part of the receiving report.

The accounting department matches its copy of the purchase order with the receiving report and holds both until the invoice is received. Invoices are checked against the receiving report to verify units shipped and unit costs. Extensions are computed and verified on the invoice. Approval for payment of invoices is given by the production supervisor, and checks are signed by the treasurer of the company only after invoice approval has been obtained.

The accounting department, in addition to processing the invoices, maintains perpetual inventory records. As raw materials are received actual costs are entered in the control account, with individual unit records kept on a moving average cost basis. Raw materials are introduced into production on the basis of requisitions, one copy of which is sent to the accounting department. Transfers from inventory to work in process are made at standard costs, and variances between standard and actual are computed and entered in the books each day on the basis of the processed requisitions. Variances are normally small in amount and are carried directly to expense for the period.

Work in process and finished goods inventories are maintained at standard direct cost; i.e., only materials and direct labor, at standard, are inventoried. All other production costs are considered period costs and taken to expense each period. Freight and purchase discounts are not entered directly to the inventory account to simplify unit record maintenance. The two items are held in a suspense account and allocated to inventories and cost of sales on the basis of relative dollar value of raw materials processed for the time period.

In addition to the perpetual records maintained by the accounting department, the stores department maintains a "quantities only" record. The stores department is responsible for initiating purchase requests through the production supervisor based upon predetermined minimum inventory levels and economic order quantities.

Jakes and Lamberti, Certified Public Accountants, were engaged for the first time this year to perform the annual audit. Preliminary investigations revealed the following information:

Due to the size and complexity of the component parts inventory the company does not take a physical inventory at year-end since that procedure results in a considerable disruption of production schedules. Therefore, the company has a team of ten men, operating in pairs, who conduct physical inventory counts on a year-round basis. Approximately one-twelfth of the inventory is counted each month.

A two-part tag, illustrated in Exhibit One, is used for inventory counting purposes. As the first pair of counters finish a particular item a tag is attached to the bin or storage area. All pertinent data is entered on the tag concerning stock number, location, and so forth. Team one enters its count on the lower portion of the tag, which is detached and retained. The second team of counters later performs a "blind" count i.e., without knowing the previous count. The team enters its count on the second portion of the tag, which is detached and retained. Later the two tag parts are matched by the supervisor in charge of inventory taking. If there is a discrepancy in the two counts, a third count is performed and differences reconciled. Once the number of items on hand has been determined, summary sheets are prepared indicating stock number and count. These are forwarded to the accounting department and stores department where the perpetual records are adjusted to agree with the actual count. At year-end, an inventory summary is prepared by the accounting department from unit record cards, and quantities are priced as described above. The audit tests of the procedures indicated that satisfactory cut-off procedures are employed before adjustments are made to unit record cards.

With respect to raw materials and finished goods inventories the company has established the following policy: If a part shows no usage or sales activity for two consecutive years, it is considered to be obsolete. At that time, a determination is made as to its ultimate value to the company and it is written down by way of an inventory valuation reserve. The reserve currently amounts to $25,000. The auditor's tests of inventories and of obsolescence indicate the amount may approximate $95,000.

A new item appeared in the inventory for the first time during the current fiscal year. It is a chemical compound used with the color photograph processing equipment. The chemical is a blend of several different ingredients, one of which is called Hotash, a generic term developed by its producers. Hotash is a commodity that is imported and refined by several domestic suppliers. But Foto-Press considers the foreign supply

unreliable because of unsettled international conditions. It has, therefore, stockpiled a large supply of Hotash to assure its own continued
operations. Hotash is a material portion of the raw materials inventory,
and the auditor has determined that the company has about a three
year supply, based upon current sales projections. Raw materials are
priced at average cost and carried on the balance sheet at the lower of
cost or market. An investigation of year-end prices of Hotash revealed
that the market price is less than Foto-Press's average cost.

Attached as Exhibit Two are financial statements for the current
year. Exhibit Three contains additional information about inventory
values. You may assume that you have been able to satisfy yourself as
to the correctness of the physical count and dollar figures of the opening
inventories.

PONDER and PREPARE

1. Considering the facts provided:
   (a) evaluate internal control realtive to inventory and purchasing.
   (b) outline a program for testing inventory quantities.
2. Discuss the problems of inventory obsolescence for the company, assuming the amounts involved are material with respect
   to financial position.
3. Discuss excess inventories with respect to the financial statements and with respect to the application of the cost or market
   rule.
4. With respect to inventories, define the overall problems involved in a first audit.
5. Given the information in the case, what kind of details would
   you include in your audit report to the board of directors?
   You may assume that the statements are found to be acceptable
   in all respects not discussed in the case.

FOTO-PRESS INCORPORATED
INVENTORY COUNTING TAG

EXHIBIT TWO

FOTO-PRESS INCORPORATED
BALANCE SHEET AS OF DECEMBER 31

ASSETS

Current Assets		
Cash	$ 120,000	
Accounts Receivable (net)	220,000	
Inventories (see Note)	1,085,000	
Prepaid Expenses	23,000	
Total Current Assets		$1,448,000
Long-Lived Assets		
Land	$ 200,000	
Plant & Equipment (net)	1,380,000	
Total Long-Lived Assets		1,580,000
Total Assets		$3,028,000

EQUITIES

Current Liabilities

Accounts Payable	$ 290,000	
Accrued Wages	15,000	
Taxes, other than Income	23,000	
Taxes on Income	52,000	
Total Current Liabilities		$ 380,000

Long-Term Liabilities

Bonds Payable, 4.5%, due 1995		750,000
Total Liabilities		$1,130,000

Stockholders' Equity

Common Stock, no par, 200,000 shares issued and outstanding	$1,000,000	
Retained Earnings	898,000	1,898,000
Total Equities		$3,028,000

Note: Raw material inventories are valued at the lower of average cost or market; work in process and finished goods are valued at standard direct costs. Amount shown is net of Reserve for Obsolescence in the amount of $25,000.

FOTO-PRESS INCORPORATED
INCOME STATEMENT FOR YEAR ENDED DECEMBER 31

Net Sales		$7,500,000
Less: Cost of Sales	$5,430,000	
Other Operating Expenses	1,420,000	6,850,000
Earnings from Operations		$ 650,000
Less: Other Deductions		220,000
Net Income Before Taxes		$ 430,000
Less Income Taxes: Federal	$ 180,000	
State	40,000	220,000
Net Income After Taxes		$ 210,000
Retained Earnings, January 1		688,000
Retained Earnings, December 31		$ 898,000

FOTO-PRESS INCORPORATED
SCHEDULE OF INVENTORIES

January 1

	Raw Materials	Work in Process	Finished Goods	Totals
Materials	$105,000	$155,000	$375,000	$ 635,000
Labor		70,000	260,000	330,000
Overhead		80,000	120,000	200,000
Totals	$105,000	$305,000	$755,000	$1,165,000

December 31

	Raw Materials	Work in Process	Finished Goods	Totals
Materials	$120,000	$170,000	$440,000	$ 730,000
Labor		80,000	275,000	355,000
Overhead		85,000	140,000	225,000
Totals	$120,000	$335,000	$855,000	$1,310,000

WAGNER WIRE DISTRIBUTORS

Wagner Wire Distributors was founded by Hans Wagner in 1922 as a wholesale distributor of various types and sizes of steel wire products manufactured by a variety of different companies. The company has grown over the years and is now a reasonably large regional distributor of wire and cable. In 1958, Frederick Wagner, Hans Wagner's son, was named president of the company. Young Wagner had been educated as a mechanical engineer and had served in a number of different positions within the company as he "learned the business."

Frederick Wagner, in his spare time, tinkered in a work area set aside for him in one part of the main warehouse. The tinkering has resulted in several patentable improvements in wire manufacturing, which have been licensed to some of the major producers. Royalties from license agreements account for about 15 per cent of total revenues of the company. Last year, he developed what he considers to be a major improvement in wire drawing machinery. When the patent was granted, he and his father discussed the possibilities of going into limited manufacturing, using the new machine. Studies of projected volume, production costs, and capital requirements induced them to start manufacturing operations in February of the current year. The production, to date, has been limited to three different gauges of medium carbon steel wire that have, in the past, accounted for about 30 per cent of the company's sales volume. The company is continuing to distribute other sizes and gauges of wire and cable to provide a complete line of products for the customer.

The company has decided to make an initial public offering of common stock to finance the current expansion into manufacturing facilities. If the manufacturing proves to be as profitable as forecasts indicate, this offering will pave the way for further public sales of stock for financing future growth. The current offering will involve a re-capitalization of the company to make stock available for public sale; future offerings, it is anticipated, will be secondary sales, in which the family will dispose of some of their holdings, retaining sufficient stock to maintain control of the company.

The firm of Reeves and Thomas, Certified Public Accountants, has been retained to supervise preparation of registration statements for the SEC as well as to perform the audit for the current year, ending December 31. In addition, Reeves and Thomas have agreed to prepare any special reports that management requests, based upon the audit. Reeves and Thomas will be replacing a local CPA who has performed the audit for the past ten years, but who does not feel qualified to cope with SEC regulations. He has assured the client of his full cooperation. Pre-audit work has revealed the following information about selected situations.

Finished Goods Inventories

There are two classes of finished goods inventories currently on hand:

(a) Wire and cable purchased from other manufacturers which are part of the distributing business; and
(b) Wire manufactured in the company's own facility.

Purchased Inventories. Wire in various gauges and grades is received from manufacturers on spools of standard measure—usually in terms of pounds per spool. While most orders are for full spools, the company will sell less than a standard spool at a slightly higher price per unit. Inventories of purchased finished goods are maintained on a periodic basis, and are physically counted at or near the balance sheet date each year.

Manufactured Inventories. When manufacturing operations were commenced, raw materials and manufactured finished goods were placed on a perpetual inventory records basis as a prelude to transferring all inventory records to the perpetual basis. In addition, a cycle physical count was instituted wherein about one-twelfth of the inventory is counted each month and reconciled to the perpetual records.

The manufacture of wire consists, essentially, of drawing raw material steel through successively smaller reducing dies until the desired gauge is produced. As a result of the new machinery, there is little or no work-in-process at any time and Wagner does not maintain formal work-in-process records. Work order sheets are maintained for each job and are used to accumulate production costs. When the job is finished, the costs are set up immediately as finished goods inventory. A tabulation of the work sheets, at any one time, would provide the necessary data for work-in-process adjustments needed for statement preparation. Both types of finished goods inventories are relieved of charges on the basis of sales orders and approved shipping documents.

Raw Materials Inventories

Raw materials for the wire production consist of coils of low and medium carbon content steel, wrapped on spools, usually 900 pounds each (exclusive of the spool). Detailed stock record cards are maintained on each gauge of coil by total weight. These stock record cards serve as a control record for the following system of inventory identification:

(a) When coils are received a prenumbered receiving report is prepared showing supplier's name, date received, coil weight and gauge description, and number of coils received. The receiving report is sent to the stock records department and is used as a basis for entries on the unit record cards.

(b) As the receiving report is prepared, individual tags are filled out and attached to each coil, showing receiving report number, date received, and coil weight and gauge description.

(c) When a coil is placed in production, the tag is removed from the coil and attached to the production report in lieu of a stock requisition. The stock records department completes the materials section of the production report and uses the tag to update the unit record cards. The tag is then stamped with date of use and filed in a "materials used" file for future reference.

To facilitate the cycle counting, coils are stored in a separate location, near the production floor, with all tags plainly visible.

Returnable Spools

The spools used for both raw material coils and finished wire and cable are so constructed as to be reusable a number of times. The useful life of these spools is between two and three years, depending upon frequency of use and type of shipment activity. When Wagner started its own production facilities, there was a necessary investment in spools and the investment was capitalized. The company has decided not to compute depreciation on the spools but will charge replacements to expense as they are made.

When a spool is shipped to a customer, a deposit is charged which is refunded when the spool is returned. In addition to its own spools, of course, Wagner has a number of spools passing through that belong to other manufacturers. Wagner pays a deposit on all incoming spools, with the deposit being passed on to the customer when the spool is shipped out. On spools not owned by Wagner, the customer may

(a) Return the spool to Wagner for refund of the deposit, with Wagner returning the spool to the manufacturer; or
(b) The customer may return the spool directly to the manufacturer.

In the latter case, the customer receives a refund when Wagner has been notified by the manufacturer that the spool has been received.

A rather complex system of bookkeeping entries has evolved over time in accounting for returnable spools. An investigation by Reeves and Thomas revealed the following pattern of entries:

(1) *Outgoing Spools to Customers:*

Accounts Receivable	XX	
Sales		XX

(2) *Incoming Spools from Customers:*

Sales Returns & Allowances	XX	
Account Receivable		XX

(3) *Incoming Spools from Manufacturers:*

Purchases	XX	
Accounts Payable		XX

(4) *Outgoing Spools to Manufacturers:*

Accounts Payable	XX	
Purchase Returns & Allowances		XX

(5) *Spools Returned by Customer Direct to Manufacturer:*
(a) When Wagner receives notice from manufacturer:

Accounts Payable	XX	
Purchase Returns & Allowances		XX

(b) When Wagner sends notice to customer:

Sales Returns & Allowances	XX	
Accounts Receivable		XX

If a spool is lost or destroyed, then cash settlement is made in the amount of the deposit. For spools owned by Wagner, a revenue account titled "Forfeited Deposits" is credited. With respect to spools owned by others, Wagner acts only as a collection agent. A suspense account "Deposits for Manufacturers" is credited when payment is received from the customer, in addition to entry number 2 above; the suspense account is debited when payment is made by Wagner, in addition to entry number 4 above. Any balance in the suspense account at statement time is carried to the balance sheet as either a miscellaneous debit or miscellaneous credit.

PONDER and PREPARE

Mr. Frederick Wagner has asked for a supplemental report evaluating the new inventory procedures and any other items that require discussion. Prepare the report for Mr. Wagner.

MEMORIAL HOSPITAL

Memorial Hospital was founded in 1872 as a ten-bed clinic operated by three doctors. Ultimately, the property was given to a non-profit corporation and today it is a 350-bed installation providing a full range of surgical and medical services to in-patients, with an extensive out-patient clinic. A cost accounting system has been installed to help in determining reimbursable costs under Blue Cross, Medicare and state welfare. No patient is refused treatment; those unable to pay for services are substantially subsidized by a large unrestricted endowment.

When the Hospital was originally given to the non-profit corporation, considerable farm land was included as a permanent unrestricted endowment together with a nominal amount of state government bonds to be used solely for out-patient services. As farming became more complex, and margins of return on investment became smaller, the Hospital started an organized program of disposing of the land and reinvesting the proceeds in securities of various sorts. The land disposal was completed in 1945 and today, the Hospital owns only the land used for present facilities plus adjacent property considered sufficient to take care of anticipated expansion over the next twenty-five to thirty years.

In 1946, the Hospital received a considerable legacy from the estate of one of the town's leading public figures. The money was to be held as a permanent endowment, with the income to be devoted to nursing and intern education, with nursing education having a prior claim on income. Also, over the years, the Hospital has accepted numerous donations and bequests all of which are dedicated to the care of the sick in one form or another.

Prior to 1960, separate investments were maintained for each individual restricted endowment, which necessitated a rather complex bookkeeping system and posed problems of custody. With so many "small" investments, the Hospital found it difficult to take advantage of changing investment opportunities because of the cost involved in shifting a large number of small holdings. As a result, in 1960 the Hospital initiated a "pooled" investment policy that combined all investments into a single portfolio for ease of management.

The pooled investment fund, in essence, has a single group of investments for all the individual endowments. The investment account is a control account and is supported by a detailed ledger of the individual endowments that have been accepted over the years.

When the pool was established, a single portfolio was started and was arranged in a manner that the board of trustees considered appropriate for the Hospital. If an investment was sold as a result of the initial re-organization, any capital gain or loss was carried to the individual trust that had provided the security. The capital gain was permanently capitalized. If a capital loss was incurred, the loss was restored to principal from income the first year before any income was distributed to beneficiaries. A policy was adopted at that time providing that future capital gains were to be capitalized and future capital losses were to be recovered from income before distribution. *Units of investment* in the pool were established with an initial par value of $10 each, and each separate endowment was allocated whole and fractional units (to three decimal places) in proportion to its contribution to the total of the trust. Subsequent endowments were given proportional interests based upon market values at date of receipt.

At the end of each operating year, all capital gains realized through portfolio management are capitalized to the individual units in proportion to their relative holdings. Net income, less an amount to cover capital losses, is then distributed much like a dividend, i.e., so many cents or dollars per unit of investment. The operations are quite similar to that of a mutual fund.

The results of the merging of investments have been gratifying to the administrator and the board of trustees. Return on investment has been measurably increased and the total investment portfolio appears to be on much firmer grounds. Beneficiaries of endowment income, of course, have been pleased with the increased funds available to them.

The treasurer of the Hospital has major responsibility for investment. He has the authority to make all investment decisions concerning portfolio management, although he submits quarterly reports to the board of trustees detailing buy and sell activities. At these quarterly meetings of the board, it may express any policy preferences for actions consistent with what the board thinks is in the best interests of the Hospital.

The securities include municipal, state, and federal bonds, corporate bonds, preferred and common stocks. Preferred and common stocks account for about 25 per cent of the market value of the portfolio while state and federal bonds account for another 60 per cent of market value. The securities, for the most part, are maintained in a safe deposit box at the local bank, although a few items are kept in protective custody with the broker. The treasurer is the only officer of the Hospital authorized to sign for admission to the lock box.

Once a month, the treasurer and his secretary visit the bank and clip interest coupons that are payable on bearer bonds. The coupons are listed on a special form the Hospital devised that indicates the serial number of the bond, the coupon number, date interest is due, and the amount. A copy of the form is attached to the deposit slip and the original plus a duplicate deposit slip is turned over to the accounting department for processing.

The accounting department maintains a subsidiary ledger of each investment owned by the Hospital, and as interest coupons are clipped and collected, this fact is noted on the appropriate record card. From the record cards, interest accruals are computed twice a year for statement preparation. Accrual entries are reversed after the statements are prepared.

Interest and dividends that are paid by check are received by the treasurer and listed on the same form as the interest coupons, identifying the security, indicating the amount of dividend or interest, and the rate. This form is processed by the accounting department in the same manner as that described above.

At the end of each fiscal year, the accounting department determines the total income received on investments. With respect to interest, the total received and accrued is reconciled to the individual investment records. Dividends received are also reconciled to the individual endowment. After providing for capital gains (and losses) the income is related to the total units of investment outstanding, weighted by the amount of time they have been outstanding if less than a year. A weighted unit is calculated and becomes the basis of distribution of income to the beneficiaries for use in the next fiscal year.

In addition to the major investment portfolio, the Hospital also has the opportunity to make short-term investments during the year. There is some seasonality of services provided as well as uneven time lags in collections. Thus, at any one time there may be funds on hand in excess of current needs. The excess tends to build up over the fiscal year since income on investments received in the current fiscal year is not made available to the beneficiaries until the next fiscal year.

In general, short-term investments are restricted to 90- and 120-day U. S. Treasury Bills. These investments are purchased by the Hospital's local bank, acting through a New York City bank. Physical custody of the Bills is maintained in New York, with custody receipts issued to the Hospital. The custody receipts list the Hospital as the owner, identify the Bills by serial number, and provide space for witnessed endorsements to facilitate negotiation. Maturities are collected by the custodian bank, and a memorandum is sent to the Hospital asking for disposition of the funds.

The Bills are readily marketable, and daily meetings are held between the administrator, the controller, and the treasurer to evaluate the cash position of the Hospital, the desirability of additional investment, or the need for redemption of Bills. Decisions reached in these meetings are carried out by the treasurer.

PONDER and PREPARE

1. Evaluate the system of internal control over both short-term and long-term investments.
2. Evaluate the investment pool procedures and indicate any changes you would institute in the accounting system. Justify your proposed changes.
3. Describe appropriate audit procedures for the investment pool.

NOBLE COMPANY

Several years ago, the Noble Company installed electronic data processing equipment. Applications include inventory processing, accounts receivable and payable processing, production scheduling, and payroll preparation. Problems have occurred with the accounts payable system and the auditors have been called in to evaluate proposed changes.

Current Procedures

The accounts payable section of the accounting department prepares punched paper tape for all vendor's invoices, which includes information about vendor's name and address, invoice number, amount due, and either an expense account identification or inventory updating data including stock number, units received, units back-ordered, and so forth. On a weekly basis, the data is used to prepare an invoice register with appropriate distributions of dollar amounts to either inventory or various expense classifications.

Twice a month the data processing center also prepares checks and a check register for the accumulated invoices. The common discount terms for Noble are 10 days after the end of the month. In order to take advantage of the discounts on the second monthly processing run, check preparation is usually scheduled for either the 8th or 9th of the month, with the result that a large batch of checks is delivered to the accounting department on the 9th or 10th.

When the checks are received, the accounting department matches them with supporting data and forwards both checks and supporting data to two authorized check signers. The supporting documents are reviewed, initialed, and the checks signed manually. Each check is countersigned by the treasurer. Under this system, checks are often not mailed until the 12th or 13th and some discounts are disallowed as a result.

Proposed Changes

To alleviate the problem, the client proposes to have all checks for amounts less than $250 reviewed by two other clerks who will be authorized to sign with facsimile plates. No further review would be required. The client presents the following points to support his belief that there are adequate controls:

1. Typical check distributions, by amounts are:

Amount	Percent of Checks	Percent of Total Disbursements
Under $50	36%	2%
$50–$249	44	5
Over $250	20	93

2. The clerks will review supporting documents. If there seems to be any irregularity, the checks will not be signed by facsimile, but will be forwarded to the regular check signing channels.
3. The signing devices will have counters. The numbers of checks signed will be reconciled to the number of checks prepared by the data processing center.
4. Bank accounts are reconciled independently of the accounts payable division.
5. The clerks will have no duties involving data preparation or matching of checks to supporting documents.
6. Checks signed with the facsimile plate will be imprinted "VOID FOR AMOUNTS GREATER THAN $250."

PONDER and PREPARE

1. Do the proposed changes include adequate controls?
2. If not, what further suggestions would you make?

FORBES ELECTRONICS COMPANY—A

The Forbes Electronics Company manufactures kits for the home market of radio and high-fidelity enthusiasts. The kits include AM-FM tuners, amplifiers, tape decks, and high-fidelity speaker systems. Included in each kit, as described by the company, are ". . . detailed instructions to enable the home craftsman to build sets with professional quality." Innovations in the form of plug-in connections and printed circuits to eliminate hand soldering have enabled the company to expand its sales activity considerably.

Recently, Forbes has been negotiating with its bank for working capital loans in order to expand production to keep up with increasing demand. Projections by the company indicate that the present rate of increase in buying should provide ample funds for repayment of all loans at maturity. The bank has examined the projections provided by the company and has requested these estimates be supplemented by audited financial statements. The firm of Bielicki, Saunders, and Sekellick, CPA's, has been retained to audit the accounts for the year ending December 31st. In the course of the audit, the following description of purchasing and materials handling was included in the working papers:

The manufacturing department, based upon current inventory levels, reorder points, and planned production schedules, authorizes the preparation of material purchase requisitions, which are sent to the purchasing department for acquisition. The purchasing department is responsible for maintaining a list of reliable suppliers and for obtaining the best possible terms without requesting competitive bids. Prenumbered purchase orders are prepared: the original is sent to the supplier, one copy is sent to the receiving department, and one copy is retained in the purchasing department files.

Material is received and counted in the receiving department. Actual quantities received are verified against the receiving copy of the purchase order and discrepancies are noted directly on the purchase order. The purchase order is then returned to the purchasing department.

When invoices are received from vendors, they are forwarded to the purchasing department. There, the invoices are compared with the purchase order received from the receiving department for prices, terms, quantities invoiced, and quantities received. Any differences between quantities invoiced and quantities received are investigated before releasing the documents to the vouchers payable section.

The invoice and receiving copy of the purchase order are sent to the vouchers payable section when approved. Voucher clerks calculate discounts, verify extensions and footings, and determine the appropriate account distribution for the payment. Coding numbers for posting are entered on the voucher and a number is assigned when entry is made in the voucher register. Unpaid vouchers are filed by due dates.

On appropriate due dates, prenumbered checks are prepared, except for signature, in duplicate. A check writing machine is used to emboss the amount on the check. When completed, the checks, with vouchers attached, are sent to the cashier who accounts for check numbers used against a master list and puts the checks through a check signing device. He retains the duplicate copy of the check for bank reconciliation purposes. The checks and vouchers are then sent to the disbursements clerk who makes entries in the cash records.

The signed checks and vouchers are finally returned to the vouchers payable section. The checks are inserted in window-type envelopes and forwarded to the mail room. The paid vouchers are cancelled by perforation and filed numerically in a paid voucher file. When the checks have been mailed, check numbers are entered in the voucher register opposite the voucher number.

Monthly, one of the voucher clerks prepares a listing from the unpaid voucher file and compares the total with a separately prepared total of unpaid vouchers from the voucher register, and with the total from the general ledger control account. Any differences are reconciled.

PONDER and PREPARE

As manager of the engagement, prepare a report for Forbes Electronics Company management discussing the system for processing purchase orders and disbursements. Suggest any supplemental or revised procedures for correcting any weaknesses in internal control you discuss.

HAYNES FOOD PROCESSORS, INCORPORATED

Haynes Food Processors, Incorporated is a large processor and distributor of convenience foods such as frozen fruits and vegetables, cake mixes, frozen pastries, complete frozen meals, and so forth. The company produces a full line under its own brand label of "Redi-Qwik" as well as under private brands for major grocery chains and other wholesale distributors. The business is highly competitive and innovation in terms of existing products and new products is essential for continued successful operations.

The company has been quite active in developing new products. Over the past year and a half, the company has been working on the development of a new food product processed by the freeze-dry method, wherein the product is both frozen and dehydrated. The addition of a suitable liquid readily reconstitutes the item, while ordinary shelf storage is possible for considerable periods of time without product deterioration. The product has been extensively test marketed in three selected locations and consumer response has been gratifying. The company has decided to market the product nationally under its own label in two sizes, "regular" and "family" size.

Extensive meetings were held with Stringham and Straightfellow, the advertising agency, to develop marketing and promotional plans. The company finally adopted a two-part promotional program involving "consumer deals." In general, the program will include various types of coupons in all products marketed under the "Redi-Qwik" label, which will be redeemable for either cash or a variety of merchandise offers. The company plans for the program to operate much like the premium coupons attached to certain cigarette brands or the various types of trading stamps redeemable for merchandise. When redeemable for cash, each coupon will have a specified redemption value and an expiration date.

To kick off the program, the first "deal" will be a coupon redeemable in cash (twenty-five cents) plus a free copy of the merchandise catalog describing future offers and the number of coupons necessary to secure each item of merchandise offered. The cash coupons are to be included in both sizes of the new product being introduced, starting October 1, this year. The cash offer will expire on March 31, next year and the company anticipates that 300,000 coupons will have been distributed for redemption. The second step in the campaign will be to include merchandise coupons in *all* "Redi-Qwik" packages after February 1, next year which, in turn, may be redeemed for merchandise from the catalog.

As part of the audit engagement, Nobel and Banter, CPA's, have been requested by the controller to submit a special report reviewing the handling of coupons. Specifically, he wants a system that will provide good internal control on a continuing basis as well as provide appropriate accounting for the premium transactions. The auditors commenced the engagement in January and a review of the accounting for coupons produced the following narrative:

An informal record of coupons received, used, and damaged is kept by the production superintendent.. As coupons are received from the printer, the number received is entered from a copy of the receiving report. The coupons are prepackaged by the printer in bundles of 1,000 and the packages are not opened to count individual coupons when received. Usage of coupons is recorded based upon the production report of the number of packages processed each day.

The coupons are kept in a file cabinet in the production superintendent's office. Daily the lead production foreman picks up a quantity of coupons based upon that day's production schedule, leaving an informal memo as to the number of coupons taken. The packaging machinery automatically inserts coupons into the packages.

An inspection of the process by the production foreman revealed that not all packages processed received a coupon. In addition, the equipment jammed periodically resulting in damaged coupons. Most damaged coupons were retrieved by the foreman but some ended up in sealed packages and were subsequently presented for redemption. Adjustments to the equipment eliminated nearly all of the damaging of coupons. Correspondence revealed that about one per cent of the packages did not receive a coupon. The damaged coupons are destroyed by the foreman by discarding them in the incinerator chute. He reports the count of damaged coupons, orally, to the production superintendent each day.

A review of the informal records kept by the production supervisor revealed the following summarized information:

Coupons received to December 31	300,000
Coupons included in "regular" packages	100,000
Coupons included in "family" packages	50,000
Coupons damaged and destroyed	4,000
Coupons on hand, December 31	146,000

The auditors made arrangements for the client to take a physical count of coupons on hand at December 31. The count indicated that 140,000 coupons were actually in the storeroom.

Correspondence containing coupons for redemption is opened by the mail room. The letters are sorted into a separate stack and sent to the cashier's department for handling. A special imprest fund has been established for purposes of handling redemption. One employee in the cashier's department has been assigned the responsibility for the coupons. She places a twenty-five cent piece, mounted on a mailing cardboard, in the self-addressed envelope sent in by the customer. After sealing, the envelopes are returned to the mail room for stamping and mailing. The clerk then cancels the coupons that have been redeemed with a rubber stamp bearing the legend "PAID" and the date.

Once a week the imprest fund is reimbursed for all coupons redeemed during the week. Expenditures are reconciled with the cancelled coupons by the same clerk who stuffs customer envelopes. After preparation of the voucher for reimbursement, the redeemed coupons are mutilated by a paper cutter and discarded. A review of the vouchers revealed that 75,000 coupons had been redeemed as of the end of the year. This reconciled with the expenditures from the imprest fund.

The controller indicated he had discussed ultimate redemption figures with several other firms that used similar coupon programs. Based upon these discussions, the controller estimated that about 60 per cent of the coupons still outstanding and to be issued would be presented for redemption.

No experience is available as yet with respect to the merchandise coupons. A purchase order has been issued for the printing of 1,000,000 of these coupons. The merchandise catalogs have been printed and are stored in a special storeroom from where they are being mailed to customers sending in cash redemption coupons. Premium merchandise has not been purchased as yet, although preliminary estimates of the number of units of each item in the catalog to be ordered have been prepared and ordering will probably commence in February. A special storeroom, under lock and key, is being prepared for the storage of premium merchandise. The clerk who is presently handling the cash redemption coupons will also be assigned the responsibility of processing the merchandise coupon redemptions when they commence. One of the production stores clerks will take care of issuing premium merchandise.

PONDER and PREPARE

1. Prepare a memorandum to the controller outlining any weaknesses in the present procedures with respect to internal control and accountability of the coupons. Suggest any recommendations you think essential in improving internal control and accountability, not only for cash redemption coupons but for merchandise redemption coupons to be issued in the future.

2. Compute the company's estimated liability for unredeemed coupons as of December 31, showing your method of computation. Based upon your calculations, prepare any necessary journal entries.

THE HAGIN CONSTRUCTION COMPANY

The Hagin Construction Company is owned and operated by Max Hagin as sole proprietor. The company operates solely within New York City and in the past few years has been able to secure a number of major construction jobs on competitive bid. It is now considered one of about a dozen major construction companies operating in the city.

Through engineering planning, the company has been able to usefully employ a permanent work force of about 200 skilled construction men on a regular basis. Additional part-time work force is supplied by the central hiring hall of the Amalgamated Construction Workers of America, as needed. Part-time employees are generally hired on a day-to-day basis. They are paid in full at the termination of employment on any given day, except that those who work as long as a week at a time are paid weekly with regular full-time employees.

The work force, generally, is organized along trade lines; i.e., carpenters, electricians, masons, and so forth. Each group works under one or more foremen who are responsible for scheduling the work to be done and estimating the number of workers needed for the scheduled job. The total work force varies from a low of about 200 "permanent" men to as many as 600 employees during the peak construction period of May through October. At the time of the audit under consideration, there were 247 employees on the job.

The nature of the construction business requires heavy cash commitments during the construction phase. These cash needs are frequently met by borrowings against the construction contract. When the structure is completed, the construction notes are retired through refinancing by the owners of the structure, usually with a first mortgage being pledged as security. Hagin Construction Company has arranged for lines of credit at several different banks for working cash as construction progresses. These banks require audited statements each six months, one for the period covering the six months ending April 30 each year, and the other for the period covering the six months ending October 31 each year.

Alden & Bacon, Certified Public Accountants, have been engaged for the first time to conduct the audit for the period ending October 31. The manager in charge of the audit, along with the senior assigned to the field work visited the construction site on September 15, for a preliminary conference with the client. Although Max Hagin maintains an office in Brooklyn, near the central hiring hall of the Amalgamated Construction Workers of America, during most of the year the office staff is located in a "construction shack" on the site of one of the major jobs, and all office routines and functions are carried out from that location. This visit revealed the following information about the payroll procedures.

Each afternoon, all foremen meet with Mr. Hagin to review the work progress and to plan for the next day's activities in particular and the next week in general. As each phase of the job is scheduled to commence, the individual foreman estimates the number of men that will be needed and the approximate time needed to complete that phase of the work. Employee needs are broken down into union authorized job classifications and the list is turned over to Mrs. Bessie Henderson, the payroll clerk. Mrs. Henderson compares the list with the employee roster and notes any job classifications indicating shortages. A second list is prepared showing the number of workers needed under each job classification.

After the list has been approved by Mr. Hagin, it is sent to the central hiring hall with a notation as to the date the men are to report to work and the approximate duration of employment. The central hiring hall secures the needed workmen and returns, on the appropriate day, a list of names by job classification, of the workers reporting that day. After each man's name is given the approved union rate of pay for his job classification. These lists along with the regular payroll lists become the basis for the permanent payroll register.

Each week, each foreman is supplied with a time sheet for the men under his supervision. He is required to enter the number of hours worked each day by each man listed on the sheet. As new men are hired, the foreman enters the names in pencil along with the date the new men reported for work. These entries are subsequently checked against the hiring list supplied by the union. At the end of each week, the time sheets are returned to the office for payroll preparation. Daily, the foremen verbally report the names and hours worked of men being terminated that day. Mrs. Henderson prepares a special payroll record for the terminated employees and they are paid at the end of that day.

From the weekly time sheets, Mrs. Henderson prepares the payroll record showing for each employee his gross pay, distinguishing between regular and over-time pay, the various kinds of deductions, and the net pay due. During the period of peak employment, she is assisted by Miss Joan Archer, Mr. Hagin's secretary. The completed payroll register is then compared to the list of terminated employees for the week and a notation is entered as to the date each was paid, with a verification of the amount. The total net payroll is then adjusted for these payments and Mrs. Henderson prepares a check which is taken to the bank and cashed. Mr. Steve Clifford, the cashier-accountant for the firm, normally makes the bank trip.

Name plates are prepared and maintained by Miss Archer for each employee showing name and social security number and providing space for payroll information. The following is a reproduction of one of the plates:

James Wilson   787 02 5596

Gross: $_____   Deductions: $_____

NET: $_____

Miss Archer prepares the pay envelopes by processing them through a printing device and she turns the completed envelopes over to Mrs. Henderson. Mrs. Henderson, with help from Miss Archer during peak seasons, fills in the appropriate figures from the payroll register. The envelopes are not added to ascertain that the total agrees with the register. Mrs. Henderson, Miss Archer and Mr. Clifford all assist in putting the appropriate amount of cash into the pay envelopes.

When the pay envelopes are completed, they are sorted by foremen groups. The foremen then pick up the envelopes and distribute them to the workers. Pay envelopes for absent workers are returned to Mr. Clifford who places them in the petty cash box. These men must then report to the office to secure their pay.

Mr. Clifford, in addition to his other duties, also maintains the petty cash. There is no attempt made to keep petty cash and unclaimed wages segregated, all the currency being kept in a single envelope. Expenditures from petty cash are recorded on any handy piece of scrap paper, with a notation as to the nature of the expenditure and the amount. Employees who are terminated prior to a regular pay day are frequently paid from petty cash funds rather than having Mrs. Henderson draw a separate payroll check as is done for the regular weekly pay.

In addition to Mr. Clifford, Mrs. Henderson, and Miss Archer, the company regularly employs two bookkeeping clerks who maintain the detailed cost ledgers. Mr. Clifford keeps all other records including the general ledger. During peak periods of activity in the summer, as many as three extra bookkeeping clerks may be employed.

In organizing the audit, the senior assigned one of the staff assistants to the cash audit, including petty cash. He arrived at the site office at 9:30 a.m. on November 1, and Mr. Clifford gave him a metal cash box which he said contained all the money and data relating to the petty cash fund. Upon examination of the contents the assistant found three envelopes containing:

1. a quantity of cash,
2. a group of empty envelopes, and
3. a number of slips of paper containing written amounts and descriptions.

A summary of the contents showed:

cash on hand	$319.10
8 empty pay envelopes, net pay totaling	590.25
40 "vouchers" totaling	571.15

The general ledger account for petty cash indicated that the fund had been created in 1959 in the amount of three hundred dollars.

Since Mr. Clifford was custodian of the fund, he was asked for an explanation of some of the items contained in the box. The first question related to the empty pay envelopes and he replied:

"Well, you see, Mr. Hagin insists the men want their pay in cash. So, when the foremen turn in time sheets, Bessie figures out how much cash we need and I take a check to the bank and get it. Then we all sit around for a few hours and stuff the pay envelopes with the cash and then I take them to the foremen to give to the men at the end of the day. Any man who is not there when the pay is passed out must come to the office and pick up his pay in person. We don't require him to sign for it. I know most of these guys.

"Well, anyway, so that I will have plenty of cash to pay out, I just empty the pay envelopes and put all the cash together, including whatever I have for petty cash. When I get down to about fifty bucks, I get another check for the petty cash fund. I fill out a form on which I list the various expenditures from petty cash and one of the gals spreads the amount to the various accounts for tax expense."

In response to a question about what happens if there is not enough cash to pay an employee whose pay envelop is being held in petty cash, the reply was: "Well, I just fill out a petty cash form with enough tickets to get the cash I need to pay him. Sometimes, if I am not real busy, I will put all of the tickets on the form and get all the money back. I don't have a regular schedule; just when I get down to fifty bucks or so."

In an effort to gain more information, a second conference was arranged with Mr. Hagin, the senior accountant, and the staff assistant. Mr. Hagin was asked about the payment of employees in cash rather than by check. He replied that most of the employees, in his opinion, preferred to have the cash rather than bother with cashing a check. He said: "You boys know how bankers are with their short hours and all; and many of my boys just can't get to a bank and the old lady needs the dough for groceries." He also indicated that he knew unclaimed wages were being used for petty cash expenditures but defended this by saying it reduced the need to write checks to replenish the fund. "Writing checks is a bother; I have to sign them all; besides, it costs money."

PONDER and PREPARE

1. Evaluate the system for payroll preparation, distribution, and unclaimed wages in terms of its strengths and weaknesses.
2. If Mr. Hagin continues to insist upon paying wages in cash, what changes in the system would you recommend to provide better internal control and information relative to payroll and unclaimed wages?

3. Prepare, in outline form, the arguments you might use to convince Mr. Hagin he would be better off paying his employees by check rather than in cash.

FORBES ELECTRONICS COMPANY—B *

In connection with a bank requested audit, the firm of Bielicki, Saunders and Sekellick, CPA's, has been retained to audit the accounts for the year ending December 31st.

In the course of the audit, payroll expense accounts and payroll taxes were investigated. The following information has been accumulated by the junior staff man on the engagement:

1. In the working papers are transcripts of the company's general ledger accounts for salary expenses and payroll taxes. These are reproduced in Exhibit One.

2. No copies of the quarterly tax returns are available. Some files were destroyed accidentally when new office equipment was acquired and many dormant files were incinerated.

3. The working papers also contain summaries of payroll taxes withheld from the employees' wages as well as remittances made by the company quarterly. These are reproduced in Exhibit Two. Calculations contained in the working papers indicate that the payroll clerk properly computed withholdings.

4. The effective Federal Unemployment tax rate for the current year is 0.3 per cent of covered payroll. The laws of the state in which Forbes does business do not provide for employee contributions for state unemployment insurance purposes.

PONDER and PREPARE

1. Assist the junior staffman in preparing a worksheet to determine the correct balances at December 31st for the general ledger accounts: Salary Expense, Payroll Taxes Expense, Payroll Taxes Withheld, Employer Payroll Taxes Payable. You may disregard any accruals for payroll at the year-end. Your worksheet should also contain any necessary adjusting journal entries to correct the accounts.

2. Suggest a payroll system that will provide reliable and useful payroll data. You may ignore cost accounting requirements.

* See Forbes Electronics Company—A, p. 93.

EXHIBIT ONE

FORBES ELECTRONICS COMPANY

SALARY EXPENSE

Date	Explanation	L.F.	Debit	Credit	Balance
12-31-68	Weekly payrolls (Total of 12 monthly summary entries)	CD	163,050		163,050

PAYROLL TAX EXPENSE

Date	Explanation	L.F.	Debit	Credit	Balance
1-10-68	Quarterly Payment	CD	13,300		13,300
4-20-68	Quarterly Payment	CD	13,590		26,890
7-14-68	Quarterly Payment	CD	11,890		38,780
10-18-68	Quarterly Payment	CD	11,865		50,645

PAYROLL TAXES WITHHELD

Date	Explanation	L.F.	Debit	Credit	Balance
1-1-68	Balance Forward			11,200	11,200

EMPLOYER PAYROLL TAXES PAYABLE

Date	Explanation	L.F.	Debit	Credit	Balance
1-1-68	Balance Forward			2,100	2,100

EXHIBIT TWO

FORBES ELECTRONICS COMPANY

PAYROLL TAXES WITHHELD

Quarter	Gross Salary	FICA	Income Taxes	Net Salary
First	$48,650	$ 1,520	$ 9,300	$37,830
Second	42,900	1,340	8,150	33,410
Third	45,790	1,160	8,580	36,050
Fourth	66,860	800	10,300	55,760

PAYROLL TAX REMITTANCES

Description	4-20-68	7-14-68	10-18-68	1-12-69
FICA (Total 6.24%)	$ 3,040	$ 2,680	$ 2,320	$ 1,600
Income Taxes	9,300	8,150	8,580	10,300
State Unemployment Taxes (2.7%)	1,250	1,060	965	570
	$13,590	$11,890	$11,865	$12,470

STUART PRODUCTS

Stuart Products manufactures a line of electrical consumer products ranging from small hand drills to electric ranges and refrigerators. Stuart does not distribute products under its own name but manufactures for private label customers. The Company operates five plants throughout the country, employing about 15,000 hourly paid workers and around 1,500 salaried personnel.

The Company is highly decentralized, with local plant management exercising considerable local autonomy within broad policy guidelines laid down by top management. Two years ago, the home office installed a high speed electronic data processing system and currently all aspects of production scheduling and control and inventory control have been centralized at corporate headquarters. Rapid communications are maintained through a network of leased-wire data transmission facilities, with sending and receiving terminals in strategic plant locations.

One of the functions centralized for computer processing is the salaried employees payroll since this group includes all top executives at the corporate headquarters and at each plant. All records necessary for the preparation of the salaried payroll are maintained in the Corporate Payroll Department under the supervision of the Chief Payroll Supervisor. Hourly payroll is reviewed by the Corporate Payroll Department, but is prepared and disbursed locally at each plant.

The Corporate Payroll Department receives data concerning salaried personnel on a special form that originates at each plant, or at corporate headquarters. The forms include information on hiring, termination, change of salary rates, promotions, and inter-plant transfers. No written policy exists with respect to approvals. The form provides space for two approving signatures and forms are received from the plants with various combinations of two signatures from among the department supervisors, plant controllers, plant managers, and the vice-president for industrial relations. All corporate headquarters personnel changes are approved by the corporate controller only.

Information concerning payroll deductions originates in the plant controller's office, with two of the plants channeling the data through plant personnel offices prior to submission. Time worked is reported on an exception basis only; i.e., days not worked because of sickness, vacation time, other authorized absences and unauthorized absences. Reductions in salary are made for unauthorized absences only.

Individual earnings records are maintained on magnetic tape on a Master Salaried Payroll file. Checks, payroll registers, and departmental cost allocation reports are prepared automatically from an output tape resulting from the payroll processing run. All changes are key-punched in the Corporate Payroll Department and forwarded to the Data Processing Center. The Master Salaried Payroll file and processing tapes are kept in the Data Processing Center library. Checks, payroll registers, and departmental cost allocations are returned to the Corporate Payroll Department after processing. In some cases such as when a check has been issued prior to the regular pay day or a last minute change has not been processed, checks are prepared manually in the Payroll Department and entered manually on the payroll register and departmental cost allocation reports.

All checks are signed with a facsimile signature plate by the Chief Payroll Supervisor. After signature, each check is sealed in an individual window envelope and sent to the appropriate plant controller along with a copy of the payroll register and departmental cost allocation report. The plant controller reviews the payroll register with his personnel records. A report is returned to the Chief Payroll Supervisor either approving the register or listing exceptions. The internal audit staff subsequently reconciles these reports to a report prepared by the Payroll Department concerning monthly payroll disbursements by plant.

Checks are distributed under the supervision of the plant controller. Unclaimed checks are returned to the Chief Payroll Supervisor for follow-up. Two payroll accounts are established at banks near each plant to cover, separately, hourly payroll and salaried payroll. For salaried payroll, prenumbered checks are issued, with unused stocks maintained in the Payroll Department. The Chief Payroll Supervisor personally reconciles the salaried payroll accounts. The internal audit staff, which reconciles all other payroll accounts, has no access to salaried payroll records or accounts, other than the reconciliation previously described. In addition, the internal audit staff does not observe check distribution for salaried personnel.

PONDER and PREPARE

1. What are the strengths and weaknesses in internal control?
2. What suggestions would you make, as auditors, for improving the system?
3. What audit procedures would you employ to satisfy yourself about the salaried payroll? You may assume the amounts are material.

PART THREE

Statement Presentation
Auditors' Reports

MATERIALITY *

by Donald Rappaport

Accounting authorities use "materiality" to qualify almost all expressions of opinions or positions. By actual count *Auditing Standards and Procedures* and the *Accounting Research Bulletins* of the American Institute and *Regulation S-X* of the SEC contain more than one hundred references to items: material and significant, immaterial, of little or no consequence, so inconsequential as to be immaterial, inconsiderable in amount, of substantial importance, of significance, material, not so significant, substantial, materially distorting, and so on. The well-known general expressions are (author's italics):

> . . . to express an unqualified opinion, he (the independent auditor) must have reason to believe and must believe that the financial statements fairly present the financial position and results of operations and that they disclose all *material* facts necessary to make them not misleading. (*Codification of Statements on Auditing Procedure*, AICPA, 1951, p. 18.)

> The committee (on accounting procedure) contemplates that its opinions will have application only to items *material and significant* in the relative circumstances. (*Accounting Research Bulletin No. 43*, AICPA, 1953, p. 9.)

> If the amount which would otherwise be required to be shown with respect to any item is not *material*, it need not be separately set forth in the manner prescribed. (*Regulation S-X*, Rule 3-02, SEC.)

Expressed in general terms in the foregoing fashion and in detail, accounting speaks of what matters and what does not matter, what is material and what is trifling. (See H. W. Fowler on "material" in *Modern English Usage*, London, Oxford University Press, 1960, p. 344.) It is not too much then to suggest that the construction of financial statements which are reasonably informative and not misleading hinges on the accountant's method of deciding on materiality.

* Reprinted from *The Journal of Accountancy*, vol. 117, no. 4 (April 1964), pp. 42–8, by permission of the publishers.

The importance of materiality criteria, it seems, would have brought forth programs or guides for materiality measurement. A search of the literature, however, discloses little effort in this direction. It has been perhaps too frequently assumed that the absence of a statutory measuring unit indicates that objectivity is unobtainable or that no visible yardstick means guesswork is involved. Thus, it is held, materiality questions are to be resolved by mere opinion, impression, or intuition with such help as may be obtained from definitions too subjective to be called guides. Take, for example:

> The term "material," when used to qualify a requirement for the furnishing of information as to any subject, limits the information required to those matters as to which an average prudent investor ought reasonably to be informed before purchasing the security registered. (*Regulation S-X*, Rule 1-02, SEC.)

But does the essence of accounting experience point to the desirability of that manner of materiality decision-making or does it point to the desirability of materiality decisions grounded in objective facts and analyses? It is an opinion held at least by some accountants that a search for more objective guides should be undertaken. This paper sets forth the findings of one such search.

First, we survey the users of financial statements and discuss the aims of financial analysis. Having established the audience and the timbre of their analytic listening devices, we search for materiality guideposts for three areas: the amount shown as net income, classification of dollar amounts in financial statements, and adequate disclosure of other essential financial information.

Our findings include three specific guideposts for materiality decisions about presentation of net income, five areas of guidance for separate disclosure of extraneous items and for disclosure of lack of comparability in income statements, eight guideposts for balance sheet materiality decisions and five for disclosure of certain other data and information.

A limitation—in the work of accountants the use of materiality may be divided into two broad classes: (1) the auditing of transactions, and (2) the preparation of financial statements. Some accounting literature closely associates these two aspects of materiality. But we believe they are largely separate subjects. For example, the materiality guides set forth in this paper cannot sanction erroneous accounting or an improper transaction. Nor do they guide the accountant in deciding the number of transactions he should test in the auditing of an account. This paper will deal with materiality from the point when the audit has disclosed no impropriety and the transactions have been recorded properly on the books of the company.

Materiality in Financial Analysis

In order that financial statements be judged fair or misleading they must be used by someone and for some purpose. Those who depend most heavily on financial information in published annual reports, particularly as a guide to the value of an investment presently held or contemplated, are the investors themselves. The chief interest of these users is in reading the future from the past. Those who use accounts as an historical record, that is, as a report of stewardship, and executives who use accounts as a guide to present and future business decisions are not insensitive to materiality criteria. All the same, in published annual reports, inadequate disclosure of some business information or accounting practice or questionable presentation of an item is most likely to be material to investors. Thus, accountants can depend on conclusions that investors might draw from financial statements to furnish the most sensitive guideposts for materiality decisions.

Financial statements are prepared not in accordance with personal doctrine but in accordance with generally accepted principles. And, the accountant's materiality decisions need not depend on rather haphazard conclusions that an average investor might draw from financial statements but on interpretations that might be expected from the application of the best methods of financial analysis. Certainly the most important investment decisions, both institutional and individual, are increasingly being made by professional security analysts. Thus, it is important for the accountant to give some recognition to financial analysis theories and techniques when considering treatment of items in financial accounts.

The aim of financial statement analysis is to translate accounting data into economic indicators. Nevertheless, this does not place on accounting a burden to conform to economic concepts. Rather, it demands that users of accounts make what adjustments are necessary to glean economic significance from accounting data. In this process we can recognize at least three stages:

1. An understanding of the nature and limitations of accounting statements; they are primarily historical and are based on convention and opinion, and the principles of accounting used to prepare particular financial statements. (This is essential to comprehension of the business activity portrayed, just as knowledge of the language used in a book is essential to comprehension of the writer's meaning.)
2. Rearrangement of dollar data found in financial statements into financial analysis tools, such as averages, trends, and ratios, which establish meaningful relationships, and drawing inferences from such relationships.

3. Association of inferences derived with general and particular economic forces affecting a business to assist in reaching an opinion on the future course of the business.

The accountant's responsibility extends to stage 2, the direct analysis of financial statements (known as financial statement analysis and interpretation). Thus, for example, growth trends or liquidity ratios should not be misleading. But the economic explanation of the causes of changes in trends or ratios is not within the area of an accountant's responsibility. To reiterate, in deciding whether a particular presentation, classification, or disclosure matters or does not matter in financial statements, the accountant should carefully study the possible interpretations of the measuring devices normally derived from such data.

It is important to observe that much information useful in the analysis of an investment is not set forth in financial statements. Security analysts will often require more information than even the highest quality financial statements contain. This makes the job of the analyst more difficult. He may need to obtain information on units sold, plant location, and products in development stage, from sources other than the financial statements. Reasonably informative disclosure in financial statements does not contemplate that such information be given. This necessarily restricts inferences that may be drawn from financial statements to those that deal principally with dollar data. It rather neatly carves out of the field of financial analysis the area for study by accountants in a search for materiality guideposts.

To begin, we must mold materiality problems into a form suitable for such a search. The three questions set forth below are the most useful and perhaps most realistic form we have been able to evolve.

1. Are misleading inferences likely to be drawn from the amount shown as net income?
2. Are the classifications of dollar amounts set forth in the financial statements reasonably informative and not misleading?
3. Is certain other information which is necessary to make the statement reasonably informative and not misleading adequately disclosed in the body of financial statements or in footnotes?

Determining Net Income *

The materiality problem in this area is whether extraneous items should be included in the results of the current year. Fowler in *Modern English Usage,* p. 162, says: "That is extraneous which is brought in, or comes or has come in, from without. A fly in amber, a bullet in one'

* *Author's note: this section should be compared to paragraphs 19–31 inclusive Accounting Principles Board Opinion No. 9, AICPA, December 1966.*

hest, are extraneous bodies; . . ." Such items in accounts develop out
of events that took place in past years or in the year covered when not
the result of usual operations. Items specifically related to operations of
prior years include elimination of unused reserves and adjustments of
income taxes of prior years. Items of the current year not likely to recur
include unusual sales of fixed assets, catastrophes, or write-offs of in-
tangibles. Now the financial analyst's interest in net income is its earning
power indications. Extraneous items may not provide such indications or
may act as misleading indicators. Further, analysts, like accountants, are
aware that no real earning power indication could ever be obtained from
study of a current year alone. Thus emphasis is on long-run analysis. The
concern is not so much about last year's earnings as about average earnings over a period of years, the stability of past earnings, and the growth
of earnings.

Although most extraneous items are excluded by analysts in considering results of the current year, in many cases these are included in
considering overall results over a period of years. All real profit and loss
items, extraneous only insofar as they relate to events which took place
entirely in past years—for example, income tax assessments—are taken
into consideration in studying average earnings over a period of years.
By contrast, profits and losses resulting from unusual sales of assets not
acquired for resale are usually excluded. One of the main guides then
in deciding on including an extraneous item in net income for the
current year is whether it properly belongs in net income of a previous
year. If an extraneous item belongs in average income over a period of
years, this evidence favors including the item in net income for the
current year. If not, presumption favors excluding the amount from net
income. (Note: It has been said that every income statement of a large
corporation will contain a certain normal amount of extraneous items.
Usually this "normal amount of abnormality," even when associated with
prior year events, can properly be included in income.)

Stability of past earnings is also an important earning power indi-
cator. The ratio of the lowest earnings for a five-to-ten-year period measured against the average earnings of the three preceding years is a gauge
of earnings stability. If inclusion of an extraneous item in the current
year's income causes or prevents an earnings decline ratio (current income to the average income of the three preceding years) that exceeds
the most serious previous setback over a given period of years, this
evidence suggests exclusion of the item from net income.

Continuing, an extraneous item's relationship to the growth of
earnings should be studied. Here accountants should compare results of
extrapolation of earning trends when current income includes an
extraneous item against such results excluding the item. Greater or less

materiality depends on the particular trend pattern, secular, cyclical or irregular. A company with steady progressive improvement in earnings should exclude extraneous income that contributes to the maintenance of the trend. On the other hand, a corporation with an erratic pattern of earnings may not need to be concerned about including a similar amount in net income.

To restate, the guideposts discovered for materiality decisions about presentation of net income are: (1) Would income over a period of years include the extraneous item? (2) Would the ability of the earnings decline ratio to shed new light on the factor of earnings stability be clouded by the inclusion of the extraneous item? (3) Would extrapolation of earnings that included the extraneous item result in erroneous inferences because the item preserves the appearance of regularity in trend where no regularity exists and conversely?

Certainly neither inclusion nor exclusion of an extraneous item will always do full justice to net income. This observation, we shall see, signifies the importance of disclosure of extraneous items determined to be part of net income.

Finally, we cannot help mentioning that consistency in the application of these guides may, somehow, be part of the subject. However, to keep this paper within manageable bounds we will do no more than state that this subject calls for attention.

Statement of Operations

Having arrived at net income, the accountant might have to decide next about what matters and what does not matter in classifications of items in the statement of operations. Conventionally, reasonably informative disclosure contemplates that this statement include at least the following: sales, operating revenues, cost of products sold excluding depreciation, depreciation expense, operating expense, selling, general and administrative expenses, other income, other deductions, income taxes, and net income. To make the statement of operations not misleading, other classifications might be required.

The accountant would probably first consider those extraneous items that were determined to be part of net income for the year. The leading question is: Should extraneous debit or credit items show separately in the statement of operations?

Second, he would consider any lack of comparability from one year to the next of amounts in conventional captions. Comparability may be affected by:

1. Change in accounting principles employed.
2. Changed conditions which necessitate accounting changes (but not changes in accounting principles).
3. Changed conditions unrelated to accounting.
4. Reclassifications.

The leading question here, for all but the first of these four classes, is: Should lack of comparability be disclosed in the notes to the financial statements? The first class, changes in accounting principles, will be discussed afterwards.

Guidance in answering these questions can be had by studying the analytical significance of the content of the income statement. Some analytical relationships under this heading are set forth below.

The most important classification affecting a view of the future of a company (other than net income) is *sales*. Analytic relationships include:

The rate of growth of sales
Gross profit as a percentage of sales
Net income as a percentage of sales
The growth of dollar sales
Sales per dollar of capital funds invested

Other common relationships obtained from income statements are:

Cost of Goods Sold
Gross profit percentage

Depreciation
Trend of dollar amounts
The rate of growth of funds derived from operations (net income plus depreciation and similar charges)

Selling, General and Administrative Expenses
Change in dollar amounts

Income Taxes
Income taxes as a percentage of income before taxes

In summary. The objective approach to the question, "Is a particular classification material?" consists of figuring if the amount in question affects the significance of common analytic relationships. Generally, only amounts affecting established historical patterns would be material. Illustrating this: Company X—because of consistent sales growth a reclassification (say the treatment of freight expense as a selling expense rather than as a deduction from gross sales) which preserves a consistent sales growth pattern is a material fact required to be disclosed. Company Y— because of absence of consistent sales growth a similar reclassification is not likely to call for disclosure because a misleading inference is not as likely to be drawn from an amplification or modification of an erratic sales pattern.

The consistency standard. Published financial statements frequently disclose changes in accounting principles from one year to the next (in response to the consistency standard of reporting), even though the current effect is trivial and there is little certainty of substantial effect in future years. These include changes from item to composite method of depreciation and changes from Fifo to Lifo method of inventory pricing. This sensitivity about the effect on comparability of changes in accounting principles beyond that displayed about such effects produced by other changed conditions may spring from any of a number of sources. It may have developed from overly cautious reading of paragraph 21 of the Institute's Statements on Auditing Procedure No. 31, "Consistency," covering disclosure of an accounting change having no effect on the current year but reasonably certain to have substantial effects in later years. Or perhaps an accounting change is set before the user of financial statements so that he may decide on the wisdom of the choice. Another possibility: sensitivity to changes in accounting principles comes about indirectly as the backwash of consideration of fair presentation. Fair presentation demands, if an accounting practice has not attained uniformity, disclosure of the particular practice be made, as with methods of inventory pricing and bases of stating plant assets. So, changes in accounting principles employed—from one acceptable principle to another—will be apparent when comparing the financial statement of the current period to the financial statements of the preceding period. Thus, being aware that comparability may be at stake, users of financial statements are, it is believed, curious about the dollar amount. Accountants have satisfied this curiosity by describing the change and its effect. Or finally, this sensitivity to changes in accounting principles simply may recognize the high virtue of consistency in financial accounting.

The Balance Sheet

Viewing the relationship of materiality to the balance sheet, certain financial analysis guideposts dominate the horizon. That any guideposts for materiality concepts in balance sheet presentation derive from financial statement analysis may come as a surprise. Undeniably, balance sheets are not ordinarily of paramount importance in appraising common stocks, but the assets of a business are integrally related to the ability of a business to attain a level of earnings at any given time. Therefore, they are entitled to more attention than they receive. This being true, simply because balance sheets are frequently ignored by average investors in publicly held companies, the accountant is not relieved from responsibility for misleading inferences drawn therefrom.

Whether customary balance sheet captions may be combined, either added together or netted, and whether changes in accounting or conditions from one year to the next affect comparability and must be disclosed in notes to the statement, are the frequent balance sheet materiality questions. Set forth below are the more important objective analytic guides for materiality decision-making for selected balance sheet problems:

Cash. Disclosure of restrictions on withdrawal of certain cash.

> *Guidepost.* Adequacy of ratio of free cash plus receivables to current liabilities, say 1 to 1.

Marketable securities. Balance sheet value when market is less than cost.

> *Guidepost.* Comparison of unrealized loss to current position and net worth, but not net income as sometimes suggested; i.e., writedown would not directly reduce future earning power of business.

Receivables. Separate captions for customers' accounts receivable, other receivables, and reserve for doubtful accounts.

> *Guidepost.* Distortion created in computation of number of days average customer receivable is outstanding (Receivable/Sales for year × 365 days) or in trend of this ratio from year to year.

Inventories. Disclosure of components, i.e., raw materials, work-in-process, finished goods.

> *Guidepost.* Whether unreasonable turnover proportions, i.e., inventory to cost of sales, etc., and adverse trends in such proportions are hidden.

Property, plant and equipment. Breakdown by major classification.

> *Guidepost.* Importance of breakdown, which enables computation of effective depreciation rate and shows the average age of fixed assets to total assets and depreciation expense to cost of sales.

Current bank loans. Disclosure separate from accounts payable.

> *Guidepost.* If borrowings are larger than cash and receivables combined, serious difficulty may be indicated through such separate classification.

Treasury stock. Disclosure of minor amount carried as an asset.

> *Guidepost.* No analytic importance; significant only if company is buying in own stock to shrink capital or to make future acquisition of assets for stock.

Current position. (1) Inclusion or exclusion in working capital of borderline classifications (deferred charges, cash surrender value of life insurance) that may not be converted to cash in the operating cycle; (2) Netting of current assets and current liabilities.

Guidepost. Effect on: suitable ratio of current assets to current liabilities (say 2 to 1), the acid test ratio of current assets minus inventories to current liabilities (say 1 to 1), the amount of working capital
per dollar of sales.

What follows from focusing on these problems is that classifications
in balance sheets may matter more when certain favorable proportions
do not exist among the particular items in the financial structure of a
business enterprise. For example, when the number of days average customers' receivables are outstanding is increasing but this fact is disguised
by a classification in the balance sheet which combines customer and
other receivables, it could be held that the classification was materially
misleading.

*The importance of disclosing potential conflict of interests even
when the amounts might be considered immaterial.* Responsible reporting may call for disclosure of a transaction between a corporation and
directors or officers not in the ordinary course of business, or a transaction between a parent and a subsidiary if separate financial statements
are prepared. Disclosure of such non-arm's-length transactions with potential conflict of interests is made by classification: "loans to officers;"
or by heading, "a subsidiary of XYZ Company;" or by footnote, ". . . the
property was purchased for XX dollars from the president and principal
shareholder. He paid XX dollars for the property in the year _____."
When special situations like these are disclosed, the purpose is usually
to enable the owners of the business to decide for themselves about the
objectivity of a particular transaction. Hard experience has proven the
salubrious effect of such a glass house. This does not mean that disclosure
itself is satisfactory in each instance. Occasionally, the substance of a
transaction may be such that the independent accountant should express
disapproval of the transaction in his formal opinion. But George O. May
said many years ago that within the limit of a reasonable difference of
opinion an auditor may properly subordinate his own judgment to that
of directors, and unless the point is of crucial importance, he can quite
properly refrain from telling the stockholders of that difference of
opinion.

Disclosure of Other Information

Having considered materiality of classification, the accountant now
may turn his attention to deciding what other information needs to be
disclosed to make the financial statements reasonably informative. This
may consist of financial data not practicable to include in the statements,
or accounting information required to interpret the statements properly.

Again the accountant can find guides for disclosure by studying the interpretive techniques of financial analysis.

The main guideposts are set forth below:

1. The manner in which a corporate obligation must be met over the years has a much more important bearing on future earning power than the mere amount of such obligation. This guidepost calls for the following type of disclosure:

   (a) Interest rate, maturity date and amount of periodic repayment of long-term liabilities or conversion rate, if convertible, into stock.

   (b) Changes in pension plans and information as to whether payments on account of past service are included in the account currently.

   (c) Amount of annual rentals to be paid under long-term leases and length of leases.

Whether disclosure of such fixed cash obligations matters in a particular situation depends on: (1) a comparison of the annual payments to funds generated from operations, the stability of such fund generation and the adequacy of working capital (Is the company vulnerable to such fixed obligations?); (2) the percentage relationship of such fixed charges to gross profit, to form a view of the potential impact of fixed interest, pension, and lease expenses on net income.

2. Studying operating results with full reflection of the company's interest in unconsolidated subsidiaries and 50 per cent-owned companies is a usual endeavor. Thus, where investments are carried at cost and only dividends received are taken into income, disclosure of the difference between cost and underlying book value and between dividends received and equity in earnings should be considered. The necessity for such disclosure would depend largely on the relationship of the cost and underlying book value of the investment to total assets. The amount of dividends received from or income earned by the unconsolidated company against net income of the parent should not be used as a measure because if only a minor amount of dividends was received or income was earned in any year, that in itself might be a material fact.

3. Guaranteed debts or notes receivable discounted or other contingent liabilities might need to be set forth. Here, if the contingency is extraneous to normal business operation, potentially unfavorable impact (and need for disclosure) is chiefly measurable with respect to working capital. Surely current net income is no direct guide to disclosure because the damage to earning power would be indirect through reduction in the assets devoted to producing income.

4. The number of shares of common stock under option and the option price may be a factor in estimating future earnings per share; however, stock option information must be disclosed on "transactions with management" grounds, and we usually need not study the quantitative relationships.

5. Accounting information is required to interpret the statements properly where choice between two or more concepts is available (or where there is a departure from generally accepted accounting principles). Lack of such information makes impossible interpretations of financial accounts. Accounting information includes method of inventory pricing, principles of consolidation, method of accounting for installment sales or long-term contracts, basis of carrying plant and equipment, basis of carrying investments. To illustrate: Suppose we were analyzing a company's earnings over an inflationary period. Certainly to extrapolate future earnings it would be essential to know among other things whether last-in, first-out or some other inventory pricing method was employed.

Summary of Findings

1. Materiality decisions should depend not only on inferences that an average investor might draw from financial statements, but on interpretations that might be expected from the application of the best methods of financial analysis. Guideposts for materiality decisions can be found in such tools of financial analysis as averages, trends, ratios that establish meaningful analytic relationships of information contained in annual reports.

2. Materiality guideposts for inclusion or exclusion of an extraneous item in net income for the current year include:

   (a) Whether an extraneous item belongs in a computation of average income over a period of years;
   (b) Whether an extraneous item affects the measurement of earnings stability;
   (c) Whether an extraneous item results in erroneous inferences from a trend because the item preserves the appearance of regularity in trend where no regularity exists or conversely.

3. Materiality guideposts for the statement of operations are found in the common analytic relationships utilizing sales and cost classifications. Essentially disclosure should be guided by a study of the effect of an item on consistent historical patterns. These materiality guides, however, are not, it was pointed out, the sole basis for disclosure of changes in accounting principles.

4. Materiality guideposts for classifications in the balance sheet are also found in financial analysis tools. Briefly, classifications in balance sheets generally matter more when certain favorable proportions do not exist among the particular items in the financial structure. Potential conflicts of interests, however, frequently require disclosure apart from such considerations.

5. Materility guideposts for disclosure of other information in financial statements or in footnoes include those which measure the importance of:

(a) The manner in which fixed obligations must be met
(b) Interests in unconsolidated subsidiaries
(c) Contingent liabilities
(d) Stock options
(e) Certain accounting information

A final word. In the practice of accounting let us all carry materiality questions as close to decision as we can, using facts and rigorous analysis before exercising final, perhaps even more intelligent, judgment.

J. H. TURNER & SONS

The accounting firm of Baker & Baker has been contacted by J. H. Turner & Sons to audit the company's financial statements. A preliminary investigation, prior to acceptance of the engagement, indicates that J. H. Turner & Sons is a small distributor of tobacco, candy, and magazines, serving retail drug and grocery stores in Jasper, Connecticut. The firm owns its own seven-story warehouse in which are located the company offices. The firm has not been previously audited by an independent public accountant. In the past, unaudited statements have been submitted to the local bank that has granted a line of credit to the company. The bank is currently in the process of re-evaluating lines of credit of certain customers, and has requested audited statements from J. H. Turner & Sons. Baker & Baker have accepted the engagement.

Unaudited statements for the three previous years have reported fixed assets at an appraised value with a corresponding credit to an appraisal surplus account. Straight-line depreciation, as reported on the income statement, has been based on the appraisal value, with the offsetting credit taken to the Allowance for Depreciation. The appraisal surplus has not been adjusted, but is still carried at the amount originally entered on the books. Exhibit One, found in the files of the company, is the letter from the appraisers accompanying their full report.

PONDER and PREPARE

Assuming that all other aspects of the audit were satisfactory, and that the client insists upon keeping the appraisal figures in the statements, prepare the auditor's short form report and any footnotes you consider necessary under the circumstances. You may assume that the net appraised value of fixed assets represents 40 per cent of total assets, and that the company, in the current year, realized a return of 10 per cent, after taxes, on total assets.

ULYSSES APPRAISAL COMPANY
827 Fairmont Road
Oleander, New York

Members of
American Appraisal Assn.   December 29, 1968

Mr. John Turner, President
J. H. Turner & Sons
5569 Maine Street
Jasper, Connecticut

Dear Mr. Turner:

Attached is a complete report of our appraisal of your warehouse property
and the fixtures inclued therein. The report details the procedures we used
in determining the appraised values and documents the authoritative support
for our conclusions.

The over-all results are summarized in the following tabulation:

Assets	Cost	Appraisal
Land	$ 3,000	$ 39,000
Building	50,000	100,000
Allowance for Depreciation*	25,000	50,000
Fixtures & Improvements	30,000	60,000
Allowance for Depreciation**	10,000	20,000

*Note: As of December 31, this year, the building is 25 years old; we estimate
its useful life to an additional 25 years; the Allowance for Depreciation, therefore, represents the figures for the end of this year.

**Note: As of December 31, this year, the fixtures and improvements are 5 years
old; we estimate the useful life to be an additional 10 years; the
Allowance for Depreciation, therefore, represents the figures for
end of this year.

Sincerely,

L. D. Ulysses for

ULYSSES APPRAISAL COMPANY

Mr. Curtiss: Please enter the appraisal values as of January 1, and compute depreciation on the appraisal.

Turner

HOMEWAY AERO-SPACE COMPANY

Homeway Aero-Space Company, located in Spacetown, California, manufactures a variety of specialty items for the aero-space industry. At the end of the current fiscal year ending June 30th, annual sales amounted to about $9,900,000, representing close to a 15 per cent increase over the preceding year. Financial statements, in condensed form, are presented in Exhibit One.

Homeway's sales increases have been averaging between 8 and 15 per cent a year for the past five years, and the company is now using its physical facilities to practical capacity. Funds have been set aside over the past three years for purposes of renovating existing plant and adding to capacity in order to take care of anticipated increased volume in the foreseeable future.

On June 25th, Homeway and Newhouse Insurance Company reached tentative agreement for a private placement of $3,000,000 in bonds. If final details are agreed upon by the parties, Homeway will deliver the bonds and receive the cash on August 15th. The proceeds will be added to funds already set aside and construction of new facilities will begin almost immediately.

On July 24th, the last day of field work, the bond indenture was finally completed and the manager in charge of the audit examined a copy and discussed the provisions with the treasurer. The major provisions, among others, included the following:

1. The bonds will mature in 20 years and will be dated July 1 of the current year.
2. Interest will be at 6 per cent per year, payable in January and July.
3. Working capital must be maintained at a minimum 1.5 to 1 ratio.
4. A sinking fund payment, to a trustee to be named, in the amount of $150,000 per year will be required.
5. Dividend Restrictions:
   (a) Dividends on preferred stock must be kept current.
   (b) Dividends on common stock may not reduce Retained Earnings below the balance on June 30th, current year.
   (c) Special provisions will govern the declaration and payment of preferred stock dividends in the event that operations result in a net loss for the year.
6. Cumulative losses in excess of $500,000 may result in a call for redemption of all bonds outstanding and not covered by balances in the sinking fund.

About 280 of the 300 stockholders live in Spacetown and substantially all of them attend the annual meeting, held on the first Monday of August, each year. The meetings are quite lively, with stockholders actively participating in the proceedings. Pointed and pertinent questions are frequently asked, often relating to the financial statements.

PONDER and PREPARE

1. Draft any needed footnotes for the financial statements, based upon the information given.
2. Is there any reason to qualify the auditor's opinion as a result of this additional information? Why or why not?

EXHIBIT ONE

HOMEWAY AERO-SPACE COMPANY
BALANCE SHEET AS OF JUNE 30, 19___

Current Assets			
Cash on hand and in banks		$ 160,000	
Marketable securities		185,000	
Accounts and notes receivable (net)		845,000	
Inventories		1,060,000	$2,250,000
Investments			
Funds held for plant expansion			1,875,000
Long-Lived Assets			
Land		$ 150,000	
Property, plant, & equipment	$6,930,000		
Accumulated depreciation	1,936,000	4,994,000	
Patents		200,000	
Other assets		75,000	5,419,000
Total Assets			$9,544,000
Current Liabilities			
Accounts and notes payable		$ 528,000	
Current portion of mortgage		100,000	
Wages payable		100,000	
Taxes payable		450,000	$1,178,000
Long-Term Liabilities			
Mortgage Payable, 5%, maturing in 12 years			1,200,000
Stockholders' Equity			
Preferred stock, par $100, 6%, 8,000 shares		$ 800,000	
Common stock, par $10, 100,000 shares		1,000,000	
Premium paid on common stock		2,200,000	
Retained earnings		3,166,000	7,166,000
Total Liabilities & Stockholders' Equity			$9,544,000

HOMEWAY AERO-SPACE COMPANY
INCOME STATEMENT FOR YEAR ENDED
JUNE 30, 19___

Sales revenue (net)		$ 9,885,000
Dividends and interest		115,000
Total revenues		$10,000,000
Less expenses		
Cost of products manufactured	$5,870,000	
Selling expense	1,126,000	
General & administrative	710,000	
Taxes other than income	100,000	
Depreciation expense	139,000	
Interest expense	80,000	8,025,000
Net income before taxes		$ 1,975,000
Provision for income taxes		900,000
Net Income After Taxes		$ 1,075,000

SHELLER-GLOBE CORPORATION *

On December 30, 1966, a new name appeared on the corporate scene: Sheller-Globe Corporation. Negotiations between the boards of directors of Globe-Wernicke Industries, Inc. and Sheller Manufacturing Corporation resulted in an agreement whereby Sheller Manufacturing was merged into Globe-Wernicke. Sheller Manufacturing ceased to exist as a separate corporate entity and Globe-Wernicke, the surviving corporation, changed its corporate name to Sheller-Globe Corporation.

The negotiations, which were approved by stockholders of both companies, reached a satisfactory agreement involving a tax-free exchange of shares. The merger is to be treated as a partial pooling of interests in the accounts. The capital structure of Sheller-Globe Corporation will consist of:

1. Common Stock, stated value, $1.00 per share, and

2. Preferred Stock, $1.35, cumulative, convertible, stated value, $1.00 per share.

* Adapted from 1966 Annual Report to Stockholders, Sheller-Globe Corporation. Used by permission of Sheller-Globe Corporation.

Also involved in the negotiations was an investment by Globe-Wernicke in 259,287 shares of Sheller Manufacturing common stock. The agreement provided that these shares of Sheller Manufacturing would be retired as part of the merger; i.e., no shares of Sheller-Globe Corporation would be exchanged for these shares.

The final agreement as approved by stockholders contained the following provisions, among others:

1. Share Exchange:
   (a) For each remaining share of Sheller Manufacturing common stock

   > 0.8575 share of new Common Stock and
   > 0.7289 share of $1.35 Preferred Stock;

   (b) For each outstanding share of Globe-Wernicke common stock

   > 0.5000 share of new Common Stock and
   > 0.4250 share of $1.35 Preferred Stock.

2. Reclassification of $1,205,985 from Accumulated Depreciation to Deferred Federal Income Taxes to reflect the use of accelerated depreciation for tax purposes.

In connection with the retirement of the Sheller Manufacturing common stock held by Globe-Wernicke, the excess cost over book value will be added to Property, Plant and Equipment. An analysis of the investment account, as recorded by Globe-Wernicke, revealed the following book values attributable to:

1. Capital in Excess of Par Value $ 862,848
2. Retained Earnings $5,161,631

Balance sheets for both Sheller Manufacturing Corporation and Globe-Wernicke Industries, Inc., as of September 30, 1966, are presented in Exhibit One.

PONDER and PREPARE

1. Assuming that the merger is to be effective as of September 30, 1966, prepare a worksheet indicating the necessary adjusting entries to the accounts of the individual companies and to provide the necessary data for combined pro forma statements reflecting a full pooling of interests treatment.

2. Prepare any necessary footnotes, in suitable form, to be attached to the pro forma statements to reflect the important facts of the merger.

BALANCE SHEET AT SEPTEMBER 30, 1966 OF:

Current Assets	Sheller Mfg. Corp.	Globe-Wernicke Industries, Inc.
Cash & Certificates of Deposit	$ 1,695,189	$ 3,109,108
U.S. Government Obligations	—	1,301,151
Receivables (net)	10,553,014	7,080,761
Inventories	12,729,877	5,676,994
Prepaid Expenses & Other Current Accounts	431,188	291,995
Total Current Assets	25,409,268	17,460,009
Investment in Sheller Mfg. Corp. (259,287 shares)	—	7,566,718
Property, Plant & Equipment	37,040,413	16,969,888
Less Accumulated Depreciations	17,985,324	8,150,471
Net Property Plant & Equipment	19,055,089	8,819,417
Other Assets	163,653	376,490
Intangible Assets		
Patents, Trademarks, Goodwill	570,165	1
Total Assets	$45,198,175	$34,222,635
Current Liabilities		
Note Payable, unsecured	$ —	$ 166,668
Accounts Payable	7,647,232	2,035,821
Accrued Expenses	2,235,555	539,075
Federal and Canadian Income Taxes	2,068,398	1,133,836
Other Current Liabilities	—	148,072
Total Current Liabilities	11,951,185	4,023,472
Deferred Federal Income Taxes	—	78,500
Long-Term Debt (unsecured notes)	6,000,000	11,541,663
Stockholders' Equity		
Common Stock, $5.00 par value	—	6,898,100
Common Stock $1.00 par value	1,089,892	—
Capital in Excess of Par Value	3,927,375	2,643,859
Retained Earnings	22,229,723	9,037,041
Total Stockholders' Equity	27,246,990	18,579,000
Total Liabilities & Stockholders' Equity	$45,198,175	$34,222,635

BEST-OF-CROP FOOD COMPANY

Best-of-Crop Food Company packages a full line of canned and frozen fruits and vegetables. The Company operates five processing plants in the United States and two plants in Canada through a wholly-owned Canadian subsidiary. Customers are serviced from warehouse facilities located at each processing plant and from eight other warehouses located in major marketing areas. The Company prides itself on being able to make quick delivery on all orders regardless of the location.

About 40 per cent of the Company's output is contracted to six wholesale grocers under private labels. The wholesale grocers service independent merchants, and labeling is individual to geographic areas. The six wholesalers account for more than 30 different private brands, some of which are full line; i.e., include both fruits and vegetables, some of which include only one or the other, with a few brands involving only a single product.

The remaining 60 per cent of output is sold under the Best-of-Crop label to an average of 400 different customers, with each customer selecting all or parts of the complete line. All sales are on credit, with terms of 2/10, n/60. Occasionally, longer terms are arranged, on a customer by customer basis. Price lists are revised at least quarterly, and more often if crop conditions warrant.

About 30 per cent of crop needs are supplied from farms owned by Best-of-Crop, operating under a separate corporation. The remaining crop needs are contracted for from a rather large group of cooperating growers. Contracts are negotiated, based upon demand analyses made by the Company, crop forecasts made by various agricultural groups, and long-range weather forecasts provided by the U. S. Weather Bureau. Contract provisions generally cover such items as planting dates, acreage, quality harvested, use of fertilizers, herbicides and pesticides, varieties planted, harvesting dates, and delivery dates. Some contracts include a guaranteed delivery price while others provide for a negotiated price at time of delivery. These terms vary by geographic location.

Over the past eight years, a percentage analysis of the income statement of Best-of-Crop indicates the following average relationships:

Sales Revenues		100.0%
Less expenses:		
Raw products	29.3%	
Plant labor, plant overhead	18.3	
Containers, cases, labels	25.4	
Other ingredients, supplies	8.3	
Selling, general & administrative	14.6	96.4
Net profit before taxes		3.6%

The senior staffman in charge of the audit has been reviewing the working papers and has made the following comments about events that have occurred since the date of statement preparation:

1. One of the six wholesale grocers who has contracted for private label packs has filed a petition of voluntary bankruptcy under Chapter XI of the National Bankruptcy Act. Receivables for contract orders shipped amount to about 4 per cent of total receivables and less than 1 per cent of total assets. It may be sometime before settlement amounts and dates are determinable, since the creditors' committee is still evaluating the financial condition of the bankrupt. Inventories of contracted packs not yet delivered may possibly be relabeled and sold to other customers. Inventories produced under this contract amount to about 10 per cent of total finished goods inventories and about 5 per cent of total current assets.

2. A severe frost damaged plantings of carrots and beans on a Company-owned farm in central Texas. Estimates are that crop yields will be about one-half of expected yields. Company officials are currently negotiating additional contracts to cover raw product needs.

3. A strike at one of the Canadian plants has been going on for the past thirty days, with settlement still uncertain. The plant normally accounts for about 20 per cent of the Company's output. Since the strike has occurred at the peak of the season for this plant, officials of the Company estimate that its annual production may be cut by more than 50 per cent.

4. Several notes receivable, which had been discounted with the Company's bank, have been repaid by the makers. The amounts involved were about 2 per cent of total assets.

PONDER and PREPARE

1. What effect, if any, would these events have on the accountants' report to the Company? If any disclosure is required, draft sample notes to be used by the Company.
2. Assume any one of the items listed was a material item, and assume that the Company refused to permit disclosure. What effect, if any, would this have on the auditors' report?

McBEDE MANUFACTURING COMPANY

George Lowell & Company, CPA's, have audited the statements of McBede Manufacturing Company for the past seven years. On December 12th, the manager in charge of the engagement, Joseph Toonis, was reviewing the working papers just prior to the completion of the field work on the current engagement for the year ended October 31st. The financial statements for the current year are given in Exhibit One. McBede Manufacturing is a family owned corporation and the audited statements are used primarily by the Martin State Bank, which holds both the notes payable and the bonds payable.

McBede has been classified in a recent edition of Smooties' Credit Investigators as ". . . a small manufacturer of component parts used by the machine tool industry." Because of its dependence upon machine tool production, McBede's own operations are subject to the same cyclical fluctuations as machine tool manufacturers, with McBede frequently experiencing a general decline before the machine tool manufacturer.

In reviewing the working papers, however, Mr. Toonis noted that sales have been expanding at the rate of about 5 per cent over the past three years and net income from operations has averaged between 10 per cent and 12 per cent of net sales for the same period. Finished goods inventory turnover has averaged about six times a year over the past two years. Similarly, accounts receivable turnover has been about six times a year.

In the afternoon mail, Mr. Toonis received an income statement for the month ended November 30th, with a request from the senior in charge of the field work that the statement be included in the working papers. The statement is given in Exhibit Two. Mr. Toonis noted that the principal records of the company are the general ledger, cash receipts record, voucher register, sales register, check register, and general journal.

PONDER and PREPARE

1. What effect, if any, would the additional information have on the post audit review of material transactions?
2. If you were preparing the auditor's opinion, what effect, if any, would the additional information have on your opinion, or on footnotes to the statements?

McBEDE MANUFACTURING COMPANY
BALANCE SHEET
AS OF OCTOBER 31, 19___

ASSETS

Current Assets
Cash $ 50,000
Accounts Receivable (net) 700,000
Inventories (FIFO)
 Raw Materials $ 60,000
 Finished Goods 500,000 560,000

Total Current Assets $1,310,000

Long-Term Asests
Land $ 100,000
Buildings & Machinery (net) 2,590,000 2,690,000

Total Assets $4,000,000

EQUITIES

Current Liabilities
Notes Payable to Bank $ 400,000
Trade Notes Payable 60,000
Accounts Payable 200,000
Taxes Payable 90,000

Total Current Liabilities $ 750,000
Bonds Payable 1,000,000

Stockholders' Equity
Capital Stock $1,500,000
Retained Earnings 750,000 2,250,000

Total Equities $4,000,000

INCOME STATEMENT
FOR YEAR ENDED OCTOBER 31, 19___

Sales (net) $4,380,000
Less: Cost of Sales $3,025,000
  Depreciation (S/L) 300,000
  Selling Expense 336,000
  Administrative Expense 144,000 3,805,000

Net Operating Income $ 575,000
Less: State & Federal Income Taxes 290,000

Net Profit for Year $ 285,000

McBEDE MANUFACTURING COMPANY

McBEDE MANUFACTURING COMPANY
Income Statement
For the month ended November 30, 19--

Sales (net)		$ 260,000
Less: Cost of Sales	$ 195,000	
Depreciation (S/L)	25,000	
Selling Expense	56,000	
Administrative Expense	12,500	288,500
Net Loss from Operations		$(28,500)
Plus: Loss on uninsured fire		(200,000)
Net Loss for the Month		$ 228,500

Mr. Toonis: The fire was on November 27.
The loss measured on book values.

Warehouse (reparable) $ 50,000
Finished Goods Inventory
*   (a total loss)   150,000*
* $200,000*

The Warehouse had a net book value
of $100,000 before the fire.
*   Jim Walters*

GETTY OIL COMPANY *

On the face of its 1966 annual report, the Getty Oil Company printed the following notice:

IMPORTANT!
This Annual Report reflects a significant change in the presentation of the consolidated financial statements of Getty Oil Company. . . .

Portions of the President's letter to the stockholders disclose the nature of the change:

To the Stockholders
The Company has substantial equity interests in two integrated oil companies, Tidewater Oil Company and Skelly Oil Company. Such equity interests at the end of 1966 amounted to 70.25 percent and 46.04 percent respectively, and are mainly the result of the Company's large holdings of shares of Mission Development Company and Mission Corporation. . . .
Prior to 1966, the Company's carrying value of the investments in Mission Corporation and its subsidiary, Skelly Oil Company, and Mission Development Company and its subsidiary, Tidewater Oil Company, was recorded at the costs of these investments plus the Company's direct and indirect share of the consolidated earnings retained by these companies.
The Company has decided to fully consolidate its financial statements with the financial statements of Mission Corporation . . . and Mission Development Company. . . .
J. Paul Getty, President

The change in presentation was foreshadowed in the 1965 annual report when Mr. Getty reported in his letter to stockholders:

Getty Oil Company and Tidewater Oil Company began discussions in January 1966 regarding a merger of the two companies. Studies are currently in progress directed towards ascertaining the details of a merger. . . .

Similar information was included in footnote 4 of the 1965 annual report. Discussions may have broken off and restarted in 1966 based upon footnote 11 appearing in the 1966 annual report:

Getty and Tidewater have resumed preliminary discussions with a view to a possible merger of the two companies.

* Adapted from 1965 and 1966 Annual Reports to Stockholders, and Notice of Meeting and Proxy Statement, dated August 14, 1967, Getty Oil Company. Used by permission of the Company.

Discussions of a merger reflected the increasing importance of the direct and indirect equity interests of Getty Oil in both Tidewater and Skelly Oil. The Company included the following information in its Notice of Meeting and Proxy Statement, dated August 14, 1967, page 10:

> The weighted average percent interest (direct and indirect) of Getty Oil in the common stock of Tidewater and Skelly during each of the five years ended December 31, 1966. . . .

	December 31				
	1962	1963	1964	1965	1966
Tidewater Oil	54.82%	59.56%	62.08%	63.02%	64.50%
Skelly Oil	34.45%	37.56%	40.16%	42.30%	44.71%

Footnote 1, Principles of Consolidation, in the 1966 annual report provides the following additional information concerning the change in accounting:

> Prior to 1966, the Company consolidated the accounts of its wholly-owned subsidiaries and recorded in its investment in unconsolidated subsidiaries, its share of the net income and special items retained by such subsidiaries. In 1966, the Company changed its consolidation principles by also including the accounts of Mission Development Company . . . and Mission Corporation. . . . Therefore the 1965 consolidated financial statements have been retroactively restated to reflect this change. Substantially all of the assets of Mission Development and Mission Corporation represent their investments in the common stock of Tidewater and Skelly, respectively. In each year all material inter-company transactions have been eliminated. In its 1965 annual report the Company reported net income of $11,765,000, share of net income retained by subsidiaries not consolidated of $45,883,000 and share of special items of such subsidiaries of $1,025,000, or a total of $58,673,000. The 1966 consolidated net income of Getty and its wholly-owned subsidiaries amounted to $12,-590,000, share of net income retained by subsidiaries not previously consolidated was $58,208,000 and share of special items was $84,047,-000, or a total of $154,845,000. . . .
>
> The Company's equity in the net assets of consolidated subsidiaries exceeded the cost of its investment by $536,995,000 at December 31, 1966, which in consolidation has been credited to retained earnings ($520,773,000) representing the share in subsidiaries earnings since date of acquisition, and to net property, plant and equipment ($16,220,000), representing the unamortized acquisition, which is being amortized over the composite life of such properties.

The inter-relationships between Getty, Mission Development Company, Mission Corporation, Tidewater Oil and Skelly Oil are given in Table One.

TABLE ONE

GETTY OIL COMPANY
INTERCOMPANY STOCKHOLDINGS

	Mission Corporation		Mission Development		Tidewater Oil		Skelly Oil	
	1965	1966	1965	1966	1965	1966	1965	1966
Percentage of Common Stock owned by:								
Getty (direct)	61.70	64.77	82.63	82.71	20.57	22.74	—	—
Mission Corporation	—	—	—	—	—	—	70.32	71.08
Mission Development	—	—	—	—	51.96	57.44	—	—
Getty (direct & indirect)	61.70	64.77	82.63	82.71	63.50	70.25	43.39	46.04

Arthur Andersen & Co., auditors for Getty Oil, reported on the consolidation in the following "Auditors' Report":

> We have examined the consolidated balance sheets of GETTY OIL COMPANY (a Delaware corporation) AND SUBSIDIARIES as of December 31, 1966 and 1965, and the related statements of consolidated income and retained earnings for the years then ended. Our examination was made in accordance with generally accepted auditing standards, and accordingly included such tests of the accounting records and such other auditing procedures as we considered necessary in the circumstances. We did not examine the consolidated financial statements of Tidewater Oil Company (a consolidated subsidiary) whose total assets and revenues represent approximately 60 percent and 65 percent in 1966 and 64 percent and 69 percent in 1965, respectively, of the consolidated amounts in those years, but we were furnished with reports of other auditors on such financial statements.
>
> In our opinion, based upon our examination and the reports of other auditors referred to above, the above-mentioned consolidated financial statements present fairly the financial position of Getty Oil Company and subsidiaries as of December 31, 1966 and 1965, and the results of their operations for the years then ended, in conformity with generally accepted accounting principles applied on a consistent basis after giving retroactive effect to the inclusion, which we approve, of the accounts of certain major subsidiaries as explained in Note 1 to the consolidated financial statements.
>
> Arthur Andersen & Co.

The companies involved in the consolidation reviewed the accounting principles and appropriate reclassifications were made in the consolidated statements. Footnote 3, 1966 annual report, disclosed that Tidewater priced inventories principally on the last-in, first-out basis while all other companies used mainly average cost. Dollar amounts were supplied, in the note, for beginning and ending inventories for 1966.

The Statement of Consolidated Income and Consolidated Balance Sheet for 1966, 1965 restated and 1965 original are attached as Exhibits One and Two.

PONDER and PREPARE

1. With respect to consolidation of subsidiaries, Accounting Research Bulletin No. 51, in paragraphs 1 and 2 sets forth the following guidelines:

> 1. The purpose of consolidated statements is to present, primarily for the benefit of the shareholders and creditors of the parent company, the results of operations and financial position of a parent company and its subsidiaries essentially as if the group were a single company with one or more branches or divisions. There is a presumption that consolidated statements are more meaningful than separate statements and that they are usually necessary for a fair presentation when one of the companies of the group directly or indirectly has a controlling financial interest in the other companies.
>
> 2. The usual condition for a controlling financial interest is ownership of a majority voting interest, and, therefore, as a general rule ownership by one company, directly or indirectly, of over fifty percent of the outstanding voting shares of another company is a condition pointing toward consolidation. However, there are exceptions to this general rule. . . . There may . . . be situations where the minority interest in the subsidiary is so large, in relation to the equity of the shareholders of the parent in the consolidated net assets, that the presentation of separate financial statements for the two companies would be more meaningful and useful.*

   a. Evaluate the consolidation policies of Getty Oil Company in view of the general guidelines stated in ARB #51, quoted above.
   b. From Exhibits One and Two, does a comparison of 1965 unadjusted figures with 1965 adjusted figures lead to a conclusion that consolidated statesments are more meaningful? Explain.
2. Evaluate the qualification of scope, i.e., relying on other auditors, in terms of the materiality of the amounts involved.

---

* "Consolidated Financial Statements, ARB No. 51," AICPA, New York, 1959, page 41, used by permission.

GETTY OIL COMPANY & SUBSIDIARIES
STATEMENT OF CONSOLIDATED INCOME [1]
YEAR ENDED DECEMBER 31

	1966	1965 as Restated (000 Omitted)	1965 Original
Revenues			
Sales & Operating Revenues	$1,218,567	$1,188,004	$66,116
Dividends, Interest & Other	17,857	12,178	11,305
	$1,236,424	$1,200,182	$77,421
Costs & Expenses			
Crude Oil, Products, Merchandise & Operating Expenses	$ 644,768	$ 619,818	$47,538
Exploration & Dry Hole Costs	28,115	25,609	1,014
Selling, General & Administrative	119,988	126,351	7,175
Taxes Other than Income	183,264	194,692	[2]
Depreciation, Depletion, Amortization	114,478	109,923	9,412
Interest Expense	8,749	10,265	1,422
Income Taxes	18,849	13,401	2,821
	$1,118,211	$1,100,059	$69,382
Net Income Before Minority Interest	$ 118,213	$ 100,123	—
Net Income Before Dividends, Earnings of Subsidiaries	—	—	$ 8,039
Less: Minority Interest, Income of Subsidiaries	(47,415)	(42,475)	—
Plus: Dividends from Subsidiaries	—	—	3,726
Share of Annual Earnings Retained by Non-Consolidated Subsidiaries	—	—	45,883
Net Income Before Special Items	$ 70,798	$ 57,648	$57,648
Plus: Special Items, Net of Taxes, Net of Minority Interest	84,047	1,025	1,025 [3]
Net Income	$ 154,845	$ 58,673	$58,673

[1] Format rearranged to facilitate this presentation.

[2] Not separately reported in 1965.

[3] This item reported in separate "Statement of Share of Earnings Retained by Subsidiaries not Consolidated" in original 1965 statements—See similar caption, Consolidated Balance Sheet, 1965 Original, Exhibit Two.

EXHIBIT TWO

GETTY OIL COMPANY & SUBSIDIARIES
CONSOLIDATE BALANCE SHEET [1]
AS OF DECEMBER 31

	1966	1965 as Restated	1965 Original
		(000 Omitted)	
Current Assets			
Cash	$ 40,567	$ 42,930	$ 7,282
Marketable Securities	15,439	37,054	280
Accounts & Notes Receivable, Net	335,535	160,222	23,998
Inventories, at Cost	71,359	92,437	9,329
Prepared Expenses, Other Current Assets	10,543	18,338	5,897 [2]
	$ 473,443	$ 350,981	$ 46,786
Investments & Long Term Receivables			
Investments & Advances	$ 57,967	$ 34,498	—
Long Term Receivables	124,667	40,582	$ 19,617
Investments in Non-Consolidated Subsidiaries	—	—	515,907
	182,634	75,080	535,524
Property, Plant & Equipment (Net)	$1,014,233	$1,088,375	$ 79,218
Total Assets	$1,670,310	$1,514,436	$661,528
Current Liabilities			
Current Portion, Long Term Debt	$ 8,904	$ 11,377	$ 955
Notes Payable to Bank	67,180	12,047	9,228
Accounts Payable, Other Accrued Liabilities	117,089	133,903	19,955
Accrued Taxes	49,109	13,459	3,233
	$ 242,282	$ 170,786	$ 33,371
Long Term Liabilities	133,796	176,499	11,401
Deferred Income & Non-Current Reserves	42,632	50,773	11,406
Total Liabilities	$ 418,710	$ 398,058	$ 56,178
Minority Interest in Consolidated Subsidiaries			
Preferred Equity	$ 56,756	$ 70,113	—
Common Equity	436,247	440,915	—
Total Minority Interest	$ 493,003	$ 511,028	—

[1] Format rearranged to facilitate the presentation.
[2] $3,972,000 of this amount reclassified as Long-Term Receivables in 1966.

	1966	1965 as Restated	1965 Original
Stockholders Equity			
Common Stock (Less 20,000 Treasury Shares)	$ 63,937	$ 63,937	$ 63,937
Capital Surplus	37,959	37,959	37,959
Retained Earnings	656,701	503,454	119,636
Share of Earnings Retained, Non-Consolidated Subsidiaries	—	—	383,818
Total Stockholders Equity	$ 758,597	$ 605,350	$605,350
Total Liabilities & Stockholders Equity	$1,670,310	$1,514,436	$661,528

PART FOUR

Electronic Data Processing
Internal Control Aspects
Selected Audit Techniques

THE INTRODUCTION OF COMPUTERS TO BUSINESS SYSTEMS *

by Richard J. Guiltinan
Arthur Andersen & Co.

Auditing the EDP System

The introduction of electronic data processing equipment to business has marked the beginning of an era of far-reaching change in business systems. Not only has this equipment provided the means for accomplishing the same work in a more effective manner, but it has also pointed up the need for a critical re-examination of existing data processing concepts. This examination will undoubtedly result in a substantial change in concept as to what a system should produce, and the form or media on which records will be maintained, as well as a redefinition of the functions which should be carried out within a well organized data processing system. Knowledge of these developments in data processing equipment and their potential impact on business systems has brought about many questions in the accounting profession as to the effect which may be expected upon the auditing work of the public accountant.

While in many respects the electronic data processing field is still relatively new, there are two important conclusions that can be drawn from existing experience with electronic equipment.

First, the use of electronic data processing equipment, in most cases, will have some effect on auditing procedures or techniques.

Second, the auditor must have a basic understanding of this equipment and how it is used in order to effectively appraise his clients' accounting procedures and system of internal control and to utilize the equipment in carrying out his own work more efficiently.

The extent to which audit procedures will be affected will vary from one organization to another, depending basically upon the type of equipment used and the manner in which it is applied to a specific problem. The practices involved in the use of electronic systems employ-

* Reprinted from *Data Processing*, Proceedings of the 1962 International Data Processing Conference, Data Processing Management Association, V, 152–58, by permission of the publishers.

ing card input and output devices are basically the same as those which have been utilized in punched card systems. Therefore, in such situations the audit procedures probably will not differ greatly from those with which the auditor is already familiar. On the other hand, electronic equipment utilizing magnetic tape and large random access memory devices provides the means for substantially different approaches to the design of business systems. With such equipment, the methods of developing the reports or records prepared by the system are likely to differ greatly from the practices which have been followed either with manual or other mechanical systems. It is even possible, in some cases, that the end product itself will differ greatly from that formerly obtained. As a result, the auditor may be faced with new situations requiring new procedures for the successful and effective completion of his work.

It is important to recognize that the sudden introduction of far reaching and dramatic changes in business systems is not a typical occurrence. Rather, these changes represent an evolutionary process during which new processing devices and techniques are developed gradually based to a large extent upon experience obtained during the previous stages of development. Thus, it is not likely that the auditor will be confronted suddenly with completely new problems which have no counterpart in his previous experience. Further, in attempting to measure the extent of potential change in audit techniques, it is necessary to recognize, also, that changes in data processing systems affect only a limited part of the auditor's activities.

Without respect to the type of equipment employed, the way in which it is used can also affect auditing procedures. Even the most advanced form of electronic device can be used simply to replace other office equipment. This often has been the case in the early stages of development in electronic data processing, and it will undoubtedly continue to some extent in the future. However, as added experience and competence are obtained in the use of this equipment, most systems will be designed to obtain the maximum benefits from its use. As this is done the changes in audit procedures or the need for such changes will become more pronounced.

Understanding of EDP Equipment

As techniques for using electronic equipment become more advanced, and as the equipment itself becomes more complex, data processing functions will be further automated and the effects of the automation will be extended into almost every aspect of business data processing and reporting systems. Even at this time, when the use of electronic equipment is still relatively new, the effects of its use are ev lent. In order for the auditor to understand and evaluate his clients' accounting procedures and controls as a basis for determining the scope of the audit work, and in order to utilize the equipment as a means of facilitating his work, it is apparent that he must acquire a basic knowledge of electronic systems and how they function.

A basic understanding of the various equipment components comprising a complete data processing system, and the functions performed by each component, is an essential part of the auditor's elementary knowledge. While the auditor need not become a computer programmer, he should have an understanding of fundamental programming techniques and the practices followed in the operation of EDP systems. This is essential to an adequate appraisal of clients' procedures and internal controls. To fully understand and analyze the possibilities of using the available equipment in his audit work, an even broader knowledge of the more detailed aspects of electronic data processing methods is required. To a certain extent, a knowledge of EDP methods can and will be obtained simply through exposure to the clients' procedures in connection with regular audit work. However, a far more effective way to acquire this understanding will be through a direct, well-planned educational program of training for auditing under electronic data processing systems.

Internal Control

Questions pertaining to electronic data processing systems often concern internal control and what constitutes adequate internal control in these systems. It is apparent that the changing nature of business systems which has come about by the use of electronic equipment has brought with it the need for changes in concept as to what constitutes adequate internal control in these systems. There are new considerations involving internal control which are brought about by both the systems utilizing this equipment and by the techniques necessary for the proper operation of such systems.

Organization has always had a very significant bearing on controls—as a practical matter real control cannot be achieved without a specific definition and separation of responsibilities and duties. At the same time, one of the greatest effects of automation will be upon existing organizational structures, particularly those functions concerned with data processing. Separation of these data processing functions, which has always been considered an important element of internal control, will be substantially diminished through the use of electronic equipment. In the past, operating departments have always performed many of their own clerical paper work operations. Now, however, there is an unmistakable trend toward combining all of these operations into a single, integrated system. As a result, the data processing function is developing as a separate entity in many organizations—a department handling all major data processing activities as a service center for the operating departments

Concurrently with this centralization of paper work functions, data processing procedures will become much more highly integrated; logically related elements of data processing activities will be combined into a single coordinated procedural process. Consider the many different step that are involved typically in the processing of a customer's order—credit analysis, inventory control, billing, sales analysis, accounts receiv able, and perhaps commission payroll. In manual and punched card systems the processing of the customer's order has been accomplished through a series of separate and distinct steps, each carried out by differ ent individuals who frequently were located in different departments Use of electronic equipment, on the other hand, has already provided the means by which all of these functions can be consolidated in a single department—the data processing center.

As a further result of the use of electronic equipment, these inte grated processing steps have become much more highly automated While the completely automatic "push-button" office still lies in the future, nevertheless an extremely high degree of mechanization already has been attained. This, in turn, has permitted a sharp reduction in personnel required for routine clerical activities. Once data have been recorded and edited into the medium for computer processing, all proc essing up to report printing is actually carried out in a completely automatic manner under control of the procedures (programs) stored in the computer's memory. One person actually directs the computer' operation from a mechanical standpoint; however, this operator need no and, in most cases, will not be informed as to the specific detailed nature of the processing steps being carried out under his direction.

In certain respects, even with many functions being carried out by one person, the internal control inherent in such systems should be stronger as the procedures built into the computer's program are no subject to misinterpretation in the course of day-to-day activities. In addition, changes to the detailed and complex instructions constituting the entire procedures are not easily made, and as a result, they are no as subject to unauthorized modification as procedures in other systems

However, with entire procedures carried out by computer pro grams, it is possible, at least theoretically, to alter any part of a program without involving the personnel assigned to the system's operation. Such an eventuality, even if remote, must be guarded against. One such safe guard would be obtained through the separation of the responsibilitie for the day-to-day operation of the system from the responsibilities for system planning, programming and introduction of procedure changes to the program library. Thus, at least two persons—the programmer and the operator—would be involved in entering any changes in the program library. Along with this separation of responsibilities, it is necessary also to establish strict procedures for the testing and validating of program changes to assure that proper and accurate changes are being made and to provide for their proper authorization and approval.

Another directly related question concerns the possibility of unauthorized changes in instructions or data being entered on either the program tape or directly into the computer's memory. This possibility also must be recognized by the imposition of control measures which minimize the likelihood of such an occurrence. As a general control measure, physical access to the tape vault or library should be strictly limited to those individuals who are directly engaged in the operation of the system. Access to tapes containing the operating program should be further limited by retaining the tapes in locked cabinets. At the same time, the possibility of program alteration by operating personnel should be minimized by (1) controlling access to operation record books containing memory utilization charts and instruction listings, (2) controls over computer usage, (3) inspection of equipment usage records, (4) the use of duplicate instruction tapes that are inaccessible during day-to-day operations which could be compared periodically with the instruction tape in current use, and (5) the use of accounting controls external to the computer system which would be used continually to check the accuracy of the system.

These measures are good operating practices for an efficiently run system, in addition to contributing to internal control. Controls over computer usage, while safeguarding against unauthorized use of the computer, also are an essential for scheduling operations of the computer and assuring the timely completion of work. A record of equipment usage, in addition to indicating the time during which the equipment is used and the personnel operating the equipment, provides the basis for determining equipment rental as well as the information needed in planning the various daily operations. These techniques, which are important to an effective system, are important also to the auditor.

Data Controls

A computer system is only as good as its controls. The system designed may accomplish a particular job faster than it has ever previously been done, may furnish more and better reports than had ever before been thought possible, and may have the enthusiastic support of management; yet in spite of speed, reports, and enthusiasm, the system may break down because the handling of controls and systems errors is poor.

In discussing data controls, we will first consider the external control of documents and data used as input to the computer system and the reports and data being created by, or the output of, the computer.

The first step in external control is to insure the accuracy of the input data. The user must be assured of clerical accuracy, that is, that names are properly spelled, that account numbers are properly assigned, that the codes assigned are correctly used, etc. Clerical accuracy must be supported by good written procedures and adequate and imaginative supervision. To facilitate the accuracy of documents entering the system, the necessity for making clerical decisions should be reduced as much as possible through the use of such standard techniques as preprinted documents, precoded lists, turn-around documents, and extensive procedural illustrations covering as wide a range of problems as is possible.

Assuming, then, that everything possible has been done to control document preparation at the source, measures must now be provided to detect the errors that will have slipped through regardless of the previous efforts. In addition, control figures must now be established in order to determine that reports prepared by the computer properly account for all items.

Use of control or batch totals has continued to be of primary importance in determining that all transactions have been recorded and processed correctly. Such controls will probably assume more and more importance with the increasing use of the more advanced equipment, since they provide an external form of control over operations of the data processing center.

Inasmuch as the purpose of batch control totals is to serve as a check over processing steps, these controls should be established as soon as possible after the source data have been prepared. In many instances, batch control totals are actually developed as a by-product of performing another necessary function. For example, in an accounts receivable application where cash is received and subsequently deposited in the bank, the development of total receipts and of proof totals for individual batches can be accomplished at the same time. These batch totals serve as a check on subsequent processing, and the sum of the batch totals is entered in the records of the company where it serves also as a control to determine that all batches were processed properly.

The technique of batch totaling is equally useful in applications where the control information does not serve a dual purpose. This would be true, for example, in a payroll or an inventory control system. For a payroll, the initial recording of a transaction would normally be in terms of hours, while for the inventory it would be in terms of stockkeeping units. Batch control totals of hours or stockkeeping units (frequently referred to as "hash totals") would be developed immediately after accumulation of the batch and would then serve to control the processing of the data in subsequent steps. At the step in the processing where a conversion to dollars is made, such as in multiplying payroll hours by rate to determine dollars to be paid, new controls are usually developed for the dollar amounts. The dollar controls are then utilized during subsequent steps as the basic control for assuring the proper handling of the transactions.

Errors not subject to detection through comparison to related documents or quantities do not lend themselves to balancing techniques. An excessive number of balances might have to be maintained; balancing might not prove the error; or the data might be alphabetic. A variety of alternative techniques have been developed to deal with such problems.

A pre-audit of the source documents, by knowledgeable clerks, will bring to light misspellings, improper codes, unrelated codes, improperly prepared documents, etc. Key verification of punched cards or punched paper tape will help detect errors in converting from the source document to a machine sensible medium.

Often, errors in transcribing numbers such as account numbers, stock numbers, or employee numbers can be controlled by use of "check digits." The digits of the number are combined together mathematically to create a unique, additional (check) digit appended to the controlling field. When this field is converted to media for tape, the control field must be properly transcribed in order to punch the related check digit; otherwise an error will be indicated.

Data transcription also may be verified by proofreading tabulating machine or other listings.

Batch totals and other control techniques, such as the use of pre-numbered documents, have long been associated with both manual and mechanized systems to provide control over the processing of day-to-day transactions and to provide assurance that all transactions were processed and in the proper manner. However, in general, such formalized procedures have not existed over the processing of documents affecting the files, such as customer files, pricing files, etc., utilized in the different procedures. Where such files are maintained on magnetic tape or on disc storage devices, as they are in many computer systems, the information recorded in the files cannot be modified in any way except by processing the files and the changes affecting them through the computer. Therefore, file maintenance procedures have become an integral and important part of all such systems. The necessity of following strict, programmed procedures for effecting such changes, in itself, provides a strong element of control. Further, since file changes must be made through the computer, the facility is provided for monitoring them to determine that they have been made correctly and that only properly authorized changes have been made. This can be accomplished as a by-product of processing the change, through the use of a printed record showing the data contained in the file both before and after the change, together with a description of the file-change transaction. Such a printed report could then be checked by the authorizing department to determine that the file changes have been made correctly and that only the proper changes were made. A control procedure comparable to this should be part of any soundly conceived electronic system.

A further consideration in the use of magnetic tape files centers around the possible destruction of files either through operator or equipment failure. While this is possible, the use of proper planning and programming techniques reduces the seriousness of such an occurrence to a matter of inconvenience rather than a catastrophe. The basic control measure to minimize such problems centers around two points: a tape retention program which governs the re-use of tapes, and the use of internal tape identification.

Tape identification, or tape labeling as it is usually known, consists simply of a set plan for recording upon each tape, as it is processed on the computer, a unique number and date which identifies the specific data on that tape. As the tape is processed in subsequent computer operations, the first step in each operation consists of checking the identification number in order to determine that the right tape, and therefore the correct input information, is actually being processed. If for any reason the wrong tape is used, this fact would be printed on the supervisory control printer and the operation would be stopped to permit correction.

If, despite the presence of tape labels, the wrong tape is processed and a file is updated with incorrect data, or if a file tape is inadvertently destroyed, the tape retention plan provides a safeguard which permits re-creation of the file with a minimum of effort. Simply stated, the basic operating procedures established under such a retention plan prohibit the re-use of a magnetic tape until the output from the computer operation, either another magnetic tape or a report, has been proved correct and usable. Typically, this is accomplished by utilizing the output tape in the next computer run, the assumption being that if the tape can be read and that if it balances to the system controls, the informaion recorded upon it is correct. Thus, in a situation in which the output is incorrect, the tapes containing the data used in preparing the output are still available for reprocessing.

THE AUDITOR'S RELATIONSHIP WITH THE ELECTRONIC DATA PROCESSING MANAGER *

by J. Kenneth Hickman

Arthur Andersen & Co.

In order to discuss the effect of electronic data processing upon "the auditor" and to appreciate the new and very different situations and relationships which it creates for him we must first identify "the auditor." Of course you will all recognize the certified public accountant who is engaged to make an annual examination and to report upon the company's financial statements. The internal auditor, a company employee, also tests the adequacy of financial reporting but places greater emphasis on the protection and proper utilization of the company's assets through improved procedures and internal controls. The revenue agent may appear less often than these other auditors, but he is no less demanding in his insistence on adequate auditable support for reported transactions. Those of you who do business with government agencies know how interested the government contract auditor can be regarding those entries and procedures which contribute to the accumulated costs charged to the contract. All these auditors will be recognized immediately by the electronic data processing manager. They may differ in their emphasis but you will find considerable similarity in their requests for data.

There are other people who are not normally characterized as auditors, but who do generate requirements for audit data from the EDP system. The Securities and Exchange Commission requires that publicly held businesses make regular reports of certain financial data. Other government agencies require special reporting from companies in regulated industries. The Federal Trade Commission may require historical analysis of costs and expenses used in setting the company's pricing policy. The company's customers, vendors, and its own employees can create the greatest demand on the system. If one of these believes, no matter how incorrectly, that there has been an error in his account, there is no satisfying him with explanations of machine controls and checks; he wants specific identification of each item making up his balance. In consideration of customer, public, and personnel relations most managements will insist that records be maintained in a manner that will

* Reprinted from *Data Processing*, Proceedings of the 1962 International Data Processing Conference, Data Processing Management Association, V, 165–70, by permission of the publishers.

satisfy these demands. Lastly, management itself is a frequent "auditor" of the EDP system; the data processing manager soon becomes familiar with requests for explanations of variations from budget and for special analyses of selected figures in the financial statements and he would do well to anticipate and plan for these requests.

These various sources of requirements for audit data are listed to emphasize that the request of an auditor is not as singular and unusual as it may at first appear. Obviously, as many as possible of these requirements should be anticipated in the initial programming of the system; however, where this was not practicable or has not been done and a special situation arises, the EDP manager should keep in mind that there are many other audit functions which subsequently may require the same information. Accordingly, he should consider the retention of the resultant report or analysis for these later requirements.

There is no doubt that as time passes and management becomes more receptive to the proper economic utilization of electronic data processing machinery, the EDP manager and the auditor will be working very closely. In order to establish the proper rapport between these gentlemen the EDP manager should appreciate the objectives and the techniques of the auditor. In this connection, the rest of my remarks will be concerned primarily with the independent public accountant. You will readily recognize the areas of similarity with other auditors.

The objective of the independent public accountant is to satisfy himself that the financial statements of the company present fairly the company's financial position and results of operations. The fair presentation in the financial statements is a basic responsibility of management, and the auditor is employed to give to management and to the rest of the financial community his independent opinion on the financial statements. In his efforts to arrive at an opinion it is not practicable for the auditor to examine every transaction. Therefore, he must resort to testing transactions on a sample basis. A test is valid only insofar as it is representative of the total to be tested. In order to satisfy himself in this connection, the auditor must take into account the adequacy of the company's procedures and systems of internal control, and the extent to which they are consistently applied.

Consequently, the first step in the auditor's examination is the review of the company's procedures and systems of internal control. This review will give him the foundation and the framework upon which he will construct his examination and build his final conclusions. Where he finds internal control strong he will tend to limit his tests; where he notes weaknesses he will bolster them with a detailed review of a greater number of transactions.

This background regarding the auditor's objectives and the sampling methods he must employ should set the stage for the introduction of the auditor to the data processing manager.

In the very early stages of his examination, the auditor will visit the EDP manager to review procedures and ask questions regarding the controls within his department. He will be interested in the limitation of access to machinery and tapes, physical control of tapes, usage log, duplicate instruction tapes, tape identification and retention program, detection and correction of errors in operation, verification of input data through control totals, safeguards against operating errors and program bugs, and other internal processing checks. Of course, the auditor will also be greatly interested in the controls established outside of the department to assure the reliability of the department's output.

It is now proper and timely for you to ask whether the auditor is equipped to articulate these questions and to understand and evaluate the answers. Until now, I and my colleagues have talked of the auditor as an individual. In fact, the company's auditor is more frequently a firm of individuals, and frequently the firm has equipped itself by employing and training data processing experts and electronic machinery specialists. There is no doubt that in the long-term the individual auditor must be trained in electronic data processing techniques and controls. However, until we have passed through this present educational and transitional period, most often you will meet the supervising auditor on this initial visit accompanied by his data processing specialist, who will help him to evaluate the controls and to design the appropriate tests to assure that the controls are actually being applied and giving the expected results.

Now, please permit me a few words concerning these controls and checks to make a point which cannot be overemphasized. We have read a great deal about why the auditor must be alert for EDP systems because they remove important controls and make data inaccessible, and why the auditor is the natural enemy of the EDP manager because he will insist upon imposing additional, costly, and frequently unnecessary controls. The case is badly overstated. It is first and foremost management's responsibility to properly discharge its custodianship and to render an accurate accounting to the shareholders. Consider then this proposition: Any system which properly serves the objectives and purposes of management must at the same time give the auditor all the assurances he needs as to the accuracy and reliability of the data. And then consider this proposition relating to the internal controls established within the EDP department: All of the controls which are listed above are essential for the effective administration, scheduling, and control of an effective EDP system. The conclusion is that in terms of operating procedures and internal controls the auditor requires no more than the company management and the EDP manager, himself.

EDP has been justly accused of having a material effect on internal control. However, this effect has not been entirely negative. Internal controls are established to protect against (1) inadvertent errors in data processing, and (2) deliberate misstatements for purposes of fraud or other irregularities. In the first case the electronic machinery with appropriate programming and operating controls and reduced dependency on manual handling of data affords much greater control than has ever existed. In the second case it has been pointed out that the concentration of duties in the EDP manager removes many of the controls that previously existed by virtue of segregation of these duties under the manual and tabulating systems. Segregation of duties gives protection because fraud then requires collusion among a number of employees. But fraud also requires access to the company's assets so that they can be diverted to the benefit of the individuals. Although theoretically the EDP manager is in a better position to alter records, he generally has little or no access to cash or other physical assets, nor to the company's customers or vendors; he would have to go out of his way to establish outside contacts which were made in the normal course of business by the employees previously discharging these responsibilities on a segregated basis.

We have talked about internal control and how the auditor's evaluation of it may limit the scope of his tests. Now let's discuss the "audit trail" about which you have heard so much. Whenever I hear this phrase I conjur up an image of an Indian brave stealthily making his way through the forest and carefully marking selected trees to establish his trail. This image slowly fades and is supplanted by the grey-suited auditor complete with white shirt, striped tie, felt hat, and attache case, carefully making his way through a maze of electronic tape and punched cards, tick marking his way back to the source document. This, in essence, is the audit trail—the thread of references leading to the original documents and relating these documents to the figures in the company's financial statements. In programming you must be cognizant of the requirement for eventually returning to the source document. This requirement arises, as I pointed out earlier, from standards of customer, public, and employee relations established by management, from subsequent legal actions, and from the requests of a rather large group of "auditors." The trail can be provided by adequate cross-referencing of input data which is carried through the system, by retention of tapes, by regularly scheduled printouts and by orderly filing of the source documents themselves. It seems that the last point is the one most frequently ignored in EDP systems. A document number was once a sufficient cross-reference because documents were filed in numerical sequence. Unfortunately, this concept has been carried into EDP systems where random access and selective interrogation in processing has removed the need to refile the source domuments in numeric sequence. Documents are now filed chronologically as they are introduced into the system. The simple addition of a date or batch number which is not lost during processing would save innumerable hours of searching at some future date.

You have heard references to the impact of EDP upon the auditor. No doubt the potential for significant change is present, but I hardly think that "impact" is the appropriate word. Generally, managements have been reluctant to accept the radical concepts proposed by EDP people and are quite willing to incur the additional costs necessary to provide the assurances of tangible evidences such as payroll registers, receivables trial balances, etc. Last September Dean J. Baroon, Director, Audit Division, Internal Revenue Service, in his remarks before the Automatic Data Processing Conference of the Internal Revenue Service suggested some of the elements which the revenue agent might require of an EDP system. Among the items listed were (1) regularly scheduled printouts of master files, (2) summary and printout of all data used to update the master files between these printouts, (3) regularly scheduled printouts of control account balances, and (4) adequate record retention facilities for storage of all these printouts. With these attitudes on the part of most managements and certain government agencies, it is unlikely that the audit trail per se will be a great problem to the auditor in the immediate future.

However, we are experiencing an evolution which will bring managements and the various government agencies to the position of accepting exception reporting from a well-controlled EDP system, and real time systems will be more popularly employed. Then the auditor will feel the effect. The more progressive auditors are preparing themselves today. In planning for the future audit of EDP systems, one factor which must be considered is the use of that very old audit technique—surprise. This audit tool has been used less frequently in recent days, but I believe its reemphasis will be brought about by the extreme difficulty and high cost of auditing the EDP system retrospectively. In the future the auditor will be familiar with the schedule of the EDP department, its programs and controls. He will appear unannounced on the day that certain data is being processed. He might very well bring his own test tape to be run against the program already in the computer. This tape will have been designed to include all of the various conditions and errors which might arise. If the program proves itself against this tape, he will then arrange for the selective interrogation of the data as it is processed. This routine is in the future, how far in the future is problematical and depends entirely on the degree of the EDP acceptance attained in the individual company.

An appreciation of the need for, an audit trail and of how the auditor must plan his tests of the EDP system emphasizes the importance of keeping the auditor advised of all changes in the system, indeed not only advised but frequently consulted. In this connection I would like to suggest that any plans for the programming and installation of an EDP system should include provisions for a review board to pass upon all proposals and to be available as consultants. This board should include the auditor (generally the internal auditor) and a tax man. A few words from these people early in the planning stages can save a good deal of headache and additional work later on.

I would like to conclude with some comments regarding the working relationship of the EDP manager and the auditor. There is great need for better understanding of each other's problems. I have attempted to give you some feeling for the auditor's objectives and techniques; the auditor in turn must gain an appreciation of the operating problems of the EDP manager. He must learn to plan in advance and to make his requests on a timely basis. Most auditors and EDP managers will be surprised at how many special analyses and comparative trial balances can be prepared through use of available machinery if only the auditor will make his requests in advance rather than asking the EDP manager to re-create information months after it has been processed. These few suggestions might be helpful to the EDP manager in establishing a better relationship with the auditor:

1. Special reports prepared only to satisfy the requests of the auditor must stand the test of comparative costs; the dollar savings to the company in terms of audit fees must be greater than the cost of producing the report. Here I should emphasize the word "only" because it is very likely that the auditor may request a printout or report not regularly produced which he feels the financial management should have on a regular basis. If this is the situation, the auditor must take his case to financial management; this is not a matter for the EDP manager to decide.

2. Generally, the EDP manager should not store additional data within the system so that it might be available for use at the auditor's election at a later date. Again here the key word is "within." Any request for retention of old tapes, punched cards, etc., should be honored so long as the quantity is not so voluminous as to be wholly unreasonable. Retention of certain data outside of the system and special processing at a convenient future

time to prepare comparisons and analyses can be extremely helpful to the auditor and not at all costly to the company. Such requests require careful planning and specific arrangements on a timely basis with the EDP manager.

3. The auditor's interrogation requests should be timed to coincide with the regular processing of the file so that they can be accomplished with a minimum of disruption to the normal routine and schedule of the EDP department.

THE EFFECT OF EDP ON INTERNAL CONTROL *
by Robert E. Schlosser and Donald C. Bruegman

The rapidity with which electronic data processing is revolutionizing our "paper work" world is amazing, if not breathtaking. EDP has exposed the business community to an environment which is unique only unto the world of electronics and computers. In fact, the presence of an electronic computer has certainly affected the accountant's traditional paper work oriented methods. Perhaps this effect is best recognized by the change in appearance of many ledgers, journals, and source documents. But methods of implementing internal control, too, have been affected. For many years internal control has been identified with such characteristics as the division of duties, a network of authorization and approvals, arithmetical verifications, and lines of responsibility; however, with the ever-increasing centralization of data processing through the use of large-scale electronic computers, there has been a tendency to consolidate many of these functions.

For example, in processing sales on account, a computer system, by just one pass of the data, can record the sale and the receivable, modify the inventory file, compute the cost of the sale, test to see if the inventory needs to be replenished, type a purchase order if necessary, and prepare an invoice and shipping documents which relate to the original transaction. Since the computer has performed all of these operations without manual intervention, not only has there been no division of duties, no authorizations or approvals, nor any lines of responsibility, but the incredible accuracy of the computer has even eliminated the need for arithmetical verifications. It seems fitting, therefore, that one examine more closely existing internal control methods

* Reprinted from *Management Services*, Vol. 1, No. 2 (March–April 1964), 44–51, by permission of the publishers.

in order to determine what real effect EDP has had upon them. The first portion of this paper will explore this. Thereafter, a discussion outlining "new methods of control" will follow. In addition to outlining a new control network for EDP, we will also attempt to show which of the traditional methods of implementing internal control are compatible with electronic data processing systems.

The American Institute of CPA's defines internal control in this manner:

> Internal control, in the broad sense, includes . . . controls which may be characterized as either accounting or administrative. . . .
>
> (a) Accounting controls comprise the plan of organization and all methods and procedures that are concerned mainly with, and relate directly to, the safeguarding of assets and the reliability of the financial records. . . .
>
> (b) Administrative controls comprise the plan of organization and all methods and procedures that are concerned mainly with operational efficiency and adherence to managerial policies. . . .[1]

On can note that the above definition delineates between internal administrative control and internal accounting control (including internal check). The committee on audit procedure resorted to this division of internal control in order to more clearly indicate the auditor's responsibility for the review of internal control. From a systems standpoint, however, the entire concept must be considered.

Internal administrative control is characterized by the organizational independence among departments and lines of delegated authority. The impact of EDP upon this group of controls has not been as far-reaching as in the case of internal accounting control and internal check. Nevertheless, some of the characteristics of internal administrative control are affected. The organizational independence which now exists between an operating department and accounting is undergoing a change in emphasis. Consider, for example, the following statement:

> . . . I believe . . . the internal control function will have excellent results in the long run by focusing attention on the essential point of control (i.e., where the transaction takes place) and away from some of what we now consider controls which are established in accounting departments.[2]

The foregoing statement might be taken as a direct violation of the premise that no department should control the accounting records re-

---

[1] Statements on Auditing Procedure No. 29: "Scope of the Independent Auditor's Review of Internal Control," American Institute of Certified Public Accountants, 1958, pp. 36–37.

[2] Arthur B. Toan, Jr., "The Auditor and EDP," *The Journal of Accountancy,* Vol. 109 (June 1960), 45–46.

lating to its own operations, but this is not the case. What is implied is that the formal preparation of source data, for processing by the EDP system, will in the future become the responsibility of operating departments as data processing becomes more integrated and the desire for up-to-the-minute results increases (consider the widespread use of the data transmission devices which transmit data by wire from outlying district offices to the home office EDP unit). Thus, organizational independence will be vested, not in the separation of the operating department and the accounting department, but in the separation of the operating department and the processing unit or computer facility. Furthermore, lines of responsibility are drawn within an organization to facilitate conformance with prescribed managerial policies. EDP, however, interferes with a management principle which recognizes that with the placement of responsibility must go the delegation of authority. In the past, lower level management has been free to interpret general managerial policies handed down from above in order to carry out the day-by-day operations of the business. With the conversion to EDP, these groups of managers tend to lose their authority to make decisions, as the computer is now being programmed to execute these decisions for them.

Internal accounting control constitutes another element of the existing internal control network. The function of this group of controls is to check the accuracy and reliability of the accounting data. The characteristics of internal accounting controls permit them to be classified under one of three major subheadings—control total techniques, authorizations and approvals, and comparisons.

Control total techniques assure processing accuracy. The provisions made for the use of controlling accounts and the fundamental practice of batching are common examples of methods now being used to assure processing accuracy. Computer systems, however, afford a means for attaining unprecedented accuracy. The element of human error is no longer present when data are processed electronically. Although control totals might no longer be necessary to assure processing accuracy, they are still required to prove that there has been accurate transmission of data to and from the computer facility. Emphasis is being placed, therefore, not upon techniques to assure processing accuracy, but upon new techniques which make certain of transmission accuracy.

Sound accounting control is also believed to be vested in a system of authorizations and approvals. The ability of the computer to make logical, comparative, "yes-no" decisions permits a set of predetermined criteria to be introduced into the stored program, thereby granting the computer the power of review. Input data can be accepted and processed, or rejected on the basis of these criteria. Since the present system of authorizations and approvals is nothing more than a review function—

judgments being based upon predetermined criteria—it is apparent that the computer, through its stored program, is capable of performing such routine tasks as: granting credit, reordering stock, writing off delinquent accounts, issuing purchase orders, approving vendor invoices, and preparing checks. These are certainly not all of the duties which might be assumed by the computer, but they are sufficiently representative to indicate how the system of authorizations and approvals is now part of the computer's program.

Control by Comparisons

The third classification of internal accounting control, which likewise attests to the accuracy and reliability of accounting data, is based upon comparisons. Comparisons take a variety of forms: time cards and clock cards are compared to prove the accuracy of the payroll; vendor's invoices and receiving reports are compared to authenticate the receipt of material; sales orders are compared with catalog prices to check quotations; and cash remittance advices are compared with accounts receivable to determine the accuracy of customer receipts. These, then, are a few examples of comparison techniques. The computer's ability to make logical comparative decisions of an "equal to," "less than," or "greater than" variety allows representative data to be fed into the computer with the result that the computer itself can make similar comparisons of data.

Internal check, another element of the present internal control system, represents the measures adopted to safeguard the assets. The division of duties (so that no one department, group, or individual authorizes a transaction, records it, and holds custody of the assets) is a well-established principle of sound internal control. The electronic data processing system, however, is designed to facilitate the consolidation of files and transactions. Payables, receivables, inventory records, credit information, salary and wage rates, and ledgers are all a part of the file system of the computer facility. Likewise, every transaction which makes use of or affects these files is processed through the computer. This mass consolidation of files and transactions certainly affects traditional internal control methods.

This, then, illustrates the effect of electronic data processing upon the existing internal control system. In almost every instance it has become apparent that many of the present methods of implementing internal control have been preempted by the computer facility. Manual techniques and decentralization have given way to electronic mechanization and consolidation. The internal control system which had been nurtured by management and accountants alike, for almost a decade, must now be re-evaluated, redesigned, and reinstituted in the terms set forth by the EDP environment. The rationale supporting such innovations has been well expressed by Arthur B. Toan, Jr.

> We should make a mistake if we thought of EDP as just a piece of equipment or technique for handling clerical and administrative work. It is also a potent psychological force in its own right which stimulates innovation and creates a degree of drive and receptivity which helps to turn ideas into realities. Those who work with EDP delight in challenging basic concepts of record-keeping, of organization, and of management itself. . . .
>
> EDP specialists have, in short, a striving for accomplishment which is not unlike that of the truly professional accountant. . . .[3]

How, then, might an internal control system be designed and wedded with the computer facility, when so many of the present methods of implementing internal control seem ineffective? EDP, however, has an answer, for it has in readiness a whole host of new methods—a few of which even represent new applications or modifications of some of the older and more familiar methods.

Internal Control by EDP

Felix Kaufman speaks of the automation of internal control via EDP and notes that the "electronic data processing system's powerful checking abilities make it a center of control." [4] He furthermore seems to lend support to a premise that control is now a part of the computer facility when making introductory remarks relative to the effect of EDP upon internal control:

> Systems employed to date, using manual and semi-automatic means for processing, have not achieved . . . internal control goals. Their controls are, in a sense, a separate procedural system, even though superimposed on regular operating procedures. The effectiveness of these controls depends primarily on the continuous vigilance of people, whereas in electronic data processing the means to integrate the procedural system and the control thereof is present.[5]

EDP takes no exception to the American Institute's broad definition of internal control. Only the present methods of implementing internal control are being affected. Since the emphasis has been placed exclusively upon the computer facility, it seems logical that these new methods might be characterized by the three elements present in any

[3] *Ibid.*, p. 43.
[4] Felix Kaufman, *Electronic Data Processing and Auditing,* The Ronald Press Company, New York, 1961, p. 146.
[5] *Ibid.*, p. 123.

EDP control system—input controls, processing controls, and output controls.

Input Controls

Source data will naturally continue to be generated from the operating departments. Input controls, however, not only ensure that all valid data are being processed, but afford the computer a means for summary checking processing accuracy. The control methods introduced here are not new; they are merely adapted to fit a computer-oriented data processing system.

Batching with a control total. Under batch accounting methods source documents are accumulated into batches which constitute economic processing groups. Control totals customarily represent dollar amounts; but if the input is not expressed in dollars, or as in the case of a random access facility where input need not be sorted into any logical transaction group or sequence, use of some other control total is desirable. These other control totals (commonly referred to as "hash" totals) represent insignificant totals of some data field which is common to all documents in the batch. Common examples of such data fields are quantities, item codes, and account numbers.

Serial numbered forms. This practice is certainly not new, but is included because of the computer's ability to control serial numbers. Serial numbers of certain documents which constitute input (such as requisitions, vouchers, and receipts as opposed to invoices and checks) might be introduced along with account codes, quantities, etc., and stored within the computer. At periodic intervals the serial numbers of those documents which had not yet passed through the data processing unit could be determined by the computer for review and follow-up. This would assure that all data are being processed through the computer facility.

Digit verification devices. Peripheral devices are available which ensure the accuracy and validity of all input data. Although many digit verification devices are not associated electronically with the EDP system, this equipment is just as much a part of the system as is the electronic computer and its components. For example, International Business Machines' 56 Verifier is one type of digit verification device. This machine checks and verifies card-punching. The operator, using the original source documents and the punched cards, re-keys the data into the keyboard of the Verifier. The machine compares what has been punched and what is re-keyed; any difference will cause the keyboard to lock. Another digit verification device is National Cash Register's Check Digit Verifier. This machine is designed to test the validity of an account number before it is recorded into tape or cards by means of a programmed mathematical formula. Thus, the presence of any one, or a combination, of these or similar devices contributes to the effectiveness of input controls.

Processing Controls

Processing controls comprise by far the largest and most important comprehensive group of new methods of controls offered by EDP. Not only is unprecedented accuracy and reliability attained in processing accounting data, but the impersonal nature of the computer permits transactions and file records to remain independent and assures that prescribed managerial policies will be carried out with a high degree of consistency. Processing controls are made up of checks built into the system by the manufacturer and checks capable of being incorporated into the computer's program. The first group to be discussed relates to the "built-in" features, or what are sometimes referred to as "hardware" controls.

Parity check. The most universal of all machine circuitry controls is the parity check. This particular check verifies each binary-coded character (a character being a letter of the alphabet, a number, or perhaps a special symbol, each of which is represented by a certain combination of zeros or ones). By adding another bit (a zero or one) to the binary-code value when characters are being converted to machine-code by some input medium, a condition is created whereby every character is made up of an even or odd number of ones. Computers designed to recognize an even parity count, for example, would process information containing only an even number of ones. The computer, therefore, is designed to check the situation continuously at every point where information is transferred in its system. Any addition or loss of a bit, thereby distorting the character, will cause the machine to stop or correct itself by switching to an alternate program.

Duplicate circuitry. Some computers duplicate the more essential circuitry of their main arithmetic unit. In this way calculations are carried out twice to ensure accuracy.

Dual arithmetic. In this case the computer does not possess dual circuits, but automatically performs every computation twice using the same circuitry. The results are then compared. A few systems are capable of performing the second calculation with the complements of the true figures.

Echo check. This method is often incorporated into the system at points where information is transferred. Here a feedback mechanism echoes a character back from the point of transmission to its source. For example, when information is to be transferred from the computer to magnetic tape, the recording device senses what has been received and a signal is echoed back to the computer from the tape unit. This signal is then compared for accuracy.

Dual heads. This is another method similar to echo checking but is used in checking the transmission of recorded information. A reading device senses recorded information and transmits it instantly back to the source for comparison. Dual heads represent a much more effective check than the echo check, since recorded information is checked, not just the electronic impulse.

Overflow check and sign check. The overflow control is designed to indicate whenever an arithmetic function causes the data to overflow the capacity of a counter or accumulator in the computer's arithmetic unit. This prevents the loss of significant digits during computation. The sign control will indicate whenever an arithmetic function is performed on an amount which does not carry a positive or negative designation.

Tape ring. When information is being written on reels of magnetic tape, old information is automatically erased. To assure that master files might not inadvertently be used on an output unit, a plastic ring is removed from the reverse side of the tape reel. Without this plastic ring no information can be written on the tape.

Preventative maintenance. Although this control method is not a part of the system per se, it is included under this section of "hardware" controls because it does make use of some of the technical aspects of computer design. Normally a schedule is followed which allows a crew of engineers to devote at least one hour a day to preventative maintenance. Test problems are fed into the computer which check all of its components. A "high-low" voltage test is applied whereby the computer is tested to detect marginal functioning of its circuitry.

These, then, represent the mechanical controls which have been built into the electronic computer's system by the manufacturer. A second group of processing controls, however, represent checks capable of being incorporated into the computer by means of coded instructions and control panel wiring. These so-called "programmed" controls are much more sophisticated than many of the "hardware" controls previously discussed. They will now be examined in greater detail.

Record count. A record consists of a group of characters which are normally considered together as a unit, such as the combination of numbers which make up a particular transaction or an account balance. The computer might be programmed to count the number of records it processes, and later this result can be compared with a predetermined total. Record counts are generally made a part of the information on every tape reel. Thus, file data can be transferred from one tape to another without fear of loss of records.

Sequence check. This program control permits master records to be checked for ascending sequence while being read for processing. Master records, for example, might be identified consecutively by customer number or account code. This control method assures that a file is processed in its proper sequential order.

Limit check or reasonableness tests. Predetermined limits (gross pay, the amount of an invoice, or the amount of a purchase order) can be established as part of the computer's program. When processed data exceed these predetermined limits, the machine can be instructed to stop and special handling techniques can be designated by the on-line printer.

Proof figures. A proof figure can be used to check an important series of multiplications. An arbitrary figure, larger than any multiplier, is selected. Each multiplicand is multiplied once by its true multiplier and then again by the difference between the multiplier and the proof figure. Upon completion of a series of multiplications, the total of the products resulting from both multiplications is compared with the product of the total of the multiplicands and the proof figure. They should be equal.

Reverse arithmetic. This is another method which might be used to ensure that a multiplication has been made correctly. A calculation of x times y equals z might be checked by multiplying y times x and subtracting z to determine that the result is zero.

Cross-footing balance checks. Cross-footings have long been used by accountants in checking the accuracy of individual postings. For example, by vertically adding the net amounts of invoices and discounts allowable, the totals, when cross-footed, should equal the total gross amount of the invoices. The computer, however, can be programmed to perform this function.

Identification comparison. This method permits comparisons to be made of common items. By programming a compare instruction, invoice amounts can be compared with predetermined credit limits to facilitate limit checks. All in all, identification comparison enables data fields to be machine-checked against one another in order to prove the accuracy of matching, coding, balancing, and file record selection.

Tape labels. A tape label is part of the records on each reel of magnetic tape. Certain identifying information can be written on the tape in the form of a lead record. Desirable types of information which might be made a part of the tape label are: nature of the information on the tape, processing directions, frequency of use, earliest date the reel might be used as a new output tape (frequently referred to as the "purge" date), control totals (record count, for example), and name of the individual responsible for the tape. The computer can then be programmed to read this information before processing the tape.

Blank transmission test. The computer system might be programmed to monitor data fields at transfer points for blank or zero positions. The blank transmission test might be used to detect the loss of data and to prevent the destruction of existing records in file storage.

Alteration test. Failure to update a file may be sensed by comparing the contents of the file before and after each posting. This test is similar to identification comparison.

Checkpoint or "rollback" and restart procedures. These methods permit the computer to continue processing from the last checkpoint, rather than from the beginning of a run, in case of an error or an interruption in the program. Checkpoints are predetermined in the program and at certain intervals input-output records, as well as the contents of certain storage areas, are recorded internally in the computer. At the same time, if desired, accuracy of processing up to the checkpoint can also be established. In the event of an error, restart procedures permit the program to revert back to the last checkpoint and resume processing.

Error routine. After a programmed check signifies an error in reading or writing (for example, the tape file may be out of sequence, or the disc file might not be properly updated through execution of the alteration test), a programmed error routine should cause the operation to be performed once again. If there is still an indication of an error, certain predetermined formal procedures should be made available to the operator outlining what action is to be taken.

These, then, represent some of the more common checks which can be made an integral part of the computer's stored program. In a sense, these "programmed" processing controls are optional, but, if there is to be sound internal control, they should be made an inherent part of every computer program. The accountant must be as equally familiar with each of these programming control features as he is with existing control applications, for in many cases, these new methods of control have superseded their manual counterparts.

Output Controls

Output controls accentuate the role of the computer facility as a center of control. Insofar as input controls ensure that all data are being processed, output controls assure that the results are reliable and that no unauthorized alterations have been made to transactions and records while in the custody of the electronic data processing unit. Output controls promote operational efficiency within the computer facility over records, programs, processed data, and machine operations.

Comparison of control totals. In reality, the most basic of all output controls is the comparison of batch control totals, after processing, with those which accompanied the source data to the computer facility. It will be recalled that the nature of these control totals was discussed under input controls.

Separation of duties. This is certainly an old method, but in new guise. Within the computer facility there should be at least four separate and distinct groups of individuals—the planners (system specialists and programmers), the machine operators, a group responsible for output controls, and a record librarian. In this way no one group has direct and complete access to the record-keeping system. For example, the planners, who are intimately familiar with the stored program and the entire EDP system, should have no contact with the day-to-day operations. On the other hand, the machine operator's knowledge of detailed programs and the historical records should be sufficient enough to enable him to perform his job as an operator effectively; too much knowledge can lead to intentional or unintentional manipulation of data, but too little knowledge might reduce the efficiency of the entire data processing unit. Responsibility for output controls might be identified with the internal audit function or could be assigned to a separate group of individuals organizationally responsible to the data processing unit. The presence of a record librarian assures that programs, as well as historical records, will be adequately controlled. By assigning one individual—one who has no relationship whatsoever with any of the other data processing activities—the responsibility for the custody of all file information, only authorized changes can be introduced into computer programs or historical records.

Control by exception. The output control group would make comparisons of control totals; they would also be responsible for investigating persistent errors, amounts which exceed predetermined limits, and any differences between file records and physical inventory counts or account confirmations. Summaries might also be prepared comparing current data with historical data to note any other significant changes.

Information retention program. Programs, transaction data, and records must be meticulously controlled. Master tapes which contain computer programs are usually duplicated, with one copy retained in a locked storage area. A formal system of authorizations might be instituted for making any program change. File records might be periodically read out of the machine, so that, in the event of losing some portion of the file data through operator error, an opportunity remains available for reconstructing the file records. A policy must also be set relative to the retention of transaction data since tape reels are expensive and they can be used over and over again. [Author's note: See Exhibit One for IRS retention and documentation requirements.]

Systematic sampling. Tests might also be made, by the control group, of selected individual items being processed. Individual transactions can be traced from the originating department, through the computer facility, to the records stored internally by the computer. Such tests would assure that transactions are being processed both accurately and in accordance with prescribed policies and procedures.

Numerical accountability. This practice is again an old one. Although invoices, checks, and all preprinted forms are presently controlled by numerical sequence, numerical accountability might be extended to all types of output—preprinted forms or otherwise, and including data generated by the on-line printer. For example, a program can be designed to print out instructions or data to the operator. If numerical control is exercised over this type of printout too, reasonable control can be assured over machine operators, as well as all the various forms of output data.

Separate runs. The ability of the computer facility to consolidate so many functions might require in some instances that the same data be run through the computer more than once. For example, McCullough [6] illustrates this by inferring that there might be three inventory runs: a run to produce accounting totals; a run to produce data for storekeepers; and still another run to provide information to purchasing. Separate runs, therefore, represent an effort to establish continuity and agreement among successive related computer runs since control totals can be established during each run and later compared.

In fact, there is another advantage to separate runs other than that of control—this being processing efficiency. Many computers are programmed to perform a number of functions by passing the data through the machine only once. The time saved by this single run, as opposed to separate runs, is not so significant when compared with the problems which could arise in the event of a data-transmission error or an error in processing. Not only are these types of errors difficult to localize during a single run, but also a great many file records are affected. Hence, separate runs might even be a more efficient way of processing data.

Control over console intervention. The likelihood of console intervention is a problem common to all computer facilities. Programmed

6 Thomas E. McCullough, "The Auditor Uses the Computer," *The Internal Auditor*, Vol. 16 (December 1959), 35.

controls are unable to prevent the operator's ability to interrupt processing and manually introduce information into the computer through the console. Likewise, even if the stored program does possess an instruction to print out all information introduced via the console, the machine operator still has the opportunity to suppress the printout. Perhaps this entire situation has been magnified beyond reality. It seems improbable that the machine operator could manipulate the records successfully when his knowledge of the detailed program is limited (if there is adequate separation of programming and machine operator responsibilities), and when there is such a large number of complex file records requiring alteration. Research on this subject, however, revealed only one reference in the literature (cited by the same author in two separate articles [7]) to a defalcation which was actually attributed to the unauthorized manipulation of a computer program. Nevertheless, if there is proper separation of duties (with the operator accounting for processing time as is customary in most computer installations), if there is rotation of operators, and if numerical accountability is exercised over all types of printout, chances for intervention will be minimized.

EDP has certainly provoked a number of new ideas with respect to internal control methodology. The talk of automation of internal control cannot be scoffed at, and the growing importance of the role of the computer facility as a center of control is gaining momentum. When accountants are instructed to review the system of internal control, they cannot afford to overlook the computer facility. They must recognize that it is now an integral part of the internal control system.

In a manual, as well as in an electronic data processing system, data must be introduced into the system (input), processed, and the resultant information (output) communicated to management and other interested parties. Thus, a sound functional internal control system is equally important in either system. However, traditional methods of implementing internal control are affected in the presence of EDP.

The foregoing discussion illustrates that: (1) traditional methods of implementing internal control need only be adapted in the input-output phases of an EDP system; and (2) separation of duties, authorizations, approvals, manual comparisons, recomputations, and the like, are either unnecessary or should be extremely modified in the processing phase of an EDP system.

7 William L. MacDonald, "The Auditor and the Computer," *The Canadian Chartered Accountant,* Vol. 81 (September 1962), p. 256, and "Audits and Audit Trails," *Data Processing, Proceedings of the 1961 International Conference of the National Machine Accountants Association,* Vol. 4, National Machine Accountants Associaton, Toronto, 1961, p. 149.

Summary

In support of conclusion (1) it has been shown how batch control totals, serial numbered forms, and digit verification methods all can be used effectively when data are introduced into the electronic system. Similarly, separation of duties, comparison of results, and numerical accountabilities are equally important, but especially in the output phase of an EDP system. Evidence has been offered as well in support of conclusion (2). It was emphasized how an electronic computer can perform so many processing steps without manual intervention. Thus, the need to superimpose control steps during processing operations becomes less important in order to ensure accurate processing due to the mental and moral frailties of the individuals in the system. It was shown that many controls have been built into or programmed into an electronic computer by manufacturers and programmers alike in order to continually test the accuracy of the processing unit. Emphasis has shifted, then, from controls which test employee integrity to those which test machine accuracy.

Accountants today must be aware of the characteristics of internal control which have changed or which have experienced a change in emphasis due to the advent of EDP. Accounting systems can neither be designed nor audited properly unless the real effect of EDP upon internal control is thoroughly understood.

EXHIBIT ONE *

The IRS, in Revenue Produce 64–12, IRB 1964–8 notes: "The inherent nature of EDP is such that it may not be possible to trace transactions from source documents to end results or to reconstruct a given account unless the system is designed to provide audit trails." In this Revenue Procedure, the IRS issued broad guidelines, outlining record retention requirements for taxpayers using data processing systems. Taxpayers are required to observe the following guidelines when implementing EDP systems.

(1) *General and Subsidiary Books of Account.* A general ledger, with source references, should be written out to coincide with financial reports for tax reporting periods. In cases where subsidiary ledgers are used to support the general ledger accounts, the subsidiary ledgers should also be written out periodically.

* *Author's note: This listing has been supplied by the text author and editor. It was not part of the article as published.*

(2) *Supporting Documents and Audit Trail.* The audit trail should be designed so that the details underlying the summary accounting data, such as invoices and vouchers, may be identified and made available to the Internal Revenue Service on request.

(3) *Recorded or Reconstructible Data.* The records must provide the opportunity to trace any transaction back to the original source or forward to the final total. If printouts are not made of transactions at the time they are processed, then the system must have the ability to reconstruct these transactions.

(4) *Data Storage Media.* Adequate record retention facilities must be available for storing tapes and printouts as well as all applicable supporting documents. These records must be retained in accordance with the provisions of the Internal Revenue Code of 1954 and the regulations prescribed. . . .

(5) *Program Documentation.* A description of the EDP portion of the accounting system should be available. The statements and illustrations as to the scope of operations should be sufficiently detailed to indicate (a) the application being performed, (b) the procedures employed in each application (which, for example, might be supported by flowcharts, block diagrams or other satisfactory descriptions of input or output procedures), and (c) the controls used to insure accurate and reliable processing. Important changes together with their effective dates should be noted in order to preserve an accurate chronological record.

GUIDE TO REVIEW OF INTERNAL CONTROL IN EDP SYSTEMS *

Generally, the system of internal control in an EDP system can be segregated into three major types: (1) organizational controls, (2) administrative controls, and (3) procedural controls. The questions included in this guide are structured according to these three areas.

The questions are not intended to form a questionnaire, to be handled with "yes" or "no" answers, but rather are intended as a guide to the auditor in his review of the system of internal control in EDP systems. The guide is limited to types of controls in the EDP portion of the system. Non-EDP aspects of computer-based systems will not generally include procedures and controls that are different from those encountered by auditors in non-EDP systems today. Of course, *the overall*

* Touche, Ross, Bailey & Smart, Technical Letter #99, October 18, 1963.   Reproduced by permission.

evaluation of the system of internal control must consider the total system, and not only the EDP portion.

Organizational Controls

1. Is the EDP department independent of all operating units for which it performs data processing functions.

2. Are the following functional units physically as well as organizationally separate:

    (a) systems and programming
    (b) computer operations
    (c) EDP program and tape library
    (d) control group

3. Is the EDP manager responsible to someone other than the chief accounting officer.

4. Are current organization charts available.

5. Are systems and programming people forbidden to operate computers on regular processing runs.

6. Is the computer room accessible to only those people having a legitimate reason for being there.

7. Are approved copies of all computer programs and necessary supporting documents maintained in the EDP library and released only to authorized personnel.

8. Is access to control data restricted to the control group.

Administrative Controls

This section of the guide is divided into two sections: (a) systems design and programming, and (2) computer operation.

Systems Design and Programming

1. What standards exist for systems development. Are such standards used.

2. Are current system flowcharts available which show the flow of information through the system and which indicate major control points of the system.

3. Is there a programming manual which sets forth programming techniques and procedures which can be standardized. Are there standards for:

    (a) program documentation
    (b) program testing procedures

    (c) tape retention procedures
    (d) halt addresses and error correction procedures
    (e) symbolic programming labels
    (f) tape labeling
    (g) initialization routines
    (h) program change procedures

4. Do program testing procedures include the following:

    (a) Are all programs tested before conversion.
    (b) Does test material test all important processing steps.
    (c) Are programs always tested after being changed by a patch (i.e., when a change is made directly to the object program, rather than to the source program and no recompiling is done).
    (d) Are programs tested after revision including all previous patches (i.e., when a change is made to source program and recompiling is done resulting in a new object program).

5. Do program maintenance or change procedures include the following:

    (a) Are program changes cleared through people of authority other than programmers directly involved in preparation of programs.
    (b) Is all necessary documentation prepared and changed as a result of any change in program.
    (c) Are programs tested after the change.

6. Do program run books exist and are they adequately documented for each computer program. Do program run books include:

    (a) specific program name and number
    (b) system flow chart showing portion of system that the program represents
    (c) agreements and minutes of meetings where decisions were made on:

        (1) availability of source of data, formats
        (2) indication as to "when" source data is to be made available for processing
        (3) required output format
        (4) when reports are to be ready in processing cycle
        (5) approximate volumes
        (6) handling of various transactions and exceptions
        (7) what codes are to be used

    (d) narrative description of the program, listing the major processing and calculations performed and the controls
    (e) general program flow charts
    (f) detailed program flow charts
    (g) listing of program (resulting from program assembly or compiling)
    (h) complete setup and operating instructions (verbal instructions should not be necessary)

        (1) identification of tape units for input and output files
        (2) description of any action required by external tape labels
        (3) console switch settings

(4) list of program halts and prescribed action for each
(5) description of restart procedures, if other than standard

(i) description of all input required, indicating where it is obtained
(j) output materials required. Form numbers, approximate quantity, number of copies should be listed
(k) disposition of input and output materials. Define exactly what is done with all input materials upon completion of the operation, how they are to be marked or labeled, where to deliver them
(l) detailed layouts of:

    (1) tape input records
    (2) tape output records
    (3) punched card input and output records
    (4) printed output. Include examples on proper form for (3) and (4) of this section

(m) layout of storage allocation showing locations of:

    (1) input, output, and work areas
    (2) subroutines
    (3) constants and variables
    (4) accumulator areas

(n) list of program switches; their designation, location, setting and purpose
(o) a program history log containing a record of changes and such matters as programming progress, dates of reassembly, etc.
(p) a description and example of any control cards, which may be used
(q) a sample printer carriage tape
(r) test data used to debug the program referenced to the subroutines on which each item is used, with manually prepared and computer prepared results of final debugging run

Computer Operation

1. Is computer usage recorded for each program showing run-time and set-up time and equipment components used.

2. Are these computer usage records analyzed and reviewed by responsible operating people on a periodic basis.

3. Are there formal procedures in the EDP library to provide information as to:

    (a) the physical location of any given tape reel
    (b) the tape reels available to be written on
    (c) the usage history of each reel of tape

4. Is there a tape retention plan which permits the reconstruction of the tape file in the event the file is inadvertently destroyed. In random access systems, is provision being made, at realistic intervals, to "dump" the random access files to provide the ability to reconstruct the files.

5. Are master files stored under conditions that provide reasonable protection against accidental damage or destruction.
6. Are all important master files and all programs stored in a fireproof off-premises storage location.
7. Are situations whereby data may be inserted or extracted by the use of the console set forth in writing and limited to circumstances which cannot be handled through the stored program.
8. Are console printouts intelligibly labeled and controlled and reviewed by responsible persons, other than computer operators, who are familiar with the data being processed.

Procedural Controls

Procedural controls are classified according to three types: (1) input controls, (2) processing controls, and (3) output controls.

Input Controls

1. Are all input documents prenumbered.
2. Are all numbered documents accounted for by the control group.
3. Are batch controls established prior to keypunching, and keypunched data compared to this control prior to processing.
4. If batch controls are not established prior to keypunching, what other control is exercised.
5. Does the control group use a document register, control log, or other positive method of recording input control totals for subsequent comparison with machine run totals.
6. Does each processing run accumulate totals that can be tied back to pre-established controls, and does the system call for such tie-back.
7. If no controls are pre-established, how does the system provide for assurance on accuracy and processing.
8. Is responsibility fixed, and are adequate procedures in effect, for tracing and correcting input errors.
9. Are input media error-correction techniques adequately controlled to verify that correction and re-entry processes have been carried out, that duplicate correction will not occur, and that subsequent audit will be possible.

Processing Controls

1. Do computer programs provide checks to detect loss or nonprocessing of data:

(a) Do programs provide for a sequence check to verify sorting accuracy of each of the following:

    (1) transactions which were pre-sorted before entry into computer
    (2) internally sorted transactions
    (3) sequenced master files

(b) Does each computer run for which predetermined totals have been established accumulate independent matching totals (or at least a record count) and compare the predetermined totals with totals developed during the run providing positive printed indication that the totals match or do not match OR provide printed output of computer developed totals (or both sets of totals), in a form suitable for an external visual matching process.

2. Is there adequate control over the process of identification, correction and reprocessing of errors after batch total matching or another checking technique indicates a discrepancy.

3. Is reasonable use being made of computer's ability to make logic data validity tests on important fields of information:

    (a) Do programs test for valid transaction codes in input data, and are halts or printouts provided when invalid ones are detected.
    (b) Are account codes, employees' numbers, and other identification data designed with self-checking digits and does the program test for these digits.
    (c) Are other valid program checks (i.e., limit checks) being used to the extent required for authentication of other significant data fields.

4. Are all machine switches being properly interrogated by programmed steps prior to processing of data.

5. Are checkpoints used to record the contents of memory at selected intervals so that if errors occur subsequently (as disclosed by the application of various machine checks) the computer may be restarted at a point prior to the error without the necessity of rerunning all the previous data.

6. Do computer programs provide checks to determine that all transactions are posted to a proper and current file:

    (a) Are magnetic tape file header and trailer label records and corresponding tests being effectively utilized to assure accuracy in file loading and processing.
    (b) Do computer programs provide for identifying each file reel with the tape label record containing the following minimum information:

        (1) file identification
        (2) data or cycle created
        (3) sequence reel number
        (4) date or cycle when data file is to be subsequently processed
        (5) earliest date tape may be erased.

    (c) Do computer programs provide for recording a tape file control record at end of each file containing the following minimum information:

    (1) total record count

    (2) hash and/or accounting control totals

(d) Are all file control records consistently and adequately checked each time a file is read and processed.

(e) Are completeness and accuracy of random access file records verified by period control checking procedures, such as control totals and record counts.

(f) Are record length and identification of each active random access file record that is read into memory for processing verified by program logic or machine checking features.

Output Controls

. Are control totals of data processed compared with control totals of data prepared as input to the computer.

. Do processing programs provide for printout of the exceptions to the programmed checks, and are these exceptions reviewed by the control group.

DECISION TABLES AND FLOWCHARTS

In the days before computers, work flowcharting, as a device for locumenting paper flow and control checkpoints, was enthusiastically ecommended even if sparsely adopted in practice. With the advent of he computer, flowcharting (along with decision tables) has become an mportant form of documentation of electronic data processing systems. The ability of the auditor to read and interpret flowcharts and decision ables represents an important tool in understanding and evaluating nternal control aspects of the system. There seems to be no general igreement, in the literature and in practice, as to whether the auditor hould have capabilities in programming techniques in order to evaluate EDP systems. And it is beyond the scope of this discussion to argue the ssue. Certainly, however, a basic knowledge of flowcharting and deci-,ion tables is an important first step in understanding EDP systems. The bility to interpret these forms of documentation will provide the auditor vith an element of expertise in dealing with EDP systems that will prove 'ery useful.

Definitions

The nature of EDP systems requires an orderly and detailed descrip-:ion of data flow from the beginning of the system to the end. Data are accumulated, processed, and summarized in various types of reports in the most usual business oriented systems. Accumulation, processing, and summarization procedures require a number of individual activities that must be organized in a logical sequence for introduction into the system One writer has noted:

> The sequence in which operations are to be executed must be precisely stated and exceptions to normal processing must be identified. Most operations are so elementary that a large number of them must be combined properly in order to carry out a meaningful processing task.
>
> Decision tables are a means of bringing together and presenting this related information to express complex decision logic in a way that is easy to visualize and follow.[1]

In some respects, flowcharts derive from the decision table. The data presented in the decision table is translated into individual processing steps and the flowchart indicates the orderly flow from a "Start" point to a "Stop" point. Two general types of flowcharts are in use today A *system* flowchart and a *program* flowchart. The system flowchart describes the general flow of information through all parts of the system (similar to the previously used work flowcharts) while a program flow chart describes the detailed processing steps included in the stored program. The brief examples described here will utilize the program flowchart in a very simplified form. Program flowcharts prepared for use in programming a particular application may become very complex and are beyond the scope of our discussion. A reproduction of program flow chart and system flowchart symbols, with appropriate definitions, i illustrated in Figure 1.

Applications

A typical decision table format is illustrated in Figure 2. Note that it contains four parts: (1) condition stub, (2) action stub, (3) condition entry, and (4) action entry. The logic of the decision table takes the form of "*if* abc condition exists, *then* xyz action will result." That is, a conditional question (or questions) is asked, and some action is taken depending on the answer to the question. Consider the following sim plified example:

> ABC Company is planning to incorporate its sales accounting records into the EDP system used for processing accounts receivable. The Company desires to check the credit limits of customers prior to shipping the order to the customer.

[1] Reprinted by permission from F20-8102—"Decision Tables: A System Analysi and Documentation Technique." © 1962 by International Business Machines Corpora tion.

FLOWCHART SYMBOLS DEFINITIONS

PROGRAM MODIFICATION	PROCESSING	DOCUMENT
An instruction or group of instructions which changes the program.	A group of program instructions which perform a processing function of the program.	Paper documents and reports of all varieties.
KEYING OPERATION	AUXILIARY OPERATION	PREDEFINED PROCESS
An operation utilizing a key-driven device.	A machine operation supplementing the main processing function.	A group of operations not detailed in the particular set of flowcharts.
PUNCHED CARD	TRANSMITTAL TAPE	PERFORATED TAPE
All varieties of punched cards including stubs.	A proof or adding machine tape or similar batch-control information.	Paper or plastic.
ON LINE KEYBOARD	TERMINAL	OFFLINE STORAGE
Information supplied to or by a computer utilizing an outline device	The beginning, end, or a point of interruption in a program.	Offline storage of either paper, cards, magnetic or perforated tape.
CLERICAL OPERATION	DISPLAY	SORTING, COLLATING
A manual offline operation not requiring mechanical aid.	Information displayed by plotters or video devices.	An operation on sorting or collating equipment.
OFFPAGE CONNECTOR	MAGNETIC TAPE	DISC, DRUM RANDOM ACCESS
A connector used instead of the connector symbol to designate entry to or exit from a page.		
INPUT/ OUTPUT	DECISIONS	CONNECTOR
Any function of an input/output device (making information available for processing, recording processing information, tape positioning, etc.)	The decision function used to document points in the program where a branch to alternate paths is possible based upon variable conditions.	An entry from, or an exit to, another part of the program flow chart.

COMMUNICATION   LINK

The automatic transmission of information from one location to another via communication lines.

FIGURE 1

CONDITION STUB	CONDITION ENTRY
ACTION STUB	ACTION ENTRY

FIGURE 2

The upper portion of Figure 3 presents a simplified decision table relating to this situation. The condition that the company desires to determine is: "Is the credit limit of the customer exceeded by this order?" If the credit limit is not exceeded, the shipping department is authorized to ship the order; if the credit limit is exceeded, the order is to be rejected. In the condition stub portion of the table, the condition "Credit Limit Okay?" is entered and in the action stub portion of the table, the two actions that can result from this condition are entered, namely, "Ship Order" or "Reject Order."

In the condition entry portion of the table, the two possible answers are entered. If the answer is "Yes," the action taken is to ship the order; if the answer is "No," the action taken is to reject the order. Actions are indicated by placing an "X" in the appropriate column. The two columns to the right of the vertical double line are called "decision rules." Note that there is only one condition that fits each action that can be taken, thus the rules are mutually exclusive. In terms of programming, the rules may be entered in any sequence and the appropriate action will always result from the existing conditions. Thus, this form of decision table ". . . defines all conditions (the prerequisites for an action) and separates them from all action. Further, it relates given conditions to the appropriate actions, with a column of entries which form a rule." [2]

The lower half of Figure 3 presents a program flowchart that could be constructed from the decision table. The flowchart presents the various steps that must be programmed, or described in machine language, in order for the computer to perform this task. Note that the general flow is from top to bottom and horizontally. The use of arrowheads to indicate the flow is generally desirable.

The program flowchart is read in much the same manner as the decision table. The computer is instructed to start the program and to read a transaction. When the transaction is read, the computer then compares information included with the transaction with information

---

[2] *Ibid.,* p. 4.

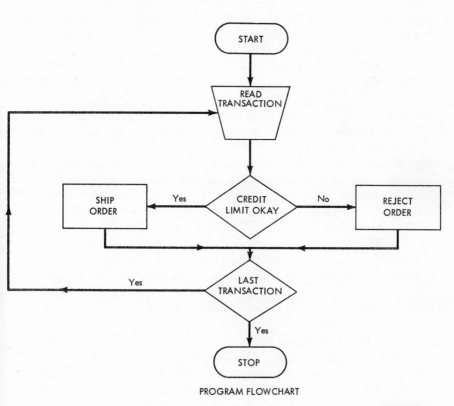

DECISION RULES ——————▶	1	2
CREDIT LIMIT OKAY?	Yes	No
SHIP ORDER	X	
REJECT ORDER		X

DECISION
TABLE

PROGRAM FLOWCHART

FIGURE 3

stored in the customer's account. If the credit limit is okay, the order is shipped; if the credit limit is not okay, the order is rejected; results are identical to those set forth in the decision table. After making the appropriate testing of the credit limit, the computer is then instructed to determine if the transaction just processed was the last transaction. If not, then the cycle is repeated by having the machine read the next transaction. When all transactions have been processed, the program instructs the computer to stop.

This flowchart is oversimplified since there are no instructions as to what the computer would do under each of the two actions considered. As shown in Figure 1, the rectangle symbol indicates a processing step. If, for example, the order is to be shipped, the processing might include having the computer prepare a sales invoice or other authorization for the physical processing of the order. If the order is to be rejected, the processing might have the computer prepare a separate document listing the reason why the order was rejected. Further, there is no indication as to how the computer will locate the customer's order or how it will determine that the transaction being processed is matched with the proper customer's account.

This example was quite simple in form. Now consider a more complex situation, in which *two* conditions must be met before any action may be taken:

> Airlines typically book two types of reservations on jet flights: first class and tourist. If the accommodations requested are unavailable, the passenger may request that his name be placed on the wait list for the next space that becomes available.[3]

Figure 4 presents the decision table for this problem. Note that if the customer requests first class reservations, the airline must be certain that

DECISION RULES ———————▶	1	2	3	4
REQUEST FIRST CLASS?	Yes	Yes		
REQUEST TOURIST?			Yes	Yes
FIRST CLASS AVAILABLE?	Yes	No		
TOURIST AVAILABLE?			Yes	No
ISSUE FIRST CLASS TICKET	X			
ISSUE TOURIST TICKET			X	
PLACE ON WAITING LIST		X		X

FIGURE 4

first class accommodations are available before the ticket may be issued. Thus, each action here requires that two conditions must be met before any action can be taken. Again, each decision rule is satisfied by only one combination of conditions; i.e., the rules are mutually exclusive.

[3] Adapted from *Ibid.*, pp. 3–4.

Figure 5 presents a simplified program flowchart for the decision table in Figure 4. As the decision table becomes more complex, the flowchart reflects this complexity. The flowchart, again, is oversimplified by having a common waiting list without designating the class of service desired.

Finally, consider a situation that is still more complex. The airlines generally will ask the passenger if he is willing to accept an alternate

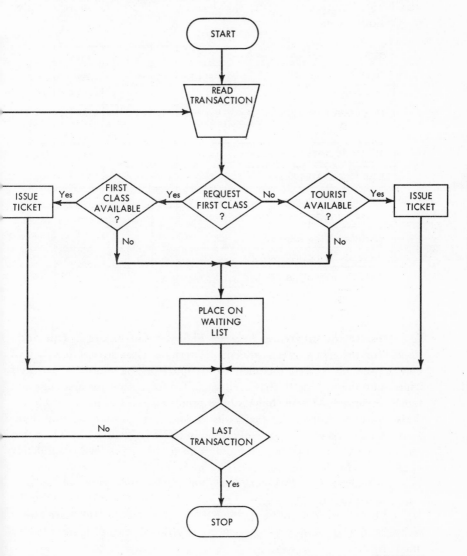

FIGURE 5

class of service if no accommodations are available for his first choice. Thus the reservation example might be amended to include:

The customer may accept alternate class of service; if neither class is available, he may request wait-listing for both classes, taking the reservation that first becomes available.

To be more realistic, we should also note that the airline must keep track of confirmed reservations to help prevent overbooking any particular flight. Figure 6 illustrates the decision table for the more complex reservation system.

DECISION RULES ⟶	1	2	3	4	5	6	7	8
REQUEST FIRST CLASS?	Yes	Yes	Yes	Yes				
REQUEST TOURIST?					Yes	Yes	Yes	Yes
FIRST CLASS AVAILABLE?	Yes	No	No	No		Yes	No	
TOURIST AVAILABLE?		Yes	No		Yes	No	No	No
ALTERNATE CLASS ACCEPTABLE?		Yes	Yes	No		Yes	Yes	No
ISSUE FIRST CLASS TICKET	X				X			
ISSUE TOURIST TICKET		X			X			
SUBTRACT 1 FROM FIRST CLASS	X				X			
SUBTRACT 1 FROM TOURIST		X			X			
PLACE ON FIRST CLASS WAIT LIST			X	X			X	
PLACE ON TOURIST WAIT LIST			X				X	X

FIGURE 6

Observe the differences between Figure 6 and Figure 4. One additional condition has been added: "Alternate class acceptable?" Two new actions have been included to account for the number of tickets issued, and the waiting list has been separated to account for first class and tourist separately. These changes have produced eight mutually exclusive decision rules. Note also, that rules 1 and 5 require two conditions, 4 and 8 three conditions, and the remainder four conditions. The table can be entered at any rule, but only one decision rule will completely satisfy a particular combination of conditions.

In general, the discussion has illustrated simple types of decision tables and program flowcharts. The basic logic of the decision table is: "*If* condition(s) *abc* is present, *then* the action is *def*." No matter how complex the combination of conditions, the essential logic remains unchanged.

PONDER and PREPARE

Consider the following short examples and prepare decision tables and program flowcharts as appropriate.

1. DEF Company needs an analysis of its employees for purposes of determining workman's compensation insurance premiums. Under the Equal Opportunities Employment Act, female employees doing comparable work must be provided with equal compensation benefits as male employees. For this analysis, the company requires a punched card printout of all female employee records; for male employees, only a printed listing of names and numbers is required.

2. Referring to the decision table in Figure 6, prepare a program flowchart.

3. Refer to the example of ABC Company on p. 178. The Company wishes to expand its sales accounting system by having the computer check the following characteristics before approving an order for shipment:

   (a) customer credit limit is okay *and*
   (b) previous payment experience is favorable *or*
   (c) special clearance has been obtained from the credit manager.

4. The ABC Company, in addition to the above checks on credit, wants to introduce an element of inventory control into the system. To help prevent errors, the company has established order limits for each customer. If an order is entered that is greater than the order limit, the computer is not to process it. In addition, the company would like to make sure that there is sufficient inventory on hand to fill the order before further processing takes place, thus the order quantity should be checked with the quantity on hand.

5. Now, for relaxation, try the following brain teaser on your friends.

   Andy dislikes the catcher. Ed's sister is engaged to the second baseman. The center fielder is taller than the right fielder. Harry and the third baseman live in the same building. Paul and Allen each won $20 from the pitcher at pinochle. Ed and the outfielders play poker during their free time. The pitcher's wife is the third baseman's sister. All the battery and infield, except Allen, Harry, and Andy are shorter than Sam. Paul, Harry, Bill, and the catcher took a trouncing from the second baseman at pool. Sam is undergoing a divorce suit. The catcher and third baseman each have two children. Ed, Paul, Jerry, and the right fielder and center fielder are bachelors. The others are married. The shortstop, the third baseman and Bill each cleaned up $100 betting on the fight. One of the outfielders is either Mike or Andy. Jerry is taller than Bill. Mike is shorter than Bill. Each of them is heavier than the third baseman.

With these facts, determine the names of the men playing the various positions on the baseball team. (*Hint*: Prepare, in decision table form, players' names vertically, positions horizontally.) [4]

MONUMENTAL MANUFACTURING COMPANY

The Monumental Manufacturing Company is now processing its inventory records on electronic data processing equipment. It uses an IBM 1401 and the master inventory file is on magnetic tape. For each item in inventory the following information is stored in the master file:

Part Name	19	characters
Part Number	4	"
Cost of Part (actual)	3	"
Quantity in Warehouse		
Current Balance	3	"
1st prior month	3	"
2nd prior month	3	"
3rd prior month	3	"
Cost Level (maximum average monthly cost permissible)	6	"

This month, for the first time since transferring processing to the computer, the Company has started a cycle physical inventory count. All parts with numbers starting with the numeral "4" have been counted. As part of the inventory taking cycle, the Company plans some additional analysis of all parts counted. For the current cycle, the following information is desired for all parts beginning with the numeral "4":

1. Calculate *Average Quantity per Month* equal to the total of Quantity in Warehouse for four months divided by four;
2. Calculate *Average Cost per Month* equal to Average Quantity per Month multiplied by Cost of Part;
3. Assign *Analysis Code A* to cards where Average Cost per Month is higher than Cost Level;
4. Assign *Analysis Code B* to all other items;
5. Punch four identical cards for each part, containing all data in the master file for that part, plus:

4 *Ibid.*, p. 1.

(a) Average Quantity per Month;
(b) Average Cost per Month; and
(c) Analysis Code.

PONDER and PREPARE

1. Prepare a decision table for the analysis of inventory.
2. Prepare a program flow chart for the analysis of inventory.

JAMESTOWN NATIONAL BANK

The Jamestown National Bank has ordered electronic data processing equipment for delivery next year. The Systems Planning Group has been reviewing checking accounts and preparing preliminary procedures to be submitted to the Data Processing Committee for approval. Approval has been received for the record format as follows:

MASTER FILE		TRANSACTION RECORD	
Positions	Name	Positions	Name
1–16	Last name	1– 9	Account number
17	First initial	10	Transaction code
18	Second initial	11–17	Amount (xxxx.xx)
19–32	Address	18	Miscellaneous
33–39	Balance (xxxx.xx)	19	Record mark
40–44	Positive/negative		
45	Flag position		
46–62	Miscellaneous		
63–71	Account number		
72	Record mark		

Master records will be sorted in ascending account number order. Transaction records will be sorted by transaction code, within account number order. Naturally, there may be more than one transaction record for a given account number in any one processing run. Transaction codes, tentatively, are as follows:

1. transaction code "1" represents a deposit;
2. transaction code "2" represents a check or routine bank debit memo such as monthly service charges or check printing charges; and
3. transaction code "5" represents any non-routine debit/credit memo to be handled separately.

Present plans are that code "5" transactions will include corrections of errors in deposits, returned (NSF) checks, corrections of errors in posting checks or other routine charge items and irregular items authorized by the depositor such as note collection proceeds and fees, and safe deposit box rentals. When transaction code "5" is encountered, the system will put the character "D" in the flag position of the master record, and write the master record and the transaction record on exception file #1 without further processing.

The Systems Planning Group has decided that a record count will be useful and should be included in the system. In addition, the system should accumulate positive and negative balances separately to facilitate decisions about reserve requirements and actions relative to overdrafts. Thus, after processing all transactions for a given account number, the account balance should be examined and:

1. if the balance is positive (or zero) it should.be added to total accumulator #1 and the updated master record should be written on the updated master output file; or
2. if the balance is negative, it should be added to total accumulator #2 and the updated master record should be written on the exception file #2.

Both balances are to be displayed on the console typewriter at the end of the processing run.

Preliminary analysis has identified at least two error conditions:

1. a transaction record with a transaction code other than 1, 2 or 5; and
2. a transaction record for which no master file record exists.

When error conditions are identified, the transaction record will be written on an error output file without further processing.

PONDER and PREPARE

1. Prepare a decision table for updating checking accounts that may be submitted with a written system description.
2. Prepare a program flow chart for updating checking accounts.
3. Are there any control weaknesses in that part of the system described here? If so, how would you correct them?

MURPHY METALS CORPORATION

The Murphy Metals Corporation acquired electronic data processing equipment about eight months ago. Since that time, the Systems & Programming Group has installed and debugged a production scheduling system which seems to be operating smoothly. A next step in systems development is to introduce an inventory control system that will operate within the framework of the production scheduling system and at the same time produce useful accounting data about inventories.

One portion of the inventory system will maintain perpetual records for each inventory item, in units only, and provide for an update run for receipts and issues. The master inventory file will be maintained on magnetic tape while transaction records, i.e., receipts and issues, will be in the form of punched cards for batch processing. Each card will contain the part number, a transaction code and the quantity involved. Transaction codes for this part of the system will be:

1. Code "1" will represent a receipt of inventory.
2. Code "2" will represent an issue of inventory.

As a member of the Systems & Programming Group, you have been asked to prepare a decision table and program flowchart for updating the master inventory file. The following procedural guidelines have been adopted:

1. The master inventory file will be sorted by part number in ascending sequence;
2. The last part number (which is a dummy) on the master inventory file will always be greater than the last part number on the transaction file;
3. The transaction file will be pre-sorted by part number and by transaction code number within each part number.

Provision should be made for at least three possible error messages to be printed out on the console typewriter:

1. An error exists if a transaction record contains a transaction code other than "1" or "2";
2. An error exists if there is no master record for a given transaction record; and
3. An error exists for any out-of-sequence condition in the transaction file as compared to the master file.

PONDER and PREPARE

1. Prepare the decision table.
2. Prepare the program flowchart.
3. Prepare a list of test transactions (test deck) suitable for the inventory update program described.

BLAZ-PRUF ASBESTOS COMPANY

Blaz-Pruf Asbestos Company has installed an IBM 1401 data processing system that utilizes punched cards as its major input-output media. One of the applications is the weekly payroll run for production workers. Transaction cards are keypunched from the following source documents:

1. weekly time cards;
2. employee exemption certificates;
3. authorized rate change forms approved by the personnel department;
4. authorized new employee forms approved by the personnel department; and
5. authorized employee termination forms approved by the personnel department.

Transaction cards, after keypunching, are not subject to key verification. Master file cards for terminated employees are removed during a pre-sort operation and are processed on a separate run.

Exhibit One provides a narrative description of a "typical" weekly payroll processing run. Exhibit Two illustrates the field layout for both the master card and the transaction card. Exhibit Three provides the field layout of the punched card output and a narrative description of the exception report and the payroll journal.

Run Functions

The computation phase of the program is designed to take account of the following aspects of payroll processing:

1. All hours worked in excess of 40 are paid at the rate of $1\frac{1}{2}$ times the regular rate of pay;
2. The first $6,600 of each employee's gross earnings is subject to an FICA rate of 4.9%; *
3. Federal income tax withholdings are computed as follows:

    (a) exempt weekly earnings = # of dependents × $13.00
    (b) taxable earnings = gross earnings — exempt earnings
    (c) taxes withheld = taxable earnings × 14%.

    The program provides for the possibility that exempt earnings may exceed gross earnings and no tax will be withheld in such situations.

4. "Other deductions" represent union dues, credit union deposits, savings bond deductions, and so forth. For any one employee, these deductions are fixed in amount, except that union dues are deducted only once a month. Since these deductions are not a function of gross earnings, the possibility exists that the total of all deductions (including FICA and income tax withholdings) will exceed gross pay. In that event, the program provides for "other deductions" to be reduced to the extent of any "negative" net pay, resulting in a net pay of zero for the current period (see Error Messages, below).

Three types of changes in input media are recognized by the program:

---

* The rate of 4.9% applies for 1969–1972. The wage base remains at $6,600 and the rate changes as follows:

1973–1975: 5.4%	1980–1986: 5.55%
1976–1979: 5.45%	1987–on : 5.65%

1. *Changes in Number of Dependents.* A change in the number of dependents for an employee will appear in field #5 of the payroll transaction card; for all other employees this field will be blank. The *new* number of dependents is used during the processing run for the current period and is punched in the updated master card for future processing runs.

2. *Pay Rate Changes.* A change in the regular rate of pay for an employee appears in field #6 of the payroll transaction card; for all other employees this field will be blank. The *new* rate is used during the processing run for the current period and is punched in the updated master card for future processing runs.

3. *New Employee.* The code digit "1" is punched in field #7 on the transaction card for all new employees; for all other employees this field will be blank. The program interprets this to mean that there is no master record for this transaction card; an updated master card will be punched for future processing runs.

Processing Controls

Processing controls are listed in Exhibit One. The first three are checks of the validity or reasonableness of the input data. Deviations, based upon the first three process controls, will result in "error messages," which are discussed below.

Both the master file and the transaction file are pre-sorted in ascending employee number sequence prior to the processing run. No duplication of employee numbers should appear in either file. The sequence check is to assure that both files are in proper sequence prior to processing the transaction.

The self-checking digits are designed to detect errors in keypunching of the employee number. In this particular application, the self-checking digits are recorded in field #2 of each transaction card. They are a function of the employee number and are computed as follows:

1. the units position of the employee number is multiplied by one;
2. the tens position of the employee number is multiplied by two;
3. the hundreds position of the employee number is multiplied by three;
4. the thousands position of the employee number is multiplied by four; and
5. the sum of the four products is computed and subtracted from 1,000 to produce the self-checking digits.

For example, assume an employee with the employee number 1105:

1. $5 \times 1 = 5$
2. $0 \times 2 = 0$
3. $1 \times 3 = 3$
4. $1 \times 4 = 4$

$\overline{12}$

5. $1,000 - 12 = 988.$

The self-checking digits, for this employee would be 988. If either an incorrect employee number or incorrect self-checking digits are key-punched on the transaction card, the computed self-checking digits will not agree with the ones recorded.

The reasonableness or limit check of gross pay calculations is designed to pick up inadvertent computational errors or keypunching errors in the number of hours worked (or provide special approval for what may be excessive overtime). The reasonableness check on gross weekly pay is $300.

The record count is a control total which is verified against pre-established numbers relating to the total number of employees included in the master file and the total transaction cards that have been processed.

Output

Exhibit Three provides a narrative description of the output of the processing run. The updated master file, of course, becomes the input for the next processing run and provides the data necessary for various periodic reports to users outside the company—federal government relative to FICA and withholding taxes, the union relative to union dues withheld, and so forth. The master cards and the payroll cards are produced by an "on-line" card punch.

The payroll cards provide the input data for two separate processing steps. Both steps are carried out on an "off-line" printer and are controlled by wired board programs. Step one is the production of the payroll journal as described in Exhibit Three. The other processing step results in the production of payroll checks. In check preparation, the payroll card deck is merged with an "employee identification deck" which contains the following information:

(a) Field 1: Employee name
(b) Field 2: Employee number
(c) Field 3: Employee social security number

The merged deck provides the input data for the payroll checks.

The error messages are printed out on an electric typewriter attached to the console. When an error message is printed out, no further processing of that transaction card takes place. The system is programmed to proceed to the next transaction card without halting. Errors are investigated, new cards punched as necessary and a second run is used to process the exceptions. The error message normally contains only the employee's number and the class of error. Details of error messages are as follows:

Error Message #1: A sequence error exists; either a duplicate employee number has been used or an incorrect ascending sequence. Print "EM #1."

Error Message #2: Incorrect self-checking digits; either the employee number or the self-checking digits have been recorded incorrectly. Print "EM #2."

Error Message #3: Sum of deductions exceed gross earnings; all the details of the gross pay and deductions are printed out in addition to "EM #3" so that "other deductions" which may have been reduced by the amount of any negative balance may be adjusted in subsequent pay periods.

Error Message #4: The limit check of $300 in gross pay has been exceeded. Print "EM #4."

Error Message #5: A transaction card without the code digit "1" for which there is no master record (new employees must have code digit "1" to indicate no master record exists). Print "EM #5."

Audit Considerations

One of the techniques the auditor may employ in his examination of an electronic data processing system is that of the "test deck" or "enquiry deck." The test deck serves the function of testing the program to see if, in fact, it does the things it is supposed to do. In general, the test deck comprises a series of simulated transactions which are processed by the client's program; they are designed to test the computational features and the control aspects of the program.

PONDER and PREPARE

If you were the auditor assigned to this client:

1. Prepare a listing of the types of transactions you would use to "test" this company's payroll program. Use a separate transaction for each item you wish to test.
2. Describe any weaknesses in the system you can recognize.
3. Suggest ways in which the weaknesses may be corrected.

PAYROLL RUN

Input

1. Master card file
2. Transaction card file

Run Functions

1. Validate data (see processing controls)
2. Calculate gross pay
3. Calculate FICA deduction
4. Calculate income tax deduction
5. Calculate net pay
6. Construct output

Processing
Controls

1. Sequence check master and transaction cards
2. Calculate self-checking digits for employee number
3. Apply reasonableness or limit check of gross pay calculation
4. Count master cards and transaction cards

Output

1. Payroll card
2. Updated master card
3. Typewriter printout of error messages

PUNCHED CARD INPUT

Master Card

Field 1: Employee number
Field 2: Number of dependents
Field 3: Regular rate of pay
Field 4: Gross earnings to date
Field 5: FICA deductions to date
Field 6: Federal withholding tax to date
Field 7: Other deductions to date

Transaction
Card

Field 1: Employee number
Field 2: Self-checking digits
Field 3: Hours worked
Field 4: Other deductions
Field 5: Change in number of dependents
Field 6: Change in rate of pay
Field 7: New employee code digit

PUNCHED CARD OUTPUT

Master Card

Same field designations as master card input, containing updated data.

Payroll Card

Field 1: Employee number
Field 2: Hours worked
Field 3: Gross earnings—this period
Field 4: FICA deductions—this period
Field 5: Income tax withheld—this period
Field 6: Other deductions—this period
Field 7: Net pay—this period

PRINTED OUTPUT

Payroll Journal

Column 1:	Employee number
Column 2:	Hours worked
Column 3:	Gross earnings—this period
Column 4:	FICA deductions—this period
Column 5:	Income tax withheld—this period
Column 6:	Other deductions—this period
Column 7:	Net pay—this period
Columns 8–15:	Gross pay broken down by cost centers based upon cost center code included as part of employee number.

Printed Error Messages

Printed error messages list the employee number and the class of error (except as noted in case) as follows:
1105—error message #2

PART FIVE

Supplemental Material,
The SEC and Disclosure,
Fraud,
Review Cases

THE SEC AND DISCLOSURE

One of the principal interests of the SEC is to *enforce disclosure of adequate information for the use of investors.* The disclosure of information, by and large, is through financial statements. Primary responsibility for the fairness and accuracy of the financial statements rests with management; the auditor assumes a secondary responsibility.

The SEC is charged with the administration of several different acts. In discharging these responsibilities the Commission exercises quasi-judicial functions, quasi-legislative functions, and administrative functions. Listed below are the various statutes administered by the SEC, with a brief summary of the intent of the act, the types of statements filed, and indication of the statements which must be certified by an independent accountant.

The Securities Act of 1933. This act is primarily a disclosure statute, with disclosure accomplished mainly through the registration statement, known as Form S-1, and through the stock prospectus. The registration statement contains, among other things, pertinent information relative to:

1. the company's business
2. its capital structure
3. the financial statements, which include:

    (a) audited statements covering the last three years, and
    (b) comparative income summaries for five years which need not be audited

4. the officers and directors of the firm and their compensation
5. the underwriting agreement.

The Securities Exchange Act of 1934. This act is primarily a registration statute that covers national exchanges, national associations of securities dealers, securities registered on the exchanges, over-the-counter broker-dealers, and various others involved in securities dealings. The act also regulates wash sales or matched orders, price stabilization, short sales, market specialists, odd-lot dealers and proxy solicitations. Banks and certain insurance companies have special regulations governing the reporting of their activities. The act requires filing certain statements, among which are:

1. Broker-dealer annual reports of financial condition (the broker-dealer must maintain a specified debt-capital relationship). Certified statements are required and some of the audit procedures are specified by the Commission.

2. Corporate insider reports (officers, directors, etc.) relative to the holding and trading of securities of the employer (short-term profits may be recoverable by the employer). Recently, this provision has been expanded to include holdings of members of insider's family where insider may have a beneficial interest.
3. Company applications for registration on a securities exchange, Form 10.
4. For registered companies, quarterly reports (Form 7-K), semi-annual reports (Form 9-K), and annual reports (Form 10-K). Form 10-K is the most formal of the reporting requirements and includes the following reports and statements:

   (a) unconsolidated balance sheet and income statement and statement of retained earnings, to be certified each year
   (b) consolidated statements of parent and subsidiary(ies), to be certified each year
   (c) certified balance sheets for each majority owned subsidiary not included in the consolidated statements
   (d) a listing of securities of affiliates pledged as collateral; a certified balance sheet and income statement of the affiliate, if not included in (b) or (c) above
   (e) special statements are required of new companies not yet in full scale operations or production
   (f) various supporting schedules dealing with plant, depreciation, and other items.

Regulation S-X details the requirements for these reports showing form and content. Forms 9-K and 7K need not contain certified statements.

The Public Utility Holding Company Act of 1935. This act is a registration statute and covers only electric and retail gas companies. The registration requirements include, among other things, details of:

1. capital structure
2. nature of business
3. corporate insider information.

The Commission also exercises regulatory powers under the act, such as:

1. Can require geographic integration of properties.
2. Can require simplification of capital structures.
3. Has considerable control over security transactions of holding companies and subsidiary companies, the acquisition and disposition of assets, intercompany loans, capital contributions, dividend payments, proxy solicitations, service and construction contracts, and accounting practices.
4. Specifies uniform systems of accounting—the only area where SEC does this regularly.

The Trust Indenture Act of 1939. This act is a registration statute covering bonds and debentures (also other debt instruments) which may not be offered to the public unless issued under a trust indenture that has been approved by the Commission. Approval usually requires an independent trustee. No certified statements are required by the act.

The Investment Company Act of 1940. This act is a registration statute under which investment companies must:

1. register with the SEC
2. file certified annual reports
3. obtain prior SEC approval of insider transactions.

The Investment Advisors Act of 1940. This is a companion statute to the preceding act, and provides for the disclosure of pertinent information about individuals who act as advisors to investment companies.

The rulings and orders of the Securities and Exchange Commission are subject to judicial review just as the rulings and orders of any other administrative agency of the government. Experience indicates, however, that the courts will not substitute their discretion for the SEC's unless the administrative view is ". . . so enirely at odds with fundamental principles of correct accounting . . . as to be the expression of a whim rather than an exercise of judgement. . . ." [1] The SEC may act as a disinterested advisor to the court (and to investors) on legal and financial matters related to companies undergoing corporate reorganization under Chapter X of the National Bankruptcy Act.

Presented below are examples of the Auditor's Report and various types of footnote disclosure taken from annual reports of companies subject to SEC regulation except for two auditor's statements illustrating foreign practice. The opinions reproduced include both "clean certificates" and illustrations of various types of qualifications. The footnotes are examples of typical disclosures, relating to various types of recurring events.

---

[1] *American Telephone & Telegraph Company* v. *The United States,* 229 US 236, 237 (Justice Cardozo).

PepsiCo, Inc. Financial Statements

ARTHUR YOUNG & COMPANY

277 PARK AVENUE
NEW YORK, N.Y. 10017

The Board of Directors and Shareholders,
PepsiCo, Inc.

We have examined the accompanying consolidated balance sheet of
PepsiCo, Inc. and consolidated subsidiaries at December 31, 1965 and
the related consolidated statements of income, retained earnings and
capital in excess of par value for the year then ended. Our examination
was made in accordance with generally accepted auditing standards,
and accordingly included such tests of the accounting records and such
other auditing procedures as we considered necessary in the circumstances.
We have received the reports of other independent public accountants
with respect to their examinations of the financial statements of certain
major operating units of the Company and consolidated subsidiaries, and
we assume responsibility for their examination in the same manner
as if made by us.

In our opinion, the statements mentioned above present fairly the
consolidated financial position of PepsiCo, Inc. and consolidated
subsidiaries at December 31, 1965 and the consolidated results of their
operations for the year then ended, in conformity with generally
accepted accounting principles applied on a basis consistent with that
of the preceding year.

Arthur Young & Company

March 23, 1966

Opinion of Independent Accountants

*To the Board of Directors
and Shareholders of*

F. W. Woolworth Co.

In our opinion, based on our examination and on the reports mentioned below of other independent accountants, the accompanying consolidated balance sheet, the related statement of consolidated income and earned surplus and the consolidated statement of source and disposition of working capital present fairly the financial position of F. W. Woolworth Co. and its consolidated subsidiaries at December 31, 1965, the results of their operations and the supplementary information on working capital for the year, in conformity with generally accepted accounting principles applied on a basis consistent with that of the preceding year. Our examination of these statements was made in accordance with generally accepted auditing standards and accordingly included such tests of the accounting records and such other auditing procedures as we considered necessary in the circumstances. We did not examine the consolidated financial statements of the subsidiaries of F. W. Woolworth Co. located in Canada, Germany and England, which statements were examined by other independent accountants whose reports thereon have been furnished to us.

PRICE WATERHOUSE & Co.

New York, N. Y.
February 14, 1966

Consolidated Statement of Source
and Disposition of Working Capital

AUDITORS' REPORT

To the Board of Directors and Stockholders of
Uris Buildings Corporation:

We have examined the consolidated balance sheet of
URIS BUILDINGS CORPORATION and SUBSIDIARIES
as of September 30, 1965 and the related consolidated
statement of income and retained earnings for the year
then ended. Our examination was made in accordance
with generally accepted auditing standards, and accordingly included such tests of the accounting records and
such other auditing procedures as we considered necessary in the circumstances. We have previously examined
and reported upon the consolidated financial statements
of the Company and its subsidiaries for the year 1964.

In our opinion, the aforementioned financial statements
present fairly the consolidated financial position of Uris
Buildings Corporation and Subsidiaries at September 30,
1965 and 1964, and the results of their operations for the
years then ended, in conformity with generally accepted
accounting principles applied on a consistent basis.

We have made a similar examination of the accompanying consolidated statement of source and application of
funds of the Company and Subsidiaries which, in our
opinion, when considered in relation to the basic financial
statements, presents fairly the sources and application
of funds of the Company and Subsidiaries for the years
ended September 30, 1965 and 1964.

LYBRAND, ROSS BROS. & MONTGOMERY

New York, November 15, 1965.

AUDITORS' REPORT

e Board of Directors and Stockholders of
Buildings Corporation:

have examined the combined balance sheet of URIS
_DINGS CORPORATION'S 50%-OWNED ENTER-
ES as of September 30, 1965 and the related com-
d statement of earnings (loss) and deficit for the
then ended. Our examination was made in accord-
with generally accepted auditing standards, and
rdingly included such tests of the accounting records
such other auditing procedures as we considered
ssary in the circumstances. We have previously ex-
ed and reported upon the combined financial state-
s of the Company's 50%-owned enterprises for the
1964, except that we did not examine the financial
ments of an operating unit of a 50%-owned company
net assets of $2,864,995, income of $24,118,026 and
nses of $18,091,448, which statements were examined
her certified public accountants whose report there-
as furnished to us. Our opinion expressed herein,
ar as it relates to the amounts included for that op-
g unit for 1964, is based solely upon such report. The

financial statements for the year 1964 have been restated
as described in Note 3 to the financial statements.

In our opinion, subject to the ultimate resolution of the
disagreement regarding the propriety of certain advertising and promotion expenses referred to in Note 11, the
afore-mentioned financial statements present fairly the
combined financial position of Uris Buildings Corporation's 50%-Owned Enterprises at September 30, 1965 and
1964, and the results of their combined operations for the
years then ended, in conformity with generally accepted
accounting principles applied on a consistent basis.

We have made a similar examination of the accompanying combined statement of sources and application of
funds of Uris Buildings Corporation's 50%-Owned Enterprises which, in our opinion, when considered in relation
to the basic financial statements, presents fairly the
sources and application of funds of the 50%-Owned
Enterprises for the years ended September 30, 1965 and
1964.

LYBRAND, ROSS BROS. & MONTGOMERY
New York, November 15, 1965.

#3. In June, 1964, a subsidiary of one of
the companies acquired title to the land
under one of the hotels. The land was purchased at a discount of $300,000 to com-
pensate for a correspondingly lower ground
rent under the acquired lease with such
hotel for the one-year period subsequent
to acquisition. The subsidiary's loss during such one-year period, arising from
lower ground rent, amounted to $269,641,
and such amount has been capitalized as
additional cost of land, including retro-
active restatement of $84,060, which had
been previously charged to expense in
1964.

11. In fiscal 1965, advertising and promotion
expenses include approximately $209,000
of charges billed by Hilton Hotels Corporation to the two hotels (approximately
$270,000 for fiscal 1964 and prior). Under
contractual agreement, Hilton Hotels Corporation manages both hotels and is also
a 25 and 50 per cent stockholder, respectively. The other stockholders have chal-
lenged the propriety of the afore-mentioned charges under the hotel management agreements. Any subsequent adjustment of such charges would correspondingly reduce combined net loss of the year
affected, as well as the accumulated
deficit.

ACCOUNTANTS' OPINION

ARTHUR ANDERSEN & CO.

SAN JUAN, PUERTO RICO

To the Trustees and Shareholders,

CENTRAL AGUIRRE SUGAR COMPANY (a Trust):

We have examined the consolidated balance sheet of CENTRAL AGUIRRE SUGAR COMPANY (a Massachusetts Trust) and subsidiaries and associated companies as of July 31, 1966, and the related statements of income and earned surplus for the year then ended. Our examination was made in accordance with generally accepted auditing standards, and accordingly included such tests of the accounting records and such other auditing procedures as we considered necessary in the circumstances. We have previously examined and reported on the financial statements for the preceding year.

In our opinion, the accompanying consolidated balance sheet and consolidated statements of income and earned surplus present fairly the financial position of Central Aguirre Sugar Company (a Trust) and subsidiaries and associated companies as of July 31, 1966, and the results of their operations for the year then ended, in conformity with generally accepted accounting principles applied on a basis consistent with that of the preceding year.

San Juan, P. R.,
September 16, 1966.   ARTHUR ANDERSEN & CO.

ERNST & ERNST

Report of Independent Accountants
To the Shareholders and Board of Directors of Northrop Corporation:

We have examined the statement of consolidated financial position of Northrop Corporation and subsidiaries as of July 31, 1966, and the related statements of consolidated income, shareholders' equity, and changes in consolidated working capital for the fiscal year then ended. Our examination was made in accordance with generally accepted auditing standards, and accordingly included such tests of the accounting records and such other auditing procedures as we considered necessary in the circumstances. We were unable to confirm by direct correspondence amounts receivable from the U.S. Government and certain other major customers, but we satisfied ourselves as to such amounts by means of other auditing procedures.

In our opinion, the accompanying statement of financial position and statements of income and shareholders' equity present fairly the consolidated financial position of Northrop Corporation and subsidiaries at July 31, 1966, and the consolidated results of their operations for the fiscal year then ended, in conformity with generally accepted accounting principles applied on a basis consistent with that of the preceding year. It is also our opinion that the accompanying statement of changes in consolidated working capital presents fairly the information therein shown.

Los Angeles, California, September 21, 1966   *Ernst & Ernst*

AUDITORS' REPORT

To the Shareholders of
HIRAM WALKER-GOODERHAM & WORTS LIMITED:

We have examined the consolidated balance sheet of Hiram Walker-Gooderham & Worts Limited and wholly-owned subsidiaries as at August 31, 1966 and the consolidated statements of income and expenses and earnings retained and employed in the business for the year ended on that date. Our examination was made in conformity with generally accepted auditing standards, and accordingly included such tests of the accounting records and such other auditing procedures as we considered necessary in the circumstances.

In our opinion, subject to final determination of the proposed additional liability for income taxes referred to under the heading "Proposed Income Tax Adjustments" on page 16, the accompanying consolidated balance sheet and related consolidated statements of income and expenses and earnings retained and employed in the business present fairly the financial position of the companies as at August 31, 1966 and the results of their operations for the year ended on that date, in accordance with generally accepted accounting principles applied on a basis consistent with that of the preceding year.

PRICE WATERHOUSE & CO.
Chartered Accountants

Toronto, October 19, 1966

PROPOSED INCOME TAX ADJUSTMENTS

An agent of the United States Internal Revenue Service has completed his audit of the federal income tax returns of the Company's affiliated corporations in the United States for their fiscal years 1958 through 1962. The audit reports include, among other items, substantial proposed disallowances of certain interest payments and several major classifications of selling expense.

The additional tax proposed by the agent for the years 1958 through 1962 amounts to approximately $26,000,000, exclusive of interest on any tax deficiencies that may ultimately be payable. Items of the same nature are present in subsequent years.

In 1958 the deductibility of the questioned interest payments with respect to earlier years was reviewed thoroughly and resolved in the Company's favor by the Appellate Division of the Internal Revenue Service. Tax counsel has advised the Company that the Appellate Division's position was sound and sees no reason why the Division's earlier position should be reversed.

Tax counsel has also advised the Company that the reporting and claiming of deductions for selling expenses was generally sound and consistent with past practice and that the positions taken by the agent should be vigorously contested.

Should all the questions raised by the Revenue Agent be resolved against the Company, the amounts involved would be substantially in excess of available tax accruals.

The proposed disallowances will be contested. It appears probable that final resolution of these matters may not be achieved for several years.

ACCOUNTANTS' OPINION

THE SHARE OWNERS AND
BOARD OF DIRECTORS OF KERN COUNTY LAND COMPANY:

We have examined the consolidated balance sheet of Kern County Land Company and consolidated subsidiaries as of October 31, 1966 and the related statements of consolidated earnings and reinvested earnings and of consolidated sources and uses of working capital for the year then ended. Our examination was made in accordance with generally accepted auditing standards, and accordingly included such tests of the accounting records and such other auditing procedures as we considered necessary in the circumstances.

In our opinion, the above-mentioned statements present fairly the financial position of the companies at October 31, 1966 and the results of their operations and the sources and uses of their working capital for the year then ended, in conformity with generally accepted accounting principles applied (except for the changes, which we approve, referred to in the note on page 20 captioned "Consolidation and Accounting") on a basis consistent with that of the preceding year.

San Francisco, December 16, 1966   *Haskins v Sells*

Notes to Financial Statements

Consolidation and Accounting. The financial statements include Kern County Land Company and all of its subsidiaries except J. I. Case Company and its subsidiaries.

For comparative purposes, certain items reported in the 1965 financial statements have been restated.

The changes, described below, in accounting for pension costs by J. I. Case Company, and in accounting for acquisition costs of unproved oil and gas properties by KCL, had the aggregate effect of reducing earnings by approximately $1,300,000.

Investment in J. I. Case Company. At October 31, 1966 the Company owned 54% of the common stock and all of the preferred stock of J. I. Case Company. At that date the investment was represented by common stock ($34,978,-000), 5¾% cumulative preferred stock ($20,000,000), 5½% subordinated debentures ($3,851,000), all carried at cost, and by equity in undistributed earnings since acquisition less an amount representing taxes which would have been applicable in absence of loss carryovers accumulated prior to acquisition ($8,038,000). The total of $66,867,000 exceeded by $416,000 KCL's equity in Case's reported net assets at that date.

Dividends paid on Case 5¾% cumulative preferred stock for the year were $1,150,000. No dividends were paid on Case common stock. Case's earnings retained are restricted by provisions relative to its outstanding debt as to the payment of cash dividends on common stock. At October 31, 1966 the amount not so restricted was $7,500,000.

Change in Accounting Practice: In its 1965 and prior fiscal years it was Case's practice to expense pension costs annually as they were paid. In its 1966 fiscal year, Case

began in addition to recognize future pension costs ᴄ accrual basis, which reduced its net income by $2,800

The following selected comparative items from ᴄ audited financial statements are presented as of Octob and for the year then ended (in thousands of dollars)

J. I. CASE COMPANY	1966	1
Net sales	$326,727	$27
Income from operations	31,213	1
Net income for the year.........	17,312	1
Inventories	97,649	9
Notes payable to banks.........	16,072	2
Accounts payable	39,794	3
Working capital................	59,726	6
Properties (net)...............	58,678	4
Long-term debt	67,333	6
Stockholders' equity..........	98,891	8
J. I. Case Credit Corporation Net income for the year (included in Case income)..	2,950	
Notes receivable	236,919	16
Total borrowings	224,155	15

For those wishing more detailed information, copi Case's annual report for the year, which contains au financial statements of J. I. Case Company and consolic subsidiary companies and J. I. Case Credit Corpora may be obtained by writing Howard G. Hawkins, Jr., S tary, Kern County Land Company, 600 California S San Francisco, California 94108.

ACCOUNTANTS' REPORT

To the Board of Directors
Polarad Electronics Corporation
Long Island City, N. Y.

We have examined the consolidated balance sheet of Polarad Electronics Corporation and subsidiary as at June 30, 1966, and the related consolidated statement of operations and deficit for the year then ended. Our examination was made in accordance with generally accepted auditing standards, and accordingly included such tests of the accounting records and such other auditing procedures as we considered necessary in the circumstances; it was not practicable to confirm receivables from the United States Government as to which we have satisfied ourselves by means of other auditing procedures. As to the foreign subsidiary, whose financial statements were not examined by us, we were furnished with the report by other accountants.

In our opinion, based upon our examination and upon the report of the other accountants referred to above, the accompanying consolidated balance sheet and consolidated statement of operations and deficit, together with the notes to financial statements, present fairly the consolidated financial position of Polarad Electronics Corporation and subsidiary at June 30, 1966, and the consolidated results of their operations for the year then ended, in conformity with generally accepted accounting principles applied on a basis consistent with that of the preceding year.

New York, N. Y.
September 9, 1966

S. D. LEIDESDORF & CO.
CERTIFIED PUBLIC ACCOUNTANTS

Accountants' Report

Board of Directors,   January 12, 1967
Gar Wood Industries, Inc.,
Wayne, Michigan

We have examined the accompanying consolidated balance sheets of Gar Wood Industries, Inc., and subsidiary as of October 31, 1966, and October 31, 1965, the related statements of net earnings and earnings retained for use in the business, and the consolidated statement of source and disposition of working capital for the years then ended. Our examinations were made in accordance with generally accepted auditing standards, and accordingly included such tests of the accounting records and such other auditing procedures as we considered necessary in the circumstances.

In our opinion, the financial statements referred to above present fairly the consolidated financial position of Gar Wood Industries, Inc., and subsidiary at October 31, 1966, and October 31, 1965, and the consolidated results of their operations and the source and disposition of working capital for the years then ended, in conformity with generally accepted accounting principles applied on a basis consistent with that of the preceding year.

Detroit, Michigan

TOUCHE, ROSS, BAILEY & SMART
Certified Public Accountants

REPORT OF INDEPENDENT CERTIFIED PUBLIC ACCOUNTANTS

To the Board of Directors and Stockholders of R. Hoe & Co., Inc.:

We have examined the consolidated balance sheet of R. HOE & CO., INC. and consolidated subsidiaries as of September 30, 1966 and the related statement of income and earned surplus for the year then ended. Our examination was made in accordance with generally accepted auditing standards, and accordingly included such tests of the accounting records and such other auditing procedures as we considered necessary in the circumstances. We made a similar examination of the 1965 financial statements which have been restated, with our concurrence, to reflect the inclusion of the wholly-owned domestic subsidiaries as described in Note 1 to the financial statements.

In our opinion, the afore-mentioned financial statements present fairly the consolidated financial position of R. Hoe & Co., Inc. and consolidated subsidiaries at September 30, 1966 and 1965, and the consolidated results of their operations for the years then ended, in conformity with generally accepted accounting principles applied on a consistent basis.

LYBRAND, ROSS BROS. & MONTGOMERY

New York, January 17, 1967.

1. The financial statements for 1966 have been prepared on a consolidated basis for the first time and now include, along with the accounts of the company, all wholly-owned domestic subsidiaries. For comparative purposes, the 1965 financial statements have been restated to reflect this change. The effect on net income for 1966 and 1965 was not significant.

Accountants' Opinion

Deere & Company:

We have examined the consolidated balance sheet of Deere & Company and consolidated subsidiaries as of 31 October 1966, and the related statement of consolidated income and earned surplus for the year then ended. We have made a similar examination of the balance sheet of John Deere Credit Company, an unconsolidated finance subsidiary. Our examinations were made in accordance with generally accepted auditing standards, and accordingly included such tests of the accounting records and such other auditing procedures as we considered necessary in the circumstances.

In our opinion, the accompanying statements present fairly (a) the financial position of Deere & Company and consolidated subsidiaries at 31 October 1966, and the results of their operations for the year then ended, and (b) the financial position of John Deere Credit Company at 31 October 1966, in conformity with generally accepted accounting principles applied on a basis consistent with that of the preceding year.

Chicago
December 19, 1966

Certified Public Accountants

Auditor's Report

Board of Directors and Stockholders,
Endicott Johnson Corporation,
Endicott, New York.

New York, New York
January 26, 1967

We have examined the accompanying consolidated balance sheet of Endicott Johnson Corporation and its subsidiary companies as of December 2, 1966, and the related statements of earnings, accumulated retained earnings, and changes in working capital for the fiscal year (fifty-two weeks) then ended. Our examination was made in accordance with generally accepted auditing standards, and accordingly included such tests of the accounting records and such other auditing procedures as we considered necessary in the circumstances.

In our opinion, the financial statements referred to above present fairly the consolidated financial position of Endicott Johnson Corporation and its subsidiary companies at December 2, 1966, and the consolidated results of their operations for the fiscal year (fifty-two weeks) then ended, in conformity with generally accepted accounting principles applied on a basis consistent with that of the preceding fiscal year, as restated (Note 5). Further, it is our opinion that the consolidated statement of changes in working capital presents fairly the information therein set forth.

Touche, Ross, Bailey & Smart

Certified Public Accountants.

(5) Upon the recommendation of the Accounting Principles Board of the American Institute of Certified Public Accountants and the Company's auditors, the Company has elected to conform with a current pronouncement of such Board. As a result, gains on disposal of facilities, which in prior years' statements have been shown as credits following the determination of net earnings, are shown as extraordinary items but included in such net earnings. Figures for the fifty-three weeks ended December 3, 1965 have also been restated.

Auditors' report

To the members,
Wankie Colliery Company Limited

In our opinion the accounts set out on pages 12 to 15, amplified by the information given in the directors' report, comply with the Companies Act, chapter 223, and give a true and fair view of the state of affairs and profit of the company.

COOPER BROTHERS & CO.
Chartered Accountants (S.R.)

Bulawayo
Rhodesia
16th September, 1966

STATEMENT BY THE DIRECTORS

We, COLIN YORK SYME and NORMAN EDWARD JONES, being two of the
Directors of THE BROKEN HILL PROPRIETARY COMPANY LIMITED,
do hereby state that, in our opinion, the Profit and Loss Account is drawn up so as
to give a true and fair view of the results of the business of the Company for the
period covered by the Account, and that the Balance Sheet is drawn up so as to
exhibit a true and fair view of the state of affairs of the Company as at the end of that
period.

Dated at Melbourne, this 5th day of August, 1966.

On behalf of the Board,

Witness — J. L. JENKINS.

COLIN SYME
N. E. JONES } Directors

DECLARATION BY THE SECRETARY

I JOHN LINDSEY JENKINS, of 500 Bourke Street, in the City of Melbourne,
Secretary of THE BROKEN HILL PROPRIETARY COMPANY LIMITED, do
solemnly and sincerely declare:—
That the accompanying Balance Sheet and Profit and Loss Account are, to the best of
my knowledge and belief, correct.

And I make this solemn declaration conscientiously believing the same to be true and
by virtue of the provisions of an Act of the Parliament of Victoria rendering persons
making a false declaration punishable for wilful and corrupt perjury.

Declared at Melbourne in the State of
Victoria, this 5th Day of August, One } J. L. JENKINS.
thousand nine hundred and sixty-six.

Before me — P. D. M. CONDELL.
A Commissioner for taking Declarations and Affidavits under the Evidence Act 1958.

AUDITORS' REPORT

We have examined the Balance Sheet of The Broken Hill Proprietary Co. Ltd. at 31st
May, 1966, and the related Profit and Loss Account for the year then ended. Our
examination included such tests of the accounting records and such other auditing
procedures as we considered necessary in the circumstances.

We have also examined the Consolidated Balance Sheet and the Consolidated Profit
and Loss Account of The Broken Hill Proprietary Co. Ltd. and its Subsidiary
Companies, in conjunction with the separate Balance Sheets and Profit and Loss
Accounts of the individual companies, certain of which were reported upon by other
auditors.

In our opinion:

1. The accompanying Balance Sheet and Profit and Loss Account are properly drawn
up in accordance with the provisions of the Companies Act 1961 and together with the
Directors' Report give a true and fair view of the state of affairs of the Company
and the results of its operations for the year.

2. Based upon our examination and on the reports of the other auditors referred to
above, the Consolidated Balance Sheet and Consolidated Profit and Loss Account are
properly drawn up in accordance with the provisions of the Companies Act 1961 and
together with the Directors Report give a true and fair view of the state of affairs of
the group and of the results of its operations for the year.

We are also of the opinion that the accounting and other records (including registers)
of The Broken Hill Proprietary Co. Ltd. examined by us were properly kept in
accordance with the provisions of the Companies Act 1961.

5th August, 1966.

J. K. LITTLE
N. K. BAKER

Chartered Accountants

Notes to Financial Statements
for the Year Ended August 31, 1965

(1) PRINCIPLES OF CONSOLIDATION: The accompanying consolidated financial statements include the accounts of The Pacific Coast Company and all subsidiaries, except three majority-owned real estate subsidiaries (which became wholly owned subsequent to August 31, 1965) the investments in which are carried at underlying book value. All intercompany transactions have been eliminated. The minority interest represents a 20% ownership of the outstanding capital stock of certain distributing subsidiaries by distributing company managers.

The three unconsolidated majority-owned real estate subsidiaries (The Pacific Coast Realty Corporation of Delaware, The Pacific Coast Realty Corporation of Indiana and The Pacific Coast Redevelopment Corporation) own the land and buildings leased to certain of the company's distributing subsidiaries for terms of up to twenty years at an aggregate annual rental of $679,120 plus real estate taxes and other expenses. Combined financial statements of the three unconsolidated real estate subsidiaries for fiscal 1965 together with the auditors' opinion are shown below:

Combined Balance Sheet—August 31, 1965

ASSETS

Cash	$ 28,558
Prepaid interest and deferred charges	46,735
Land and buildings, at cost, less reserves for depreciation of $379,765 (Note B)	6,177,465
	$6,252,758

LIABILITIES

Current liabilities—	
4¾% notes payable to bank (Note A)	$ 742,000
Current portion of mortgage notes payable	165,668
Accounts payable	107,614
Accrued Federal income taxes	63,009
Total current liabilities	$1,078,291
Deferred Federal income taxes	$ 56,596
5½% to 6½% mortgage notes payable, secured by land and buildings, payable in monthly installments to 1985, less current maturities above (guaranteed by The Pacific Coast Company)	$4,662,967
Capital stock and surplus—	
Common stock	$ 220,583
Earned surplus	234,321
	$ 454,904
	$6,252,758

Combined Statement of Income and Earned Surplus
For the Year Ended August 31, 1965

Rental income		$552,698
Costs and expenses—		
Depreciation (Note B)	$120,942	
Interest expense	199,470	
Other	18,051	338,463
Income before Federal income taxes		$214,235
Federal income taxes		94,000
Net income for the year		$120,235
Special credit—gain on sale of property, less $12,000 related Federal income taxes		37,112
Net income for the year and special credit		$157,347
Earned surplus, beginning of year		76,974
Earned surplus, end of year		$234,321

NOTES: (A) Notes payable to bank represent unsecured short-term borrowings pending completion of construction and mortgage financing.

(B) In 1965 the estimated depreciable lives of buildings were extended as a result of an Internal Revenue Service examination. Accordingly, combined net income in 1965 was increased by approximately $22,000 based on revised depreciation rates for the year.

Auditors' Opinion

We have examined the combined balance sheet of The Pacific Coast Realty Corporation of Delaware, The Pacific Coast Realty Corporation of Indiana and The Pacific Coast Redevelopment Corporation as of August 31, 1965, and the related combined statement of income and earned surplus for the year then ended. Our examination was made in accordance with generally accepted auditing standards, and accordingly included such tests of the accounting records and such other auditing procedures as we considered necessary in the circumstances.

In our opinion, the combined financial statements referred to above present fairly the financial position of the companies as of August 31, 1965, and the results of their operations for the year then ended, in conformity with generally accepted accounting principles applied on a basis consistent with that of the preceding year.

ARTHUR ANDERSEN & CO.

October 21, 1965.

Accountants' Report

TO THE STOCKHOLDERS AND BOARD OF DIRECTORS
JEWEL TEA CO., INC.

We have examined the accompanying consolidated balance sheet of Jewel Tea Co., Inc. and subsidiaries as of January 29, 1966, and the related statements of income and accumulated earnings and source and use of funds for the fifty-two weeks then ended. Our examination was made in accordance with generally accepted auditing standards, and accordingly included such tests of the accounting records and such other auditing procedures as we considered necessary in the circumstances.

Jewel Tea Co., Inc. leases a number of its properties from affiliated real estate companies. Opinion Number 5 of the Accounting Principles Board of the American Institute of Certified Public Accountants contemplates that such properties (leased since September, 1964) and the related obligations be included in the consolidated balance sheet of Jewel Tea Co., Inc. Instead, this information has been included in the summarized data presented in a note to the consolidated financial statements. This difference in the treatment of leases has no effect on consolidated net earnings.

In our opinion, except for the method of presenting lease data as explained in the preceding paragraph, the financial statements referred to above present fairly the consolidated financial position of Jewel Tea Co., Inc. and subsidiaries at January 29, 1966, the consolidated results of their operations, and the source and use of funds for the fifty-two weeks then ended, in conformity with generally accepted accounting principles applied on a basis consistent with that of the preceding year, restated to include the earnings of affiliated real estate corporations.

March 16, 1966

Touche, Ross, Bailey & Smart

Real Estate Affiliates

Jewel leases a number of operating properties from 100 affiliated real estate corporations whose common stock is owned by the Jewel T Foundation. Jewel owns the preferred stock having conversion rights which, if exercised, would result in Jewel owning more than 99% of the common stock of these real estate corporations. Jewel's investment in this stock, formerly carried at cost, has been increased by the amount of accumulated earnings attributable to Jewel's investment, assuming conversion, and net earnings for fiscal 1965 and 1964 and accumulated earnings as of the beginning of 1964 have been restated accordingly.

Each real estate corporation has obtained debt financing generally for a twenty-year term at rates varying from 4⅜% to 5½% with provisions for prepayment after five years. Interest on this indebtedness amounted to $1,536,000 for 1965. Jewel has executed a net lease with each corporation at a rental sufficient to repay the amounts borrowed plus interest over the term of the lease and the leases have been assigned to secure the debt.

Aggregate annual maturities of long-term debt of the real estate corporations are as follows:

1967—$1,587,000
1968—$1,648,000
1969—$1,710,000
1970—$1,776,000
and the balance through 1989.

The following condensed balance sheets set forth the combination of the accounts of Jewel with those of the real estate affiliates as they would appear if Jewel's preferred stockholdings were converted into common stock interests:

	Jewel Tea Co., Inc. and Subsidiary Companies Jan. 29, 1966	Real Estate Affiliates Jan. 1, 1966	Combined
ASSETS	(In thousands of dollars)		
Current assets:			
Cash, marketable securities and certificates of deposit	$ 35,739	$ 2,162	$ 37,901
Other current assets	97,259	166	92,480
	132,998	2,328	130,381
Deferred charge	1,565		1,565
Other investments	9,554		5,474
Property, plant and equipment, at cost	142,833	42,174	188,217
Less allowance for depreciation and amortization	(63,778)	(3,663)	(67,441)
	79,055	38,511	120,776
	$223,172	$ 40,839	$258,196
LIABILITIES			
Current liabilities:			
Long-term indebtedness, due within one year	$ 3,126	$ 1,505	$ 4,631
Other current liabilities	64,358	2,077	64,700
	67,484	3,582	69,331
Long-term indebtedness, due after one year	30,811	32,421	63,232
Deferred federal income taxes	8,351	744	9,095
Jewel T Foundation equity			12
Stockholders' investment:			
Preferred stock issued	5,100	1,037	5,100
Common stock issued:			
Jewel	37,614		37,614
Real estate corporations (after elimination of intra-group holdings)		2	
Accumulated earnings	74,126	3,053	74,126
Treasury stock at cost	(314)		(314)
	116,526	4,092	116,526
	$223,172	$ 40,839	$258,196

1. CONSOLIDATION POLICY

Company A

Note 1—Principles of consolidation   The Company acquired the business and assets of Frito-Lay, Inc. in June 1965 and of Lease Plan International Corp. in January 1966, in exchange for a total of 3,609,371 shares of its capital stock and the assumption of substantially all of the liabilities of these two companies. These transactions have been treated as poolings of interests and are included in the accompanying financial statements on the following basis: (1) the accounts of Frito-Lay are included for calendar year 1965 and for its fiscal year 1964 which ended August 29, 1964, the difference between such fiscal year 1964 and calendar year 1964 being not material in relation to consolidated net income and (2) the accounts of Lease Plan are not consolidated and separate financial statements are included in this Annual Report; however, the Company's equity in Lease Plan's net assets and net income as of and for the years ended December 31, 1965 and 1964 are included for these years. As part of the pooling with Lease Plan, the Company contributed its wholly-owned non-consolidated subsidiaries, Pepsi-Cola Equipment Corp. and Margdave Realty Corporation to the new Lease Plan subsidiary.

The accounts of all other active subsidiaries are included in the accompanying consolidated financial statements except for certain insignificant overseas subsidiaries which are carried principally at the Company's equity in these net assets. With respect to one of the Company's consolidated domestic subsidiaries, a net provision of $260,000 has been included in "Other expenses" for estimated costs and pre-production and start-up expenses of the Montezuma, New York sugar refinery, after reduction for applicable federal income tax benefit of $1,348,000 and for investment credit of $1,200,000.

Foreign currency items have been translated at appropriate rates of exchange. The total assets, total liabilities and net current liabilities of consolidated foreign subsidiaries and branches (other than Canadian subsidiaries) stated in terms of United States dollars were $52,800,000, $23,900,000 and $600,000 respectively, at December 31, 1965.

Company B

Note A – Principles of Consolidation   The consolidated financial statements include the accounts of the Company and a wholly-owned subsidiaries. All material intercompany account transactions, and profits have been eliminated in consolidation The Company's equity at July 31, 1966, in the net assets of consolidated subsidiaries was $1,506,635 more than the fair valu assigned to the related investments. Upon consolidation, th amount has been distributed as follows:

Credited to retained earnings . . .		$5,175,57
Charged to other assets.	$ 963,043	
Charged to additional capital paid in .	2,705,900	3,668,94
		$1,506,63

Company C

(1) Principles of Consolidation

All of the subsidiaries are wholly-owned and their accounts have been included in the consolidated financial statements after elimination of intercompany accounts and transactions.

Company D

NOTE A—POOLINGS OF INTERESTS AND PRINCIPLES OF CONSOLIDATION

During 1966 the Company acquired all of the stock or assets of certain other companies in exchange for 724,436 shares of convertible preferred stock and 995,088 shares of common stock (including 16,000 shares of preferred and 90,101 shares of common held in treasury). These transactions have been accounted for as poolings of interests, and accordingly, the financial statements for 1966 include the results of operations of the acquired companies for the full year and the financial statements for 1965 have been restated on a comparable basis.

The adjustment of $1,978,810 to consolidated earned surplus arising from pooling transactions represents the difference between the cost of common treasury shares exchanged over the par value of such shares and the capital surplus attributed thereto.

The consolidated financial statements include the accounts of all domestic and Canadian subsidiaries. Foreign subsidiaries other than Canadian are not significant and are not consolidated. The Company's equity in the underlying net assets of the unconsolidated foreign subsidiaries was approximately $1,250,000 more than the amount at which the investments were carried at September 30, 1966, and the Company's equity in net earnings and dividends received from such companies for the year were not significant.

SUBSEQUENT EVENTS

Company A

8 SUBSEQUENT EVENTS:

On September 1, 1966, the Company acquired all of the outstanding capital stock of Victor Manufacturing & Gasket Company for $24,000,000 of which $12,000,000 was paid on that date and the remaining portion, evidenced by unsecured 5½% notes, is payable in two equal installments on September 1, 1967 and 1968.

During September, 1966, $18,000,000 was borrowed from banks under a $24,000,000 credit agreement dated July 5, 1966. The revolving credit notes are payable September 30, 1968, and bear interest at the rate of 5¾% per annum payable quarterly. The Company has the option to convert these notes into term notes which are payable in ten consecutive equal semi-annual installments. Under the agreement (a) consolidated net current assets cannot be less than $75,000,000, (b) cash dividends and purchases of the Company's stock are limited to 75% of consolidated net income from August 31, 1966, plus $10,000,000, and (c) there are limitations on additional borrowings.

Company B

Note 7—Subsequent events In March 1966, PepsiCo Overseas Corporation, a wholly-owned subsidiary of the Company, issued outside the United States $30,000,000 of 4½% guaranteed debentures, due in 1981. These debentures, which are guaranteed as to principal and interest by the Company, are convertible after September 1, 1967 into 322,581 shares of capital stock of the Company at a price of $93 per share, subject to adjustment under certain conditions.

Company C

10. SUBSEQUENT EVENTS

During September 1966, the Company agreed to acquire all of the capital stock of the A.B.C. Grain Corporation and Delphos Soya Products Company in exchange for approximately 35,000 shares of Central Soya Company, Inc. capital stock. These exchanges will be treated for accounting purposes as poolings of interest.

On September 7, 1966, the shareholders approved an increase in authorized capital stock of the Company from 5,000,000 shares to 10,000,000 shares and a stock split on a two-for-one basis by the issuance of an additional share for each share outstanding. The additional shares were issued on October 12, 1966.

All references to the number of shares in the consolidated financial statements and notes are based on shares authorized and outstanding as of August 31, 1966—prior to the two-for-one stock split mentioned above.

Company D

Note J—Event Subsequent to July 31, 1966: On August 25, 1966, the Company entered into an agreement to purchase certain assets and assume certain liabilities of The Hallicrafters Co. in exchange for shares of convertible preferred stock. The authorization of the new class of preferred stock is subject to the approval of the Company's shareholders.

ACCOUNTING PRINCIPLES

Company A

(2) Accounting Principles

In order to present the accompanying financial statements in conformity with generally accepted accounting principles, the following adjustments have been made therein (but not on the books which are maintained in accordance with accounting principles prescribed or authorized by the Interstate Commerce Commission):

Provision has been made for deferred federal income taxes attributable primarily to the difference between use of accelerated methods of depreciation for tax purposes and straight-line or mileage basis for book purposes.

The income from the investment credit provided by the Revenue Act of 1962 is reflected in miscellaneous income ($60,000) over the useful life of the acquired property while for book purposes the entire credit was recorded as income in the year used to reduce federal income taxes.

As to the investment credit under the Revenue Act of 1964, the company has adopted the policy of crediting the investment credit direct to income as a reduction to federal taxes. As a result the federal income tax provision for 1965 has been reduced by $326,000 ($37,500 in 1964).

The 1964 net earnings have been restated to reflect the federal income tax reduction ($860,000) resulting from the utilization of loss carryforwards of Steffke Freight Co. as special item rather than a reduction of the federal income tax provision.

Company B

1 In accordance with the general practice of the sales finance business, all retail notes receivable are shown as current assets regardless of maturity. On 31 October 1966 retail notes included $187,525,978 maturing after 31 October 1967 of which $84,394,937 will mature after 31 October 1968.

2 The balance sheet is prepared on the accrual basis of accounting. The books are kept and the tax returns are filed on the cash receipts and disbursements basis except that provision is made for a reserve for doubtful receivables. The provision for Federal income tax has been computed on income determined on the accrual basis and the accrued Federal income tax in the accompanying balance sheet includes an amount not currently payable of $6,400,000 on 31 October 1966 and $6,700,000 on 31 October 1965.

Company C

5. For financial statement purposes, the company recognizes income on contracts for the manufacture of printing equipment on the percentage-of-completion basis.

Since the company files its federal income tax return on a completed contract basis, provision for deferred income taxes has been made with respect to taxes which may be payable in the future on the additional income recognized on the percentage-of-completion basis. Such deferred federal income taxes are classified as a current liability in the accompanying balance sheets.

Company D

NOTE G—ACCOUNTING APPLICABLE TO CERTAIN COSTS

The Company's policy is to capitalize for book purposes and to amortize on a unit of production basis the intangible drilling costs of producing wells and the costs of lifting that portion of oil and gas dedicated to production payments. Such costs are deducted as incurred for income tax purposes.

ƆNTINGENCIES

ɱpany A

ƆTE F—CONTINGENCIES AND ƆMMITMENTS

The Company is contingently liable for certain ɪns and commitments payable by other companies ɖ in the opinion of management no material loss will

ɹlt from any such agreements. These include ɵunts payable as guaranteed rentals under through-agreements for the use of pipeline facilities, ter-ɪals, and service stations at an annual rate of ap-ximately $850,000 aggregating over a 20 year ɪod approximately $16,500,000 and guarantees of ɪs of unconsolidated foreign subsidiaries of ap-ximately $2,400,000.

ʰhe Company also has numerous long-term leases various equipment and facilities, for which the ɔunt of minimum annual rentals is not considered ɪificant.

ɱpany B

ɮe G—Renegotiation: Certain business done by the Com-ɪy and its subsidiaries is subject to renegotiation; however, ɑarance has been received from the Renegotiation Board ɔugh July 1964. It is not anticipated that renegotiation for ɪsequent open years will result in any determination of ex-ɕive profits.

Company C

Note J—Contingent Liabilities

At October 31, 1966, the Corporation is defendant in several lawsuits relating to product liability. The aggregate amount of damages claimed in such suits is $1,000,000 in excess of insurance coverage. Management believes that the Corporation's liability for such excess, if any, should not be material in amount.

FBI INVESTIGATION OF FRAUD

by John Edgar Hoover *

The cost of crime in the United States is conservatively estimated to be a staggering $27 billion a year. Varying estimates as to the annual losses resulting from fraud and embezzlement alone run into billions of dollars. The seriousness of these so-called "white collar" crimes is illustrated by an FBI analysis of data furnished by local law enforcement agencies for inclusion in the Uniform Crime Reports, which disclosed that in 1963 local authorities made almost 80,000 arrests for embezzlement and fraud. This estimate does not include arrests made by the FBI and other federal investigative agencies.

The term "fraud" in its generic sense includes many acts of trickery, deceit, and misrepresentation. Members of the accounting profession are usually concerned with those commercial-type frauds wherein manipulation of books and records took place either in furtherance of, or to effect concealment of, a fraudulent scheme. The FBI, during investigation of the various federal crimes under its jurisdiction, has encountered almost every conceivable type of fraud situation. These include fraudulent check schemes, securities frauds, confidence game swindles, embezzlements, false bills of lading, fraudulent bankruptcies, false claims, and various frauds perpetrated against the government.

Since the subject of fraud is so all-embracing, this article will be confined to FBI investigations in three general areas: frauds by employees, frauds by customers, and frauds by suppliers of material.

Frauds by Employees

Investigations by the FBI of frauds by employees are normally concerned with embezzlements and other violations of the Federal Reserve Act and related statutes which make it a crime for officers and employees of banks and certain other financial institutions to convert employers' property to their own use. During the fiscal year ending June 30, 1964, an all-time high of 2,728 alleged banking-type frauds were reported to the FBI. Shortages in these cases amounted to more than $19 million. There were 596 convictions in Federal Court, and fines and recoveries exceeded $16.8 million during the same fiscal year.

* Reprinted from *The Journal of Accountancy*, Vol. 120, No. 1 (July 1965), 34–
by permission of the publishers.

Many employee frauds are made possible either because the company lacks an adequate system of internal control or it does not follow reasonable precautions in using the services of internal auditors and/or public accountants. While some employee frauds are ingeniously contrived to avoid detection during audits, others are relatively simple schemes. In one of the largest bank frauds investigated by the FBI it was found that an official and customer of the bank had conspired to embezzle more than $3 million over a period of several years. The fraud was perpetrated through the simple expedient of issuing cashier's checks to the customer and to companies in which the customer had an interest. The embezzlements were concealed by false debits to the accounts of correspondent banks. The situation was not brought to light until after the officer was promoted and transferred, making it impossible for him to continue to cover up the scheme.

A considerable number of bank frauds involve the manipulation of savings account records. Since some of these accounts are relatively inactive and no periodic statements are sent to customers, they are particularly susceptible to fraud. It is interesting to speculate how many fraudulent schemes involving savings accounts would have been detected earlier if confirmations had been requested.

One embezzlement was not discovered until a customer came to the bank to check a savings account balance. The ledger sheet could not be located in the file. During the search an officer produced the missing ledger sheet, claiming that he had the record in connection with a loan inquiry. The sheet was returned to the proper ledger file, and at the close of business that day it was found the savings account ledger and the control were out of balance in the exact amount of the ledger sheet returned by the officer. This caused a bank employee to become suspicious and the matter was brought to the attention of the bank president. The officer who had produced the missing ledger sheet was confronted and admitted embezzling more than $30,000 over a period of ten years. The embezzler had withdrawn four legitimate customers' savings accounts ledger sheets from the file and had inserted two fictitious or "dummy" sheets in their place.

The FBI investigation revealed that the culprit had also prepared fictitious signature cards for the dummy accounts including false social security numbers. He prepared fictitious withdrawal slips for these accounts and withdrew the money after transferring balances from legitimate ledger sheets. The manipulations were made by him during non-banking hours, using a typewriter and the bank's posting machines. To decrease the chance of detection, the officer would periodically rotate the shortages among various legitimate savings accounts. During the last five years that the scheme was in operation almost eighty withdrawals had been made from the dummy savings accounts. The officer subsequently entered a plea of guilty in a U. S. district court and was sentenced to five years' imprisonment.

A long-time trusted employee of a firm doing business on a global basis took advantage of the confidence reposed in him to fleece his employers out of more than $300,000. He would prepare memorandums to the accounting department of the company requesting that checks in amounts ranging up to several thousand dollars be issued for commissions on foreign sales. He would indicate that the amount was to be charged to the account of one of the company's foreign export agents and request that the check be made payable to an out-of-state bank or an individual known to the employee. It was not unusual in this particular business for foreign firms entitled to commissions to request that checks be sent to third parties in the United States. After the checks were approved and signed they were returned to the employee who originated the transaction. He had an account at the out-of-state bank and would send the checks payable to this bank for credit to his personal account. He later obtained money or merchandise from the individuals to whom company checks were sent.

In order to conceal his peculations, the employee did not charge the checks to accounts of the foreign export agents since the fraud would have been detected when these agents received their monthly statements. The employee created other improper entries and adjustments in order to keep the books in balance. When the company was alerted to the employee's affluence, through a routine credit inquiry, a certified public accounting firm was called in to make an audit, and the matter was reported to the FBI. The employee was sentenced to imprisonment on state charges and also was convicted in a Federal Court for interstate transportation of stolen property.

In some instances an employee will deceptively manipulate records or reports for reasons not connected with a theft or embezzlement of the assets of the company. The FBI investigated one such case where the company manager caused false inventory reports to be submitted to a federal lending agency for the purpose of making it appear that the company was making a profit. By so doing, he was able to conceal the fact that the company had been operating at a loss and was able to retain his position of manager.

The false inventory and other overstatements of assets presented favorable financial picture and the company directors continued to pay dividends to its stockholders. The corporation had actually experienced a total loss in operations during a ten-year period of approximately $600,000. The investigation did not show any financial gain to the employee except for the retention of his position as manager as a result of the submission of the false financial figures.

The company maintained a perpetual inventory; however, it was not the practice to take physical inventories on a regular basis. The employee caused the book inventory to be overstated by several hundred thousand dollars through a series of understatements of the amount of raw material used in production over the years. The employee hoped that the company's profits would improve in the future and that he would be able to bring the inventory into line. The situation, however, went from bad to worse, and the overstatements continued to grow year after year until the company found itself in financial difficulties. The shortage was disclosed when representatives of the lending agency supervised the taking of a physical inventory.

It was necessary for the FBI special agent accountant handling the investigation to make a detailed examination of the company's records. This involved a tedious reconstruction process of working back from the actual physical inventory to the correct book inventory figures for comparisons with some of the reports submitted to the government lending agency. It was also necessary to have charts prepared in order that the variations could be understandably explained to the jury. The manager was found guilty after a trial in Federal Court.

Frauds by Customers

Bad debt losses resulting from either insolvency of customers or schemes to defraud are a constant plague to the American businessman. FBI investigations of frauds by customers usually concern criminal provisions of the National Bankruptcy Act which make it unlawful for bankrupts to conceal property or use bankruptcy proceedings as a cover in cheating creditors.

During the fiscal year ending June 30, 1964, a record high of 171,719 bankruptcies were filed in Federal Court, according to figures compiled by the Administrative Office of the United States Courts. Ninety per cent were nonbusiness bankruptcy filings and 10 per cent were business filings. In the overwhelming majority of bankruptcy filings the parties involved are conscientiously working toward just settlements and the FBI conducts investigation only in the small percentage of cases where fraud is alleged.

The FBI has noted that the hoodlum element has recently increased its participation in the so-called "racketeering" or professional type of planned bankruptcy. In one common method of operation the hoodlum will have a front man set up a business and establish a good credit rating by making prompt payment on a number of small purchases. The front man will then make large purchases of merchandise on credit and either abscond with the merchandise or dispose of it quickly at prices substantially below cost, before disappearing from the scene. The defrauded creditors will eventually place the business into involuntary bankruptcy and be able to realize only a small fraction of the amounts owing to them. The businesses most frequently involved have been furniture stores, jewelry stores, discount appliance outlets, and produce companies.

In another scheme frequently used by hoodlums, a legitimate businessman who cannot meet his obligations, possibly due to gambling debts or sudden business reversals, finds himself with a racketeer silent partner who uses the businessman's established credit to carry out a fraudulent bankruptcy scheme.

Planned bankruptcies are a challenge to the ingenuity and perseverance of our special agent accountants. In no other violation is the accountant required so frequently to develop supplementary information to bridge the gaps left by the missing, altered, or incomplete records. Many fraudulent bankruptcy schemes have been artfully contrived to avoid detection and prosecution, and in many cases substantial amount of sales and purchases have not been recorded on the books. Large withdrawals of cash from the business are often concealed by false charges to expense or inventory accounts. In securing credit some bankrupt have mailed false financial statements to banks, factors, and other credi grantors, making it necessary for our accountants to conduct a detailed audit to prove the truth or falsity of the various items covered in th financial statements.

Public accountants, by providing management and audit service to clients, could help reduce the loss from fraudulent bankruptcies an other customer schemes by recommending sound, workable credit pol cies. An alert credit department making maximum use of financial in formation available from credit agencies and other sources can ofte prevent overextensions of credit to firms in obvious financial distres

Frauds by Suppliers

The United States government and other purchasers of goods an services are vulnerable to many types of frauds perpetrated by supplier These include shipment of merchandise inferior to that specified in th contract and various false claims concerning the cost of goods and servic rendered. In dealing with frauds arising out of government contrac it has been our experience that false entries are frequently made in th records in connection with the schemes. For example, billings may made for salaries or wages of personnel not actually employed by t contractor. False payroll records and supporting data are prepared and the checks issued to the "dummy" employees and cashed by those responsible for the fraud. In other situations employee time and/or material actually used in the performance of civilian work may be falsely charged to government contracts.

Most FBI investigations of frauds by suppliers relate to violations of the Fraud Against the Government statutes growing out of procurement contracts. During the fiscal year ending June 30, 1964, a total of 611 persons were convicted in Federal Court for violations of these statutes, while fines, savings, and recoveries, including civil fraud cases, totaled almost $4 million. In addition, information developed during investigations was of assistance to other government agencies in designing controls to correct weaknesses.

One rather common fraud perpetrated by suppliers of material is the substitution of goods less expensive than those originally contracted for, accompanied by billings for the more costly material. The government and business organizations both must set up reasonable controls through inspection of materials received, together with examination of shipping documents, to keep losses from these "switching" operations to a minimum. Public accountants should consider recommending inspectional procedures to their clients, when appropriate, in connection with the review of the client's system of internal control and in providing management services.

Several years ago another government agency called the attention of the FBI to a situation where goods shipped from the United States to an overseas point under government financing were claimed to be of United States origin, whereas in fact the merchandise had been manufactured overseas. The government agency was alerted to the irregularities because of discrepancies in the unit price and the fact that inspection of a sample of the merchandise indicated that it was of foreign origin.

The FBI investigations, which included an examination of the records of companies handling the transactions, verified that the merchandise was manufactured abroad, shipped to this country, and then transshipped to the Orient. It was necessary to request investigation in several foreign countries to develop the case properly, and our investigation was further complicated by the fact that certain of the accounting records were in a foreign language little known in this country. Our inquiries also showed that an official of one of the companies involved made written statements that certain of the merchandise was of United States origin, which resulted in the government's making payments for the goods. Following our investigation, one person and two of the companies involved entered pleas of guilty in Federal Court. Fines and recoveries by the government were in excess of $200,000.

FBI Auditing Standards and Procedures

FBI auditing standards, which must be understood and adhered to by all special agent accountants, closely parallel the generally accepted auditing standards of the public accounting profession. Our accounting investigative operations and the results thereof are under constant evaluation to insure that these standards are followed and are compatible with our goals. Third-party reliance on FBI accounting reports requires that our personal standards, standards of field work, and standards of reporting be maintained at a high level. FBI reports are transmitted to other government agencies and U. S. attorneys, and the information in them becomes the basis for criminal, administrative, and civil action. Portions of the reports may be produced in court and our agents are subject to intensive cross-examination by opposing counsel on the results of our audits.

FBI accountants use the auditing procedures normally followed by the public accounting profession. The various writings of the profession have been helpful to us in this regard, and, in addition, we have our own manuals on the preparation of working papers and auditing procedures to be used in specific types of investigations.

The climate of an FBI audit in a fraud case is somewhat different from that of the usual audit engagement of the public accountant. Prior to our examinations, there have been definite allegations of fraud and/or collusion. While the FBI accountant will reconcile bank statements, for example, in the same manner as the public accountant, he will pay particular attention to the endorsements on the cancelled checks, since he knows that these will occasionally establish patterns of fraud. In one case the agent noted that checks payable to several different payees were all cashed at the same place. Further investigation showed that some payees were fictitious and this helped to establish that large amounts of cash had been siphoned from the business.

Both FBI and public accountants review and analyze ratios and trends during the initial stages of the engagement to pinpoint areas requiring further examination. The FBI accountant is particularly interested in such matters as: unusual fluctuations of expense accounts, comparisons between fixed assets and depreciation expense, relationships between purchases and sales, and the existence of classifications such as "exchange" accounts, which experience has shown, can easily be manipulated for fraudulent purposes. The gross-profits test and related analyses are among the standard preliminary techniques used by FBI agents to determine if an inventory shortage is indicated.

In many instances the perpetrator of a fraud will only partially conceal his crime by making false entries or using spurious documents in an attempt to avoid detection by auditors. We have had several cases where invoices purporting to be for items of inventory and supplies were used as a cover for personal and other expenses not properly chargeable to government work. In some instances regular invoice forms with the printed letterhead of a legitimate supplier were used and in other cases blank invoice forms were filled in by typewriter. These invoices would be processed in the usual course of business, false entries made as to the reasons for the transactions, and checks issued to the vendors. The vendor who sells personal articles to an official or employee of the company may be unaware that a fraud is being perpetrated and payment by company check will not necessarily create suspicion.

The person committing a fraud of this type does not always follow through to insure that the records support the false entries made in the books. For example, while the invoice may specify that certain raw materials were purchased, there may be no record of the actual receipt of the goods and no entry in the inventory records. When our test checks show that the supporting data is incomplete, it may be necessary to contact certain vendors to determine the true nature of the expense.

The use of blank invoice forms would, of course, be a red flag to the agent investigating a case where allegations of fraud have been made. On one occasion an FBI accountant examining the records of a customer of the firm under investigation noted that the handwriting on certain invoice forms was similar to that of the principal suspect. This resulted in uncovering several thousand dollars in unrecorded sales under a fictitious name. The nature of the supplier's business as compared with the type of material ostensibly purchased is another factor. An extreme example of this would be an invoice from a jewelry store for office supplies.

Confirmations of assets and liabilities by FBI personnel, whether by letter or otherwise, must be positive confirmations. We cannot afford to have the agent testify in court until he has uncovered all available facts. In a criminal trial for fraud it is necessary for the government to prove guilt beyond a reasonable doubt. Forewarned with this knowledge, the FBI agent must use auditing procedures designed to determine the full facts in a positive fashion, regardless of the outcome. Our men take as much pride in clearing a wrongfully suspected employee as they do in unraveling the tortuous machinations of a skillful, experienced embezzler.

I would like to thank again those members of the accounting profession who have reported violations to us and who have assisted our agents by supplying information needed during investigations. One effective deterrent to the individual contemplating a fraud is the sure knowledge that his crime will be reported to the authorities promptly upon discovery. Business and professional people can do much to make embezzlements and similar crimes a risky business by co-operating with those agencies whose duties are to investigate these schemes.

MARSHALL GLASS WORKS

The Marshall Glass Works manufactures and sells a variety of pane glass products including flat glass, plate glass, textured glass and wired or laminated glass. The company was established by Edward Marshall in 1922 and was incorporated under the laws of Delaware in 1928. It has been under continuous family management until about six months ago when Mr. Marshall died. In settling the estate, a syndicate headed by Albert Farmer and Robert L. Hallstead purchased the 700,000 shares included in Mr. Marshall's estate. Mr. Farmer was elected President and Mr. Hallstead was elected Vice President of Production and Controller.

Company Background

The company has been moderately successful over the years and has grown steadily to its present size. The new owners are convinced, however, that with aggressive production and marketing, the company can become an even more important part of the industry. Part of their program involves a public offering of securities in the near future to obtain financing for planned growth. The public offering will probably include both long-term debt and capital stock.

As the company grew from its small beginnings, Mr. Marshall gradually relinquished control over the production end of the business and concentrated on sales and financial matters. He maintained strong personal control over these aspects of the business and much of the data flow procedures have not changed appreciably since the company was a "one man" operation.

Much of the company's production is to customer order and specification, with flat glass accounting for about 40 per cent of total sales activity. Flat glass is a translucent or transparent pane of glass up to one-half inch in thickness. Its primary uses are as glazing medium in buildings and vehicles and as protective coverings for such items as desks, table tops, doors and vending machines. It is also used in the manufacture of mirrors and laminated glass.

Production involves fusing, at high temperatures, various compounds including silica sand, scrap glass and soda ash. The components are delivered to, and mixed in, the melting furnaces and then processed through a continuous drawing machine which produces a long ribbon of flat glass. At the end of the drawing process, the glass is cut into panes of workable size, inspected, graded for clarity and sorted by thickness.

Flat glass becomes the raw material for making plate, wired and laminated panes. Plate glass is produced by grinding and polishing the surface of flat glass. Wired and laminated panes are made by sandwiching wire or plastic sheets between two panes of flat glass and fusing the sandwich to produce a single pane. Textured panes are produced by using embossed rollers rather than smooth rollers in the drawing machine.

The company has maintained a small engineering department that works on product improvement and development. In the past, this department has also worked with customers in developing special panes to meet new requirements of the customer.

Manufacturing activities are carried out in two separate buildings. One houses the production of flat glass and the other houses production of special panes produced from flat glass. A third building, erected five years ago, houses the sales and administrative personnel. In addition to the home office, the company maintains four branch sales offices. All shipments are made from the warehouse located at the home office.

The accounting functions are under the direct supervision of the Chief Accountant, Mr. James F. Delansky, who reports to the Controller. A partial organization chart is attached as Exhibit One.

The new owners are aware of the need for considerable modernization throughout the organization and have contracted with a firm of certified public accountants to review the activities of the company. The consultants are to make any recommendations they feel necessary and are to supervise the installation of any changes that may be accepted by management. The same firm has been engaged to perform the first audit of the company in sufficient detail so that registration statements can be filed with the Securities and Exchange Commission.

As part of the review of company activities, the CPA firm has prepared a detailed description of paper flow activities and is now preparing a list of recommendations to submit to management. The audit manager for this engagement has received the following description of selected activities from the consulting team.

Billings

All orders are prepared on a three-part sales order form which is forwarded to the accounting department of the home office by both home office salesmen and branch office sales force. Two copies of the sales order are retained by the accounting department and one copy is sent to the sales department for sales analysis purposes. There are generally two types of orders received: (1) orders for stock items; and (2) orders requiring special production runs.

Stock Items

Orders for items normally carried in inventory—restricted to standard sizes of flat glass and limited quantities of plate, wired and laminated panes—are routed to Miss Ann Bodine, the billing clerk. She phones the stores area to see if there is sufficient stock on hand to fill the order. If there is, verbal authority is given over the phone to process the order and Miss Bodine reads the list of items that have been ordered to an inventory clerk. No perpetual inventory records are maintained.

When the order can be filled from inventory, one copy of the sales order is forwarded to the shipping department for use in preparing shipping documents and dispatching the order. The billing clerk then prepares an invoice, in duplicate, one copy of which she sends to the customer. The duplicate invoice with a copy of the sales order attached is used as posting media for the customers' account. The original copy of the invoice is held by the billing clerk until the shipping department forwards the bill of lading. Several copies of the bill of lading are retained by the carrier, one copy is retained in the shipping department, one copy is forwarded to the customer with the invoice, and the final copy is attached to the file copy of the invoice. All merchandise is shipped FOB shipping point, with freight and insurance prepaid by the company and billed to the customer.

Special Production Orders

Orders for plate, wired and laminated panes normally require a special production run for the customer. Only in slack production periods is there any manufacture of these items for inventory, and then only in standard sizes. When special orders are received, a four-part production order is prepared by Miss Bodine, the billing clerk. Three copies are sent to Mr. John Crystol, the production supervisor, who is in charge of scheduling. The fourth copy is sent to the credit and collection department.

The production supervisor returns two copies of the production order to the billing clerk indicating when the order has been scheduled for manufacture and providing an estimated shipping date. An acknowledgment of the order is sent to the customer indicating the estimated shipping date and, where possible, the shipping carrier. One copy of the production order is attached to the sales order and filed, by customer name, to await the completion of production and shipment. Another copy of the production order, with a copy of the sales order attached, is sent to the shipping department, with a notation of estimated shipping date. The shipping copy is used to prepare shipping documents and expedite shipment. The original of the production order is retained by the production supervisor.

When the order is completed, it is moved from the production floor to the shipping department for transmission to the customer. Shipping then prepares shipping documents and arranges transportation. The bill of lading is sent to the billing clerk for invoice preparation. In preparing the invoice, Miss Bodine checks the customer's account to determine if there have been any deposits made on the order; these are deducted on the invoice showing the total still due and payable.

If the stock items are not available for shipment, the billing clerk prepares a production order as described before. The production supervisor then schedules production based upon minimum-maximum inventory quantities established by his office. The billing clerk is notified of the estimated shipping date and an acknowledgment is sent to the customer. The excess production is put into inventory.

Shipping

The shipping department receives a duplicate copy of the sales order from the billing clerk. This department oversees the filling of the order, either from inventory or from production runs, determining that the order is properly packed to reduce risk of breakage.

Materials returned from the customer are received by the shipping department. The department prepares a memo indicating when the shipment was received and from whom. When possible, the quantity of returned material is determined and entered on the memo. Since many returns involve breakage, it is not always possible to determine exact quantities. Broken returns are weighed and an approximation of quantities is determined from the weight. The memo is sent to Mrs. Barbara Shaefer, the accounts receivable clerk who retains the memo and notifies the credit and collection manager.

Credit and Collection Department

The credit and collection department, under the supervision of Mr. Phillip Pratt, approves all credit sales and when necessary arranges for deposits to be made by the customer prior to completion of large special production orders. In addition, all correspondence concerning breakage and returned panes not meeting quality specifications is handled by the manager. Mr. Pratt initiates credit memos for returns and allowances which are transferred to a Returns and Allowances suspense account. Bad debt write-offs are initiated by Mr. Pratt, but must be approved by the Controller. When breakage is covered by insurance, Mr. Pratt handles all details of filing claims and receiving remittances. Checks are sent to the cashier, Mr. Thomas Bishop, who prepares a credit memo for posting to the Returns and Allowances suspense account.

Accounts Receivable

After notification is received that goods have been shipped, the duplicate copy of the invoice is used as a basis for posting to the customers' accounts. The accounts receivable ledger is maintained by Mrs. Shaefer, the accounts receivable clerk. The ledger comprises a tub file of about 400 individual accounts. Posting is done on an accounting machine that produces a Sales Analysis—Sales Journal as a by-product of the posting operation. For example, by positioning the customer's ledger card in the carriage properly, the entry is posted to the customer's account and is also entered in the appropriate product column on the Sales Analysis—Sales Journal sheet. The machine produces individual column totals, a grand total column and proof of item postings as well as proof of cross-footings of individual column totals. The Sales Analysis—Sales Journal also provides space for entering the customer's identifying number so that individual transactions may be traced from the Journal to the customer's account. A copy of the Sales Analysis—Sales Journal is sent to the sales department where it is reconciled with the sales orders received to develop a daily back-log of orders outstanding.

The tub file is maintained in alphabetical order and each day the previous day's sales are sorted into alphabetical order, assigned a number in sequence, starting with the date and ascending from 001, as follows: 11-20-001, 11-20-002, etc. This numbering system indicates that invoice number 001 was posted on November 20th. The totals accumulated in the Sales Journal for product sales, total sales and total billings to customers' accounts are posted to the control accounts by Mrs. Shaefer. The tub files are balanced to the accounts receivable control at least once a year and oftener at the request of Mr. Delansky. Cash receipts and non-cash credits are posted by the accounts receivable clerk on the basis of documents prepared by the cashier and Mr. Pratt. She also posts summary totals to the appropriate general ledger accounts.

Purchasing

Mr. Delansky, the chief accountant, acts as purchasing agent for the company. Purchase requisitions are initiated in the production supervisor's office. Sometimes these take the form of a handwritten memo indicating the type of material or supply required and the quantities usually ordered. At other times, the information is transmitted verbally by telephone.

Purchase orders are prepared by Miss Roberta Turner, vouchers clerk. The original copy is sent to the supplier, one copy is sent to the receiving department and one copy is kept in a pending file until receipt of the invoice from the vendor.

Receiving

The same personnel act as both receiving and shipping. Copies of the purchase orders are routed to the receiving desk and when the order comes in, the quantities received are verified against the quantities shown on the purchase order. Where quantities differ, the receiving department amends the purchase order to indicate actual quantities received before returning the order to Miss Turner. Quality testing, when necessary, is performed in the receiving department and test reports are sent to Mr. Delansky. Seldom is a shipment rejected for reasons of quality.

When items are returned to the vendor, the receiving department prepares a memo that is attached to its copy of the receiving report indicating what material and quantities were returned and for what reason. When material has been returned, the vouchers clerk prepares a debit memo and attaches it to the file copy of the purchase order. The debit memo is authority to adjust the vendor's invoice, if the invoice has not been adjusted by the vendor.

Vouchers Payable

The cashier, Mr. Bishop, receives all invoices and other requests for disbursement. He matches invoices against purchase orders in the pending file and sends all items to Miss Turner, the vouchers clerk. The invoice is verified against the purchase order and receiving report as to items ordered and quantities shipped. Unit prices are checked against the purchase order and extensions are verified as to amount. If purchase discounts are offered, the discount is calculated by the vouchers clerk and subtracted from the total shown on the invoice. If any debit memos are attached to the purchase order, extensions are verified and the total deducted from the invoice.

After verification Miss Turner enters the invoice in the voucher register with the debits being spread to appropriate accounts such as raw materials purchases, manufacturing supplies, travel expenses, etc. The vouchers are filed in an open voucher file by due date. It is the practice of the company to take all discounts offered and due dates are checked daily and payments rendered on time.

The company does not maintain a separate ledger for vouchers payable. The file of unpaid vouchers represents the detail of amounts owed. Weekly summary postings are made, by the vouchers clerk, to the vouchers payable control account and the cash account from the voucher register and the cash disbursements register. Monthly statements received from vendors are not verified regularly, since vouchers are filed under date of payment rather than under the vendor's name.

Cash Disbursements

On payment dates, vouchers to be paid are selected from the open voucher file and a voucher check is prepared by Miss Turner. The voucher check is a two part document, the upper half representing the check itself and the lower half providing space for itemizing the particular invoices being paid along with any supplemental information concerning discounts, returns or other allowances. The voucher check is prepared on an accounting machine that prepares a check register as a by-product. As invoices are entered in the voucher register, pre-printed numbers in the register are manually entered on the voucher and the same number is manually entered on the check. A check protector is used to emboss the amount of the check.

All checks are signed by Hr. Hallstead, the Controller. Supporting documents are submitted with the checks and are reviewed by Mr. Hallstead. After signature the checks are returned to the vouchers clerk who inserts the checks in window envelopes and mails them. She also stamps the vouchers paid along with the date. Paid vouchers are filed by vendor's name.

Blank, unnumbered checks are maintained by the cashier and are issued to the vouchers clerk each day as vouchers are prepared for payment. Unused blank checks are returned to the cashier each day.

Cash Receipts

Mail is opened by a mail clerk and all receipts from customers are sent to the cashier. The cashier pulls file copies of the customer's invoice and matches them against the checks received. Any deviations in the amount received and the amount billed, except for normal cash discounts, are noted on the invoice which is sent to the credit and collection department for further investigation and processing.

If the payment is satisfactory, the cashier initials the file copy of the invoice and sends it to Mrs. Shaefer, the accounts receivable clerk for posting to the customer's ledger card. The posting is done on an accounting machine and a cash receipts journal is prepared automatically. Accumulated totals are posted to the accounts receivable control account, sales discounts account and cash account by the accounts receivable clerk.

All checks received that have been cleared for posting to the customer's ledger are deposited at the end of each day. The cashier retains those checks relating to disputed invoices that have been sent to credit and collection. When the credit and collection department certifies that the balance paid is appropriate, the checks are deposited and the invoices are cleared for posting to the customer's account. Credit memos prepared by the credit and collection department are attached to the approved invoice as a basis for clearing the total balance from the ledger account. Any miscellaneous summary totals are posted to the general ledger by Mrs. Shaefer.

If the check has not been cleared by the credit and collection department within a week, it is deposited and a memo account is prepared by the cashier indicating the customer's name, number, amount of check, amount of invoice, the difference, and a note indicating a dispute over the difference. The posting to the customer's account is withheld pending settlement by the credit and collection department. When settlement has been reached, the memo account is released to the receivables clerk for posting to the customer's ledger card.

Daily, the cashier computes the cash balance and prepares a report of cash receipts, cash disbursements and ending cash balance that is sent to the Controller. Weekly bank statements are received from the company's bank and are reconciled by the cashier. Copies of the reconciliation report are forwarded to the Controller.

Payroll

Timekeepers are employed in the production areas and all hourly paid employees clock in and out using standard time cards. In addition, where an employee works on more than one production process, the employee prepares daily time cards indicating the time spent on each process. The timekeepers accumulate total hours for each employee and weekly forward a time sheet to the payroll section indicating employee's name, clock number, regular hours, overtime hours and total hours worked. A weekly report is also supplied to the cost clerk indicating hours worked on various production processes for cost analysis purposes. The timekeepers are responsible for reconciling hours paid with hours charged to various production processes and idle time by departments.

In the payroll section, Miss Susan Landis, payroll clerk, calculates hourly payroll from the time sheets using a schedule that lists each employee and his hourly rate of pay. Prenumbered payroll checks are obtained from the cashier and are prepared on an accounting machine. Checks contain a stub indicating gross pay, net pay and the various withholdings. A payroll register is prepared as a by-product of the check writing. Individual employee earnings records are posted separately, from the completed time sheets. After check preparation, the amount of the check is embossed with a check writing machine. The check is then signed by the cashier.

Using the payroll register totals, Miss Turner, the vouchers clerk, prepares a series of vouchers and checks for total net pay and the various withholding remittances such as federal and state income taxes. A special voucher register for payroll purposes is maintained and totals are spread according to a departmental breakdown provided by the cost clerk. The vouchers clerk posts summary totals to the various labor accounts in the general ledger.

The vouchers and checks are sent to the Controller for signature and when signed, are returned to the cashier. The net payroll check is deposited or mailed as appropriate. When the net payroll check has been deposited, weekly payroll checks are released to the production foremen for distribution to the employees.

Salaried employees are paid twice a month and the checks and payroll register are prepared from a standard listing of salaried employees showing gross pay, various deductions and net pay. Individual payroll checks, vouchers and other checks are processed in the same manner as for hourly employees. Salaried employees pick up their checks from the cashier, or have them mailed in the case of branch office personnel.

When new employees are hired, the personnel department sends the appropriate information to the timekeepers for hourly employees and to the payroll clerk for salaried employees. The timekeepers add new names to the lists as received and then forward the data to the payroll section. Miss Landis updates her hourly and salaried schedules accordingly. Terminations are also reported by the personnel department and final payroll checks for terminated employees are mailed by the cashier.

Inventories

As noted previously, perpetual inventory records are not maintained. Three inventory clerks maintain visual observation of inventory levels on finished products. When an item reaches or nears pre-determined minimum levels, Miss Bodine, the billing clerk, is notified and a production order is initiated as described before. With respect to raw materials, the production supervisor's office maintains an informal record of quantities and when a minimum level is reached, this is verified by visual observation and a purchase order requisition is sent to Mr. Delansky. On the average, about three or four times a year production schedules must be rearranged due to a shortage of raw materials.

While no formal cost accounting records are maintained, production orders showing quantities of raw materials used are forwarded to the cost clerk's office. Labor hours are added and informal cost reports are prepared for submission to the production supervisor. The cost clerk notes such items as price increases in material costs, overtime amounts and other increases in labor costs for comparative purposes.

Physical inventory counts are made once a year just prior to the end of the fiscal period. Cost information for purchased inventory items is calculated on the first-in, first-out basis while average production costs are used for manufactured items. The cost clerk also makes estimates of cost of sales and inventory amounts for monthly financial statements. Other production information is maintained in quantities only and monthly production reports, in quantities, are prepared for the production supervisor and the Vice President of Production.

Miscellaneous Items

Plant Ledger

Mr. Delansky, the chief accountant, maintains a file card for each item of plant equipment owned by the company. Annually a depreciation schedule is computed from the file. When an asset has been completely depreciated, the asset card is transferred to a pending file where it remains until the asset is disposed of by either sale or abandonment.

As new assets are acquired, a file card is prepared indicating date of purchase, name of asset, department location and total cost. Depreciation is calculated, one-half year in year of acquisition and one-half year in year of disposition, and is added to the depreciation schedule. When assets are disposed of, any cash received is recorded as miscellaneous income and the asset file card is removed from the file and a journal entry is made to record its retirement. No attempt is made to identify cash proceeds for recording gains or losses on disposal except as required by the Internal Revenue Service. There has not been an inventory of plant assets in fifteen years.

Capital Stock

There are about 750 stockholders and a stockholder's ledger is maintained by Mr. Bishop, the cashier. Stock transfers are first authorized by the Board of Directors before being entered in the stockholder's ledger. Prior to the new ownership, major stockholdings were held by Mr. Marshall and members of his family.

When dividends are declared, a special bank account is opened, with a voucher and a check being prepared in a manner similar to other disbursements. Miss Landis, the payroll clerk, prepares the individual dividend checks and a dividend register which indicates the name of the stockholder, the number of shares owned and the total dividend. The dividend register is filed with the voucher prepared to withdraw cash from the regular bank account. The vouchers clerk posts summary totals to the general ledger. The dividend bank account is reconciled by the cashier and a report filed with the Controller.

Investments

Periodically the company makes short-term investments of excess cash balances. Securities are maintained in joint custody with the company's bank, requiring a company officer and a bank official to gain admission to the deposit box. Both Mr. Farmer and Mr. Hallstead are authorized to act for the company. Payments for purchases are authorized by the cashier on the basis of a memo from the Controller. Dividends and interest revenue are received directly by the bank and a notice of deposit is sent to the cashier who prepares the necessary cash records to enter the items.

Personnel

The four clerks reporting to Mr. Delansky have specific titles and duties associated with those titles. Each is able to perform other duties and frequently fills in during necessary absences. The cashier, Mr. Bishop, has an assistant, Mrs. Alice Abnell. All duties described as belonging to the cashier are performed interchangeably by both individuals except for signing of payroll checks which is performed by Mr. Bishop. Miscellaneous postings to the general ledger not previously discussed are handled by Mr. Delansky.

MARSHALL GLASS WORKS

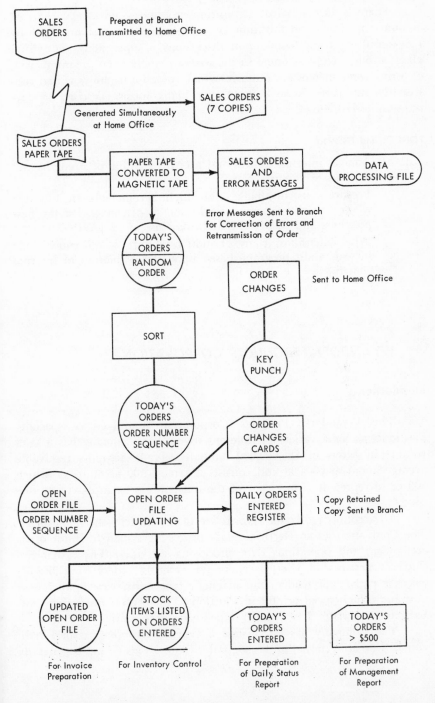

Other Items

There is no manual of accounting procedures, no formal chart of accounts or formal organization chart. Exhibit One was prepared by the consulting team based upon discussions of operations and visual observations. Except as noted in the write-up, there is no pre-numbering of forms, some memos are quite informal, some forms are not used consistently and there is no control over blank forms exercised by any responsible individual.

PONDER and PREPARE

1. Analyze internal control and prepare a listing of strengths and weaknesses you find.
2. Prepare a list of changes you might recommend. In any area where you recommend the addition of personnel, list the new positions and justify the addition, insofar as possible.
3. What extensions, if any, of audit procedures would you include in your audit program, based upon the evaluation of internal control?

WYANDOTTE PRODUCTS CORPORATION

Introduction

The Wyandotte Products Corporation manufactures specialty plastic items for a variety of different users. The Company has a sales volume in excess of $25,000,000 annually. Trade accounts receivable average about $3,000,000 and consist of some 5,500 accounts of which 500 or so represent 75 per cent of the outstanding balances at any one time.

All accounts receivable records are maintained by the home office. The Company uses an electronic data processing system for most of its accounting and operations data processing activities. The system includes a network of teletypewriters for entering orders from branch offices, a paper tape reader, four magnetic tape units, a card-punch-read unit and a high speed printer in addition to the central processing unit. Each teletypewriter has a paper tape read-punch unit.

The Company has established a Control Group of several individuals who are external to the computer center. This Group is generally responsible for initiating and maintaining controls over input and output of the computer center.

Credit limits for each customer are approved by a member of the Control Group on the basis of published ratings and credit reports from organizations such as Dun and Bradstreet. The Control Group also authorizes the sending of statements to customers who request them; about 200 statements are mailed each month.

Cash discounts are allowed for prompt payment of invoices and average about two per cent of billable charges, with varying amounts granted on different products. The discount date for billings issued during the first half of the month is the 25th of the same month. Billings covering the last half of the month carry a discount date of the 10th of the following month.

The accounts receivable system consists of three identifiable subsystems:

1. Order Entry
2. Invoicing
3. Accounts Receivable Updating.

Receivables are maintained on two magnetic tape files. One tape is the Basic Record File which contains data records for each customer. The make-up of the Basic Record File is illustrated in Exhibit One. The other tape file is the Open Items Record File and contains the details of unpaid invoices, unidentified cash payments, and other items supporting the Basic Record File account balance. In general, these two tape files are retained for three days before being written over.

The next several sections present the details of the sub-systems used to maintain the accounts receivable records for Wyandotte Products Corporation.

Order Entry System

Exhibit Two presents a flowchart describing the order entry system. Orders from all branch offices are transmitted by a teletypewriter network to the home office. Orders are usually received in the branch office by phone or mail and are entered manually on the Company's standard order form. The branch office is responsible for pricing the orders, based upon catalog prices for standard items. For special items of a non-standard nature, prices are based upon estimates prepared by the home office. In addition, the branch is responsible for determining the shipping warehouse if it is unable to fill the order from its own stock.

The standard order form is used to prepare a punched paper tape for transmission of the order to the home office. While the punched paper tape is being prepared, a two-part copy of the sales order is produced on an automatic typewriter. One copy of the sales order is kept in an open order file pending proof from the home office that the order was received properly. The second copy is distributed to the salesman.

The branch office maintains master paper tapes for all its customers. The master tape contains uniform customer information such as name, address, number, geographic code, credit class, branch office and salesman. In transmitting an order, the customer information from the master tape is transmitted first, followed by the order tape containing variable information, such as shipping point, items ordered, quantities and cash discounts. The order tape also indicates whether the order will be filled from branch stock or whether it must be shipped from another branch.

The receiving station at the home office receives orders in random sequence from the entire network and produces a punched paper tape of the information sent by the branch. While the teletypewriter is receiving the order and preparing a punched paper tape, it simultaneously prepares a standard seven-part sales order form. When validated and approved, the sales order form is sent out:

1. To division sales office for information purposes.

2. To branch office to be matched with the control copy retained by the branch. Both copies are placed in regular open files at the branch.

3. To customer as acknowledgement of receipt of order.

4. To Shipping and Stores Department as authority to release goods. After shipment, this copy is returned to the computer center in the home office to be keypunched for the Invoicing system.

5. To district sales office for information purposes.

6. As delivery receipt signed by operator of delivery vehicle.

7. As packing list included in shipment.

The paper tapes created at the home office, which contain all orders transmitted by the branches, are placed on the paper tape reader and a magnetic tape is written. During the conversion process (see point 1 on the flow chart), certain input validity checks are made on the input data. For example, a test is made to determine whether the customer number is numerical. Warehouse codes, order numbers and salesmen's codes are tested to see whether they are for the correct branch. If the order is to be split between two locations or two salesmen, the program determines that the per cent relationship adds to 100.

During this process, another sales order form is produced on the high-speed printer. Any order not meeting the input checks is rejected as an invalid order. An error message is printed at the top of the order form and the order is then printed as read off the paper tape.

The computer center's copy of each valid order produced by the high-speed printer is maintained in the files for reference. Invalid orders are matched manually with the seven-part standard order and both are returned to the branch office for correction and re-transmission. Only valid orders are placed on the Open Order File.

The Today's Order File, then, contains all valid orders in random order number sequence. The tape is sorted by the computer and a new tape is written with daily orders in order number sequence. A record count is maintained throughout the program and is recorded on the trailer label of the sequenced tape.

Order changes are received from the branch offices on the same tele-typewriter network except that a punched paper tape is not prepared. Order change cards are keypunched, keyverified and processed with Today's Order File, in order number sequence, and the Open Order File, also in order number sequence. Order change cards are also used in the Accounts Receivable Updating system.

In the Order Entry system, the computer operations produce both machine-readable output and visible output for subsequent use and distribution. Machine-readable output includes:

1. Updated Open Order File, on magnetic tape.
2. Stock Items Listed on Order File, on magnetic tape.
3. Today's Orders Over $500, on punched cards.
4. Today's Orders Entered, on punched cards.

The updated Open Order File is used in the Invoicing system while the Stock Items Listed on Order File is used for inventory updating and control and for production scheduling.

During the Open Order File updating processing, a Daily Orders Entered Register is prepared on the high-speed printer. This register lists, by branch, all orders entered on the Open Order File for the day. The listing shows the order number, customer name, shipping point, items, quantities, and sales price. This register also shows a full print-out of every order that is rejected because of a duplicate order number. One of the two copies of this register is mailed to the branch office entering the orders and is used by the branch to determine that all orders entered by the branch have been processed. The other copy is sent to the Control Group where the total of all orders entered by all branches is compared to the total orders entered that appears on the Daily Status Report (discussed in next section).

The order change cards are also used to produce a Daily Order Change Register, which is a listing, by branch, of all changes made to orders on the Open Order File. The register shows order number, the change made, the kind of change, and the sales value of the change. This report is mailed to the branch offices daily.

Today's Orders Entered cards are used in subsequent processing as part of the Invoicing system and Accounts Receivable Updating system. Today's Orders Over $500 cards are used to prepare a report for the Vice President of Sales.

Invoicing System

The home office prepares billings for all shipments using the updated Open Order File prepared as part of the Order Entry system and shipment data supplied by the Shipping and Stores Department. Exhibit Three is a flowchart of the Invoicing system.

From the processing of the Order Entry system, one copy of the standard sales order is forwarded to the Shipping and Stores Department. When an order is sent, shipping personnel indicate the number of pieces shipped, the quality control batch number, shipping method, freight charges and any other special charges related to the order. This information is in addition to the data printed on the standard order form.

These documents arrive at random from all possible shipping points and are reviewed by a member of the Control Group concerned with invoicing. After review, the forms are sent to be keypunched and key-verified; no batch or control totals are developed at this point. After punching and verification, the cards are transferred to the computer center for processing.

The shipment cards are first sorted into order number sequence and merged with the Open Order File and processed with the invoicing program. This processing step results in the following machine-readable output:

1. Updated Open Order File, on magnetic tape.
2. Stock Items Shipped, on magnetic tape.
3. Billings, on punched cards, two cards for each item shipped.

The updated Open Order File is then used for the next day's processing of orders to be entered while the Stock Items Shipped tape is used to prepare sales analyses and for inventory updating. One of the Billings punched cards is used in the Daily Status Report processing program and the other is used for the Accounts Receivable Updating system (see next section).

The only visible output from this processing program is a six-copy invoice. Three copies of the invoice are sent to the customer and one copy each is sent to the Control Group, the salesman, and the branch office which originated the sale. The original copy of the invoice includes a payment coupon which the customer is requested to return with his payment. The coupon is used in the Accounts Receivable Updating system also.

In a second processing run, the Billings card deck is read into the computer with the Daily-Monthly Status Report File on magnetic tape and Today's Orders Entered card deck, produced by the Order Entry system. The Daily-Monthly Status Report File is in product code sequence and both card decks are sorted into the same sequence before processing with the Status Report program. Machine-readable output includes:

1. Updated Daily-Monthly Status Report File, on magnetic tape.

2. Invoice Control Card, a punched card.

The updated Daily-Monthly Status Report File is used in processing the next day's Daily Status Report while the Invoice Control Card is distributed to the Control Group for review and follow-up as required. The Invoice Control Card includes the following information:

1. The total number of shipment cards read by the computer.

2. The total number of billings cards punched by the computer.

3. The total number of invoices prepared by the computer.

4. The total number of shipment cards read but not invoiced because there was no order number in the open order file.

5. The total number of invoices prepared for partial shipments.

6. The total dollar amount of invoices written.

7. The total dollar amount of open orders in the open order file.

The visible output from the processing run is the Daily Status Report. This report indicates, by product, orders entered today, month-to-date and last month-to-date; billings today, month-to-date and last month-to-date; backlog today and a month ago. The report also shows total orders entered today and total billings today and total backlog. The total orders entered today can be compared with total orders shown on the Daily Orders Entered Register (see Order Entry section) and total billings for today can be compared with the total billings shown on the

Daily Cash Receipts and Sales Register (see next section). In addition to the Daily Status Report, a Monthly Status Report is prepared at the end of each month.

Accounts Receivable Updating System

The Accounts Receivable Updating system, in one processing operation, records daily billings, daily cash receipts, non-cash credits and other changes to the Basic Record File and the Open Item Record File. Exhibit Four presents a flowchart describing the Updating system.

All cash is under the control of the Treasurer and collections are received at the home office. The Company maintains four general checking accounts and various branch and divisional accounts handled on the imprest basis. All mail, except pieces addressed to specific individuals, is opened in the mail room. There, checks and payment identity coupons are separated. A clerk makes a record of checks received without identity coupons. The coupons are sent to the computer center for keypunching and keyverification of cash receipts cards. The register of No Coupon Receipts is sent to the Accounts Receivable Supervisor in the Control Group who prepares the documents for keypunching if the payment is for an open account. No listing of checks is prepared prior to forwarding to the cashier; he prepares an adding machine tape of the amounts received.

Sundry cash receipts are included on the register of No Coupon Receipts and source documents for these items originate with the Accounts Receivable Supervisor and are approved by the General Ledger Bookkeeper of the Control Group. Billings cards are output from the Invoicing system and Today's Orders Entered cards are output from the Order Entry system.

Credit memoranda for returned material are initiated by the Control Group based upon receipt of a returned material receiving report. Branches forward their receiving reports, approved by the branch manager, to the home office daily. All credit memoranda in excess of $1,000 must be approved by the Controller and Divisional Vice President before being processed. All other credit memoranda must be approved by the General Ledger Bookkeeper and the Inventory Supervisor. Miscellaneous credits originate in the Control Group and are approved by the General Ledger Bookkeeper before processing. Usually these credits are to correct invoicing errors.

In addition, punched cards are prepared for new accounts, changes in customer name, number, address, credit limits, order cancellations, increases or decreases in orders and so forth. Other activity input consist of month-to-date cards showing sales by division, sales tax by taxing body and sundry cash receipts by account. These cards are subsequently used in printing monthly totals for posting to the general ledger.

All activity cards are first sorted into customer number order and are processed by the computer against the Basic Record File and the Open Item Record File. The processing produces the following machine-readable output:

1. Updated Accounts Receivable Basic Record File, on magnetic tape.

2. Updated Open Item Record File, on magnetic tape.

3. Updated month-to-date cards, on punched cards.

4. Exception Report Cards, on punched cards.

The updated magnetic tape files are used in the next day's processing of the Accounts Receivable Updating system as well as being used to prepare aged trial balances. Monthly statements are prepared from these files for customers who request them and the statements number about 200 per month.

The aged trial balance is prepared weekly and at the end of each month by computer processing of the accounts receivable master tape files. The aged trial balance lists, in customer number sequence, all invoices, credits and debits by date, number and amount. All open invoices are aged according to 30-day, 60-day, 90-day and over-90-day categories.

Visible output from the processing run is:

1. Daily Cash Receipts and Sales Register.

2. Cash Deposit Slip.

The Daily Cash Receipts and Sales Register is prepared in customer number sequence and shows, for each customer having transactions that day, the cash receipts and/or billings information applicable to that account. If there is no activity in the account, it does not appear on the statement. Cash receipts information includes gross amount of the billings, discount earned and net amount paid. The billings information includes invoice number, gross amount of billings with the amount applicable to material, transportation, and sales tax shown separately. The balance in the customer's account after the transactions have been posted is shown, along with grand totals for cash receipts and billings. Total sundry cash receipts are shown separately as well as the total balance of all accounts receivable and the number of invoices processed during the day.

The Cash Deposit Slip itemizes each receipt and is prepared in duplicate. Both copies are sent to the cashier for agreement with the remittance adding machine tape he prepared and for use in depositing the daily collections.

The Control Group compares the total billings printed on the Daily Cash Receipts and Sales Register with total billings shown on the Daily Status Report and the Invoice Control Card, prepared as part of the Invoicing system.

The Exception Report Cards punched by the computer as part of the Updating system are processed through the high-speed printer to produce the Daily Exception Report. The exception cards are produced by programmed controls in the Updating system and fall into three types of exceptions:

1. Exceptions to operational policies.

2. Errors in input data.

3. Information only.

The exception codes and descriptions are presented in Exhibit Five.

PONDER and PREPARE

1. Prepare a list of the strengths and weaknesses in internal control in the system.

2. Describe how you would test the existence and effectiveness of the controls you have described.

3. Prepare any recommendations you would make to improve the system.

Note: In preparing your answers, it may be helpful to deal with each of the three sub-systems separately.

EXHIBIT ONE

WYANDOTTE PRODUCTS CORPORATION
ACCOUNTS RECEIVABLE BASIC
RECORD FILE

Data Field	*Number of Characters*
Customer number	7
Current Accounts Receivable balance	9
Amount on order, in dollars	27
Credit Limit:	
Amount, in dollars	7
Date limit established	6
Credit history:	
Date account opened	6
Highest credit extended	9
Date highest credit extended	6
Original credit limit	9
Date original credit limit established	6
Previous credit limit	9
Date previous credit limited established	4
Number of months previous credit limit	2
Number of items currently delinquent	3
Amount, in dollars, currently delinquent	9
Delinquency history:	
Months reporting	2
Months delinquent	2
Consecutive months delinquent	2
Last month delinquent	4
Highest delinquency:	
Number of items	3
Amount, in dollars	9
Date	4
Date of last sale	6
Sales history (by product line):	
Third prior year	9
Second prior year	9
First prior year	9
This year to date	9
This month	9
Potential	9
Profit at standard rate, year to date	9
Payment history:	
Payment ratings (established by company, scale is	
0–9 based on payments each quarter):	
Third prior year, by quarter	4
Second prior year, by quarter	4
First prior year, by quarter	4
This year, by quarter	4
Dollars paid this quarter, by discount date	9
Dollars paid this quarter, by due date	9
Customer name and address	136

EXHIBIT TWO

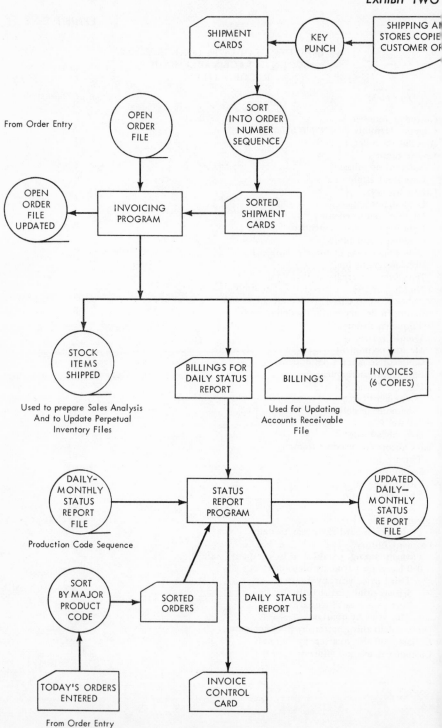

SHIPMENT CARDS

KEY PUNCH

SHIPPING AN
STORES COPIE
CUSTOMER OF

From Order Entry

OPEN ORDER FILE

SORT INTO ORDER NUMBER SEQUENCE

OPEN ORDER FILE UPDATED

INVOICING PROGRAM

SORTED SHIPMENT CARDS

STOCK ITEMS SHIPPED

Used to prepare Sales Analysis
And to Update Perpetual
Inventory Files

BILLINGS FOR DAILY STATUS REPORT

BILLINGS

Used for Updating
Accounts Receivable
File

INVOICES (6 COPIES)

DAILY-MONTHLY STATUS REPORT FILE

Production Code Sequence

STATUS REPORT PROGRAM

UPDATED DAILY-MONTHLY STATUS REPORT FILE

SORT BY MAJOR PRODUCT CODE

SORTED ORDERS

DAILY STATUS REPORT

TODAY'S ORDERS ENTERED

From Order Entry

INVOICE CONTROL CARD

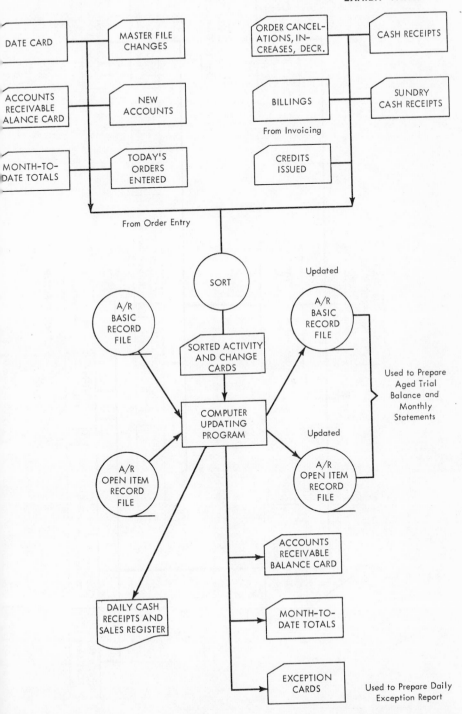

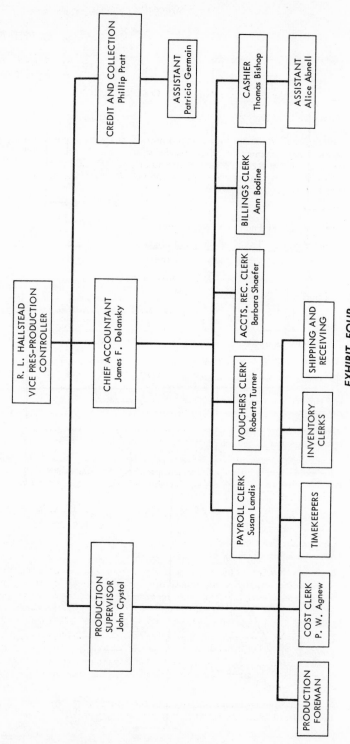

EXHIBIT FOUR

WYANDOTTE PRODUCTS CORPORATION

Code	Explanation of Exception Code

Code   *Explanation of Exception Code*

A   Order Received Today over Credit Limit—a credit limit check is not made until the order is received, processed for shipment and posted to the accounts receivable Basic Record File. The computer program then compares the total of the customer balance and orders entered with the amount of the credit limit on the customer record

B   Order Received Today—new customer

C   Order Received Today—no credit limit on Basic Record

D   Order Received Today—delinquent account

E.   New Account Opened Today—no activity

F   Inactive Account—no sales in last three years

G   Account with Credit Balance

H   Item Coded "Do Not Age"—a balance over which there is customer disagreement

J   Item Delinquent Today

K   Delinquent Item Paid Today

L   01 (subcode) Cash Discount Not Taken, Allowable, Within 5 Day Grace Period
02 (subcode) Cash Discount Taken, Not Allowable
03 (subcode) Cash Discount Not Taken, Allowable, Less Than $1.00

M   Unassigned Payment in Item Record—customer remits payment without payment identity coupon and payment cannot be identified by other means

N   Unassigned Credit in Item Record—all credits, except those which are for the same amount as on invoice, are processed unassigned until payment is received for the remaining amount due on the invoice for which partial payment applies

P   Difference in Amount Between Basic Record Balance and Total of Items in Item Record

Q   Confirmation of Changes—change is printed out, i.e., address, credit limit, or other basic record changes

R   Customer Number Change, Record Deleted—when the customer number is changed a change in the order sequence of customers on the sequential file is necessary. It is not possible to back up the tape and insert the customer where it belongs on the file. Therefore, cards are punched when a customer is to be deleted which show all information for that customer

S   Customer Number Change, Record Inserted—on the following day, the punched cards resulting from Code R are processed and inserted on the master record file and a print out of the information inserted appears on the exception report for comparison against information deleted the previous day

T   Answer to Query—the card(s) contains the listing of the customer information, from the basic record file, requested in query

Code	Explanation of Exception Code
U	Error Card—this card shows, by code, the type of error in the punched card input and information on the input card which is not processed because of the error. Several of the errors relate to program checks for proper date, proper sequence of customer numbers and valid transaction codes